Learn the Secrets of the Secret War . . .

- The true content of Soviet maneuvers in espionage and intelligence

- The achievement of "perfect cover"—Richard Sorge and the Soviet espionage ring in Japan

- The coup de grace of deception—the British corpse that made the invasion of Sicily the ultimate secret operation

- The critical distinction between "covert" and "clandestine"—the two diverging paths to secret operations

- The facts of counterespionage (CE)—the making of a mole and the "turning" of an enemy agent

- The "open-faced" American—our biggest headache in the secret war

. . . AND MUCH MORE ABOUT THE TACTICS, STRATEGY, AND DAY-TO-DAY OPERATIONS OF THE WORLD OF SPIES

"This book should be, and will be, I feel sure, a revelation to a great number of 'open-faced' Americans."—*Best Sellers*

Also by Christopher Felix

Three-Cornered Cover, a novel
(with George Martin)

A Short Course in THE SECRET WAR

Christopher Felix

Annotated with a new introduction
by the true author,
James McCargar

A DELL BOOK

Published by
Dell Publishing
a division of
The Bantam Doubleday Dell Publishing Group, Inc.
1 Dag Hammarskjold Plaza
New York, New York 10017

To J. G. and T. F. M.
—skillful and generous allies
in the secret war of the individual

Dell ® TM 681510, Dell Publishing, a division of the
Bantam Doubleday Dell Publishing Group, Inc.

ISBN: 0-440-20085-7

Reprinted by arrangement with Brandt & Brandt Literary
Agency, Inc.

Printed in the United States of America

May 1988

10 9 8 7 6 5 4 3 2 1

KRI

CONTENTS

INTRODUCTION
TO THE SECOND EDITION
WASHINGTON 1987

WHAT'S IN A NAME?

I have been asked, more times than I would care to tally, the meaning of "Christopher Felix," or how I chose that name for the original 1963 edition of this book. I would be unhappy with the tally because it shows how penetrable, at least after time, is the armor of a pseudonym. (Already in the late 1960's I received a letter from the President of the British Crime Writers' Association —until then I had not considered myself a *crime* writer—the envelope properly addressed to me, and the enclosed letter opening, "Dear Christopher Felix." In replying I asked how the writer had obtained my identity and address, to which he answered, "Simply by two London telephone calls." The man left me suspended in midair: I still don't know what those two calls were.)

When in a flippant mood—a dangerous springboard—I have sometimes answered, "It means 'Christ! Am I happy to be out of that work!'" Good for a laugh by some, offensive to others, and hardly faithful to the original Greek and Latin. The truth of the matter is that the name came to me—as many fictional names do— in my sleep, or rather, I awoke with it one morning in my mind. I promptly adopted it. One New York friend thought it was "chic" (not my intent). Another congratulated me on the choice: "I rather like it," she wrote. "It would do just as well for an Irish ferryboat."

The suggestion has been made to me—not by editors or publishers, but by a distinguished scholar—that the historical value of this second edition might be increased by revealing various true identities in the book. Apart from my own, already abundantly done by others elsewhere, I have not done this.[1] A sad proportion of those named herein, particularly in Part II of the book, are no longer with us. Even so, to name most of them, at any point, would expose them to the vagaries of later judgments by those with their own biases and purposes. The right to reveal identity should belong to the rightful owner.

The introduction to the original edition pointed out that I had used true names and places wherever possible, but that where this was not possible, I tried to maintain the pertinent point or principle while altering the names, personalities, and circumstances involved. I concluded, "The reader will appreciate that it is one of the rules of the game that I cannot say which is true and which is false." While this is still, in general, the case, I have added endnotes in this edition that reveal some original falsifications, update some of the original observations, and, thanks to a number of attentive and communicative readers, correct some errors in the original. I hope not too many remain.

WHAT HAS HAPPENED SINCE?

In the original introduction to this book I commented that American critics of the failures of the U-2 and Bay of Pigs operations in 1960 and 1961 displayed not "even an elementary knowledge of the conduct of such operations." I observed, "It is of no benefit to those responsible for American secret operations that partial ignorance or lack of understanding of the principles of these operations should be characteristic of the public." And I added that "a general awareness" by the public "that these operations are being conducted" on their behalf, "accompanied by a basic understanding of the principles governing secret operations, produces further understanding of precisely why such operations must remain secret," which is a "prerequisite to a tacit but still essential public support for these vital operations." I concluded that it was "the purpose of this book to contribute to such an understanding."

What then happened, beginning in the middle 1960's and continuing to the present day, was an outpouring, a deluge, of literature on the subject throughout the Western world (that ultimately even had a slight echo in the Soviet Empire). Serious studies, some only ostensibly so, in these twenty or more years, were in the high hundreds. If fiction is included, the output is in the high thousands. (And fiction, to my mind, should be included: a CIA friend once gave it as his opinion that the true substance of secret operations can only be captured in fiction.) What has been the result? Has there been a growth in understanding?

I believe there has been. The immediate press comment, at least in the major dailies and weeklies that might be described as "national," on the faults and defects of the 1985–86 Iranian and Nicaraguan operations run out of the National Security Council showed a basic understanding of technique, and, best of all, a grasp of the administrative and constitutional issues involved. Criticism on moral grounds seemed to have been largely replaced by attention to the more pertinent national and international political consequences of error. Twenty-five years had accomplished something in the United States.

I exclude from contributions to this understanding much of the "investigative journalism," principally in book form (which began well before Watergate). A large part of this output has been erroneous in content and intended either to establish the author or authors as experts or to grind particular axes. Talented writers of fiction, experienced in the field, such as John le Carré or Charles McCarry, have, in my estimation, made much more valuable contributions—even if that was not their primary aim.

Of course, there has been a vast amount of material to work with in these years. In the United States there were numerous revelations concerning CIA operations in both the 1960's and 1970's. In Great Britain the Soviet penetration of the British services surfaced over two decades. In France in the 1960's the Ben Barka affair and the refusal of the SDECE's Washington representative to return to France when ordered brought scandals of the French services into the open. (It is significant that the only high French official obliged to resign as a result of the 1985 uncovering of the French operation in New Zealand against the *Greenpeace,* which resulted in a death, is frequently mentioned as a potential candidate for the French Presidency.)

In Germany a succession of revelations of East German and Soviet penetrations of the *Bundesnachrichtendienst,* of arrests and flights from East to West and West to East, turned searchlights on the operations of that service and the West German domestic security services. Even the Russians were not exempt: the Penkovskiy case and a steady series of defections from both the KGB and the GRU, eventually widely publicized, brought to public attention the scope of Soviet secret operations. (And the Russians modified their own stance in these matters: Soviet agents such as Richard Sorge and Colonel Abel were publicly honored, and some books published about their exploits and those of the Soviet services.)

When this book was written communications intelligence was already a fully developed field. But the exploitation of space was just beginning. The prospects space offered led to grandiose pronouncements about machines replacing man in the world of secret intelligence, as elsewhere. Notwithstanding the enormous strides that have been made in collection of intelligence by space satellites of various kinds, those predictions have not been fulfilled. The information sought, now vastly multiplied in quantity, still needs to be evaluated by the human brain. And there is always the basic question of intentions. A 1986 interview with Michael R. Beschloss, a rising young historian, whose study of the U-2 affair, *Mayday,* was published that year, made the point: "Richard Bissell, deputy director of plans for the CIA from 1959 to 1962, told Beschloss that in the late 1950's the U-2 provided 90 percent of U.S. hard intelligence about the Soviet Union. Today, its sources are much better, Beschloss says, 'but the problem is that we don't necessarily have a better grasp of Soviet *intentions.* That's something a satellite can't show you.' "

I have not myself worked in intelligence or secret operations for thirty years now. But an occasional glance at the papers is sufficient to show that certain verities continue to reign. While there have been vast technological changes in that time—computerization has accomplished marvels in quantity and speed, but done little if anything for quality—the basic elements of intelligence and secret operations that I sought to outline in this book remain valid. Those changes noted in this edition mostly concern a changing external world. The principles and procedures of the internal world of secret operations are largely constant, as a former Director of the CIA has implied in reference to this book.

One of the great changes of the past quarter century that I discern, though still in its beginnings, does alter some of the emphasis in this book. It is set forth in a note added to this edition:

While the conflict "between the Communist and non-Communist blocs" continues, the world is no longer governed exclusively by this "single conflict." The "two great power centers" are no longer in a position to dictate unilaterally within their own spheres without recourse to force (which increasingly involves greater risks). Neither is even in a position in today's world to solve its own domestic problems with purely domestic solutions. (Note the Soviet Union's difficulties with productivity, and the United States' transformation in three years in the early 1980's from the world's greatest creditor nation to the world's greatest debtor nation.) No "other nations or combination of states" have yet achieved "some parity with them" in terms of power, but the West European GNP now exceeds that of the United States—which has long exceeded that of the Soviet Union. While both superpowers meddle in the Middle Eastern conflicts, they certainly cannot now "divide" that "world between them," and the major shifts in the balance of power now originate in East Asia.

THE SPECIAL AMERICAN PROBLEM

The trend in the United States over the past twenty-five years has been toward increasing Congressional control of initiatives in the field of secret operations. This has resulted in increasing frustration in the Executive Branch. (Open debate in the Congress of so-called "covert" operations in Angola or Nicaragua makes a mockery of the word "covert" and a tragic farce of the operations themselves.) There are solid citizens with experience in these matters who feel that the President is now hamstrung in his conduct of the nation's foreign relations.

The manner in which the "debate" on this issue has progressed over the years has worsened rather than clarified the situation. In response to the performance in the Nixon White House, as well as to revealed illegalities and excesses of the CIA, a new President in effect co-operated with the Congress in limiting the scope of action of the CIA—and, without the President apparently realizing it, his own possibilities of action. A succeeding Administration, frustrated in action by the established restrictions, and in policy by the Congress, took matters into its own hands, and centered secret operations in the White House itself—an alternative decisively rejected by clearer thinkers already in the period 1946–48. The result is "chaos" in the White House, baleful glances from the Congress at the CIA, and the potential for further restrictions on the Executive Branch not only in secret operations but in foreign relations generally.

This is the "special American problem." For both parties to this conflict between the Executive and the Legislative have right on their side. The Executive *is* too restricted by current legislation and practice, and the Legislature *does* have a right to consultation and knowledge, and in specified cases, decision, with respect to foreign policy and the expenditure of funds in furtherance thereof.

I would not venture to prophesy future developments in this conflict—which is not new to the Republic, though exacerbated during the past forty years by the development of secret operations as an authorized arm of Executive action. It is clear, however, that under our system this conflict will not disappear, because it is a part of the balance of powers built into that system. It can therefore be rendered manageable only by the sole instrument available to reconcile the irreconcilable—compromise. Spineless, ugly word to ideologues and extremists, but to those who understand, compromise is the daily cement of a democratic system—along with observance of the law and at least occasional and genuine humility (however clandestine). All three are as indispensable to and within the Executive as within and to the Legislature.

BALANCING THE WHEEL

Besides some fields of private endeavor, in which the touchstone has always been international relations, I have had considerable and varied experience in both secret operations and diplomacy. There is no question about it, secret operations is a fascinating field. This book gives only a partial taste of the excitement and the hold on one of the work. So, even though spoken flippantly, was I *really* "happy to be out of that work" when it ended thirty years ago? The answer is, "For a time, no." It takes a while to appreciate the valley after one comes off the mountain.[2]

But my feelings are not the point. What my experience over some forty-five years offers is the much more important opportunity for a comparison, in terms of contribution to the national interest, of secret operations and diplomacy.

In both fields I made lasting friendships that continue to grow with the passage of time. The people in both the CIA and the Foreign Service, give or take the customary leaven of knaves, are of high caliber. As organizations, of course, both the State Department and the CIA are monsters—though the CIA has a slight advantage in greater flexibility. Walter Lippmann used to speculate that the basic problem facing certain powers in this century was the adaptation of social organization to great size, and he considered the American contribution to this problem unique. It was only the United States, he said, that was successfully reconciling size with liberty and democratic processes. Both the State Department and the CIA are examples of institutions seeking to reconcile great size with excellence and efficacy, although for much of the past two or three decades their efforts have not met with great organizational success (as distinct from individual or personal excellence, not always recognized or rewarded). The State Department has fallen into the hands of administrators and managers, and the CIA, as an Inspector General of the agency once said to me, "is now run by lawyers and accountants."

There is no love lost between the two, to the point that Foreign Service people of the generations now retired and retiring find it almost impossible to believe that a Foreign Service Officer could be detailed—as I once was—to the CIA. (These skeptics have a point: my detail was to the Office of Policy Coordination, which was only administratively in the CIA. The OPC operated independently of the Director of Central Intelligence, under the authority of the National Security Council and the guidance of the Policy Planning Staff of the State Department—an arrangement to which General Walter Bedell Smith, when Director of the CIA, put an end, and to which many writers on these matters, and some State Department officials, pay all too little attention.)[3]

As a CIA friend observed, "The Foreign Service's feelings about the CIA were well earned. We destroyed the careers of a whole generation of Foreign Service Officers." And as a Foreign Service friend remarked of the political outcome of covert operations over the years, "I never saw the CIA do anything that we couldn't have done better."[4] As usual in such cases, there is some truth in both statements.

But again, personal feelings, in this case rivalries, are not the point. The point is how the United States is best served. Plainly there is not only room but a role, a need, for both services. Good intelligence is fundamental to diplomacy and the elaboration of foreign policy. Secret political, economic, and, when necessary, paramilitary operations are an adjunct to diplomacy.

All this is, of course, elementary. But if I felt in 1961–62 that wider and greater understanding of intelligence and secret operations was desirable and even necessary in order that the requisite support in public opinion for those activities be forthcoming, twenty-five years later I feel that the wheel is again out of balance.

There is too much attention paid by the public to the fascination of secret operations—perhaps as a result of that deluge of literature on the subject—and too little to the primacy of diplomacy in the conduct of our foreign relations. The Executive is too much absorbed in the possibilities offered by secret operations, and not enough in the elaboration of effective diplomacy. The Congress's suspicions of the CIA have too much to do with observance of the Legislature's prerogatives and not enough with ascertaining an appropriate balance between diplomacy and secret operations. The interview with Michael Beschloss cited above went on: "You can get some help from human espionage, but that's a weak reed. Each side needs a very subtle understanding of the other's decision-making process, its interests, ambitions and anxieties." That is in the province of diplomacy.

It is appalling to compare the penury characteristic of our representation abroad, such as the closing of important American consulates around the world, with the capabilities of our secret establishment. In the 1940's and 1950's the Congress couldn't do enough for the CIA—or little enough for the State Department. Bit by bit functions of the State Department were eroded and transferred to the CIA, communications, cartography, and some foreign management operations among them. The imbalance, conceptual and functional, persists. (Even today, the old "cookie-pusher" image of diplomacy, so dear at one time to the American media, lingers in the halls of Congress, particularly among very conservative Members, and colors votes on the resources to be devoted to it. The saying in those same halls is that foreign affairs have no constituency, a belief shared, to judge from the actions and attitudes of the great majority, even by the millions of Americans who owe their livelihoods to our export industries.)

It is appalling to realize that the total expenditures of our diplomatic establishment amount to two-tenths of one per-cent of the Federal budget. The failures of conception and execution in this domain, of attention and values, that the relevant facts and figures reveal cannot be laid at the door of one or the other of our political parties, or the Congress or Executive alone. The fault, of long date, is bipartisan and shared by the two branches of government—and the public. Who will right the wheel?

—James McCargar

1. For some of the prior revelations of my own identity, see Patrick Seale and Maureen McConville, *Philby: The Long Road to Moscow.* London: Hamish Hamilton, 1973; Nicholas Bethell, *The Great Betrayal.* London: Hodder & Stoughton, 1984; Henry S. A. Becket (Joseph C. Goulden), *The Dictionary of Espionage.* New York, Stein and Day, 1986 (name misspelled and professional affiliation—CIA—wrong); Charles Gati, *Hungary and the Soviet Bloc.* Durham, Duke University Press, 1986; Robin W. Winks, *Cloak & Gown, Scholars in the Secret War 1939–1961.* New York, William Morrow and Company, 1987.

2. And then shadows can last long in the valley. One example: When I had been a mere twenty-five years out of intelligence and secret operations, a tyro in international affairs who, as an academic, had written one good book of domestic history, and then, astride a giant ego, rode into Washington and the bright glow of foreign relations (where his own light ultimately faded), decreed my exclusion from private work of lively interest and promising opportunity with the dictum, "We can't use him. He's an intelligence officer." Neither the first nor the last time.

3. Bill Colby, Director of Central Intelligence 1973–76, in his memoirs gives a slightly different version of the status of OPC: "The matter [of secret political operations] was put to Truman. He agreed. In June 1948 the National Security Council issued Directive 10/2 authorizing the CIA to undertake secret political and paramilitary operations. A special unit, euphemistically entitled the Office of Policy Coordination (OPC), was set up to carry them out, under the direction of the Secretaries of State and Defense with the Director of CIA. . . . Frank Wisner . . . was named to head it. . . ." (William E. Colby and Peter Forbath, *Honorable Men: My Life in the CIA,* New York, Simon and Schuster, 1978, p. 73.) The difference between this and my version (we were informing and consulting the Joint Chiefs of Staff from the earliest days of OPC) lies in the role of the Director of CIA. Colby came to OPC after I had returned to more standard diplomatic functions in the Foreign Service. In the period while I was at OPC, then-Director of CIA Admiral Roscoe Hillenkoetter was not consulted by Frank Wisner. The Director of CIA only assumed what was to be his commanding role with the entrance on scene of General Smith.

4. Those considering a career in either the Foreign Service or the CIA should be aware of dangerous shoals. Navigational skill consists in avoiding the cross fire between two organizational monsters. During one difficult passage in my affairs, long out of the government and without pension rights, I sought relief on the basis of my past services. The Director of Central Intelligence wrote to a senator who had kindly taken an interest in my problem: "Mr. McCargar worked at the CIA . . . but he was actually on detail from the Department of State. Hence, this does not give us any basis for qualifying him for retirement privileges. The closest he came to

working for us was when he was employed by [Free Europe Committee] . . . but his employment there does not meet the tests of federal employment. He was the employee of what has been decreed by the Civil Service Commission Board of Appeals and Review as a nongovernmental entity . . . I wish we could help . . . but I'm afraid it's out of our hands." Two months later, when the State Department also refused any assistance, a journalist whom I had known well in Hungary approached a panjandrum of the Division of Foreign Service Personnel, suggesting something ought to be done. The official replied, "It is the CIA's responsibility, not ours." When it was pointed out to him that the CIA has said I should address myself to the State Department, and that I was thus being whipsawed between the two organizations, his answer was, "That may be. But that is our position." And so it has remained to this day.

INTRODUCTION
TO THE FIRST EDITION

The techniques of secret operations are as old as the human race; they are by no means diabolical inventions of the Russians or symptoms of a human spiritual decline. The intensity of their application in the past fifteen years is simply the result of the principal form taken by the historical conflict of that period. But it was only in 1960, with the U-2 case, followed by the failure of the American-directed Cuban invasion in 1961, that the secret war, and the American part in it, came actively to American popular attention. Until then, general American awareness of these operations, at least in comparison to other people's, had been remarkably slight. Understanding was largely limited to surface impressions gained from melodramatic films, spy thrillers, and surcharged memoirs. Secret operations were mostly viewed as an exotic growth, something that went on elsewhere, certainly not a part of the daily atmosphere and facts of American life.

How many Americans have seriously had to consider to whom they would turn in exile or how they would behave under occupation? These questions, closely related to some aspects of secret operations, have been part of the practical, daily thoughts of every resident of at least all of Europe and Asia, more than three-quarters of the human race, at some time—or times—in the last thirty years, and for centuries before that.

It was two defeats that brought, not without shock, some sense of the scale, prevalence, and importance, even gravity, of secret operations to the attention of the American public in 1960 and 1961. Discussion and comment were widespread. Nowhere, however, in the public prints—with the exception of a few analysts who singled out political ineptitude in the Cuban operation—have I seen good, competent, constructive understanding of the reasons for these failures. A man who had some responsibility in the Cuban operation said to me afterward that while there was plenty to criticize, and plenty of criticism, he had yet to read one American critic who displayed even an elementary knowledge of the conduct of such operations, of the type which would produce a valid commentary useful to a public which he admitted had every right to be concerned. This may perhaps be an exaggeration; but it would seem fair to state that naïveté in these matters is far from unusual among Americans.

It is of no benefit to those responsible for American secret operations that partial ignorance or lack of understanding of the principles of these operations should be characteristic of the public. Quite the contrary. An at least elementary public awareness and understanding is a positive asset. A public more sophisticated in these matters is less prone to ill-conceived and purely emotional reactions in the event of error or failure. The Cuban operation warranted vigorous criticism, but a sometimes deliberate, sometimes merely ill-informed confusion of moral, morale, policy, and technical questions could not clarify specific error; it could only complicate the general unease.

It is my impression that every American failure in the secret war which could be qualified as serious—and serious is to a considerable extent synonymous with publicly known—has either been caused or compounded by those responsible ignoring or brushing aside the classic principles of secret operations. So much for those directly responsible. But the citizen has a responsibility too. It is in no way connected with knowledge of the details of any specific operation. It is connected with, at the minimum, a general awareness that these operations are being conducted, in his name and on his behalf. Such an awareness, if accompanied by a basic understanding of the principles governing secret operations, produces further understanding of precisely why such operations must remain secret. Such understanding is the prerequisite to a tacit but still essential public support for these vital operations. It also gives the citizen the possibility of seeing more clearly the world conflict around him; it enables him to recognize more easily the true content of Soviet maneuvers in the field; and it helps to insure that his reaction in the event of failures is a direct response to the facts of the case, not a misguided emotional outburst to be exploited by either demagogues or the enemy.

It is the purpose of this book to contribute to such an understanding.

This is neither a scholarly treatise nor a historical survey nor a textbook. It is simply a record of my own recollections, experiences, impressions, reflections, and conclusions resulting from some sixteen years in secret operations, all in the service of the United States, and in a variety of countries and organizations. It is my hope that from this informal collection there will gradually emerge for the reader that understanding of the principles of secret operations which is the purpose of the book. Beyond that, it is my hope that, from the personal opinions, criticisms, and comments which occur throughout, and for which I take sole responsibility, the reader will gain some idea of the hard realities and problems which face those responsible for these activities. Lastly, it is my hope that the unconventional perspective from which this book is necessarily written will contribute, however indirectly, to that most desirable objective, the American's realistic understanding of himself and of America's place in the world.

Because secret operations deal with the relations between men, they are a subject as complex as man himself. The most important single fact to be borne in mind about them is that everything concerning them is relative. There are no absolutes. There are, however, certain classic principles which reflect centuries of experience in secret operations and which are in turn applications of historical human insights into human nature. But precisely because secret operations involve the application of human insights into human nature in constantly shifting and changing circumstances, these classical principles can never be observed to perfection. They are ideals which the professionals of the secret war forever seek and never find. Compromise, invention, adaptation govern their decisions and actions. But the measure of their competence and skill is the degree of their perseverance and success in bringing their compromises, inventions, and adaptations to a relative approximation of the classic principles.

The explanation of secret operations is complicated by the obvious fact that nothing can be said which will give the enemy some information or advantage he does not already possess. The appearance of this book under a pseudonym is therefore less for my own protection and convenience than to safeguard certain existing operations with which I was associated in the past. Throughout Part I —which discusses the generally recognized categories and aspects of secret operations—and Part II—a detailed account of a particular operation in which I participated, being a concrete illustration of the complexity of the work—I have used true names and places wherever possible. Where that has not been possible, I have tried to maintain the pertinent point or principle, while altering the names, personalities, and circumstances involved. The reader will appreciate that it is one of the rules of the game that I cannot say which is true and which is false.

PART 1

Fundamentals and Forms of Action

VIENNA 1956

At 3 o'clock Sunday morning, November 4, 1956, I returned to the hotel in Vienna where I had been staying for three days. I paused to leave a call and exchange a few idle words with the hall porter. Nostalgic early morning music from the radio behind the telephone switchboard echoed through the empty lobby. I went to my room, and within a few minutes after getting into bed, was asleep. At five minutes past 4 the telephone rang. Switching on the light, I reached sleepily for the receiver, my brain stumbling through possible reasons for a call at such an hour. It deliberately side-stepped the possibility that was all too real.

Knowing but discreet, the hall porter's voice came through to me. "Sir," he said, "there is an emergency broadcast coming from Hungary. Imre Nagy, the Prime Minister, is speaking. I thought you would be interested. Just a moment, I'll put the telephone next to the radio." And so I lay in the Vienna night and listened to the voices of Nagy and interpreters announcing, in terse and stricken but courageous tones, that the Russians had attacked Budapest at 2 o'clock that morning. They were recordings, made less than an hour before, and were repeated continuously in Hungarian, Russian, French, English, and German. I turned cold; I continued to listen, stunned, hoping for a word that it was not true. Over and over, the Magyar accents repeated the brief and terrible announcement in the five languages. I lay there, picturing the columns of Russian tanks advancing through the darkened streets, firing mercilessly into the crowded apartments, into the proud and poignant city only four hours' drive to the east—a city I had known well.

The porter's voice brought me to my senses. I thanked him, put down the receiver, and considered what I had to do. The answer was nothing. As the Russians well knew, if anyone had fomented the

*Hungarian Revolution of 1956, that astounding moment of truth
shared by a whole people, it was the Russians themselves and their
handful of Hungarian servants. We, the Americans, had had nothing to do with it. In the two weeks since its eruption, the United
States had substituted baffled wonderment for a policy, and was
headless besides: the President was campaigning for re-election; the
Secretary of State, who carried foreign policy in his hat, had had to
temporarily hang it up while undergoing surgery; the Department of
State was being run by a first-rate petroleum engineer. The Russians, it must be said, were equally baffled; they hesitated and vacillated. The night's news meant that they had finally estimated the
American reaction—correctly, as it turned out—and had therefore
found a policy—now being put into effect with the guns of the Red
Army.*

*My own purposes at Vienna were simple enough. The political
operations in which I was engaged concerned Hungarians outside of
Hungary, and my principal tasks had to do with the tens of thousands of Hungarian refugees pouring over the border into Austria.
So far as events in Hungary were concerned, my mission was purely
that of an observer; if a contact should develop with the new Hungarian revolutionary regime, I would maintain it while seeking new
instructions. Indeed, only eight days before, an exiled Hungarian, a
former very high postwar politician and Cabinet Minister, had told
me that he had telephoned Budapest and spoken to members of the
new Imre Nagy Cabinet, who had said simply, "Speak for us in the
West. Make them understand our neutrality." I had assisted this
man then to travel to Vienna, not with the intention of his re-enter-
ing Hungary, but only so that he could be in closer contact with his
colleagues and compatriots now in the Government. He had, on
arrival in Vienna, been immediately deported to Switzerland on, of
all things, the representations of the American Ambassador to Austria. I had, therefore, on my own arrival in Vienna, sent word to one
of his henchmen who was now somewhere in Hungary carrying a
letter from the former Minister to the leading non-Marxist political
personality in the new Government.*

*There was nothing I could or need do about this courier. I tele-
phoned to a post near the Austro-Hungarian border, where I learned
only that the border was still open, refugees were still crossing, and
that the sounds of heavy gunfire could be heard on the other side,
from the direction of Györ, the nearest large town. That done, I
think I briefly lost my reason. A boiling rage overcame me; it was as*

*though a fever swept through my brain. I did not curse the Russians
—I seemed to feel almost that I knew them too well for that. I did
not rant at our own impotence—the American Government seemed
to me somehow pitiful and irrelevant at that moment, hardly to
blame for its troubles. My anger instead was vented upon the British
and French, whose adventure at Suez I wildly blamed for giving the
Russians the pretext for their action in Hungary. I swore, in a kind
of momentary delirium, that I would never again set foot in France
or England, I would devote myself to exposing their monstrous cynicism in sacrificing Hungary for Suez, and so on. (Secret agents are
not necessarily coldly unemotional, and the secret agent's objectives
are to him, necessarily, of paramount, and highly personal, importance.) None of this had anything to do with the facts, of course. The
British and French operation at Suez was conceived and prepared
well before the Hungarian Revolution of October, which took the
British and French, as I well knew, as much by surprise as it did the
Russians and Americans. I realized all this in the morning, after a
few hours' sleep—and I also remembered the past, which did much
to explain the seizure which had overcome me in the night. But the
preface to that story of the past is—a short course in the secret war.*

CHAPTER I

The Secret War

At the end of the Second World War the American public generally
felt that the fighting was over. Postwar problems were recognized
to exist, but they seemed, to most Americans, to involve such
things as rehabilitation, economic questions, some political negotiations—but nothing of conflict. Organized mothers' groups in 1946
cornered the Chief of Staff of the United States Army—later to
become President—in the halls of the Capitol, preventing him from

attending Congressional hearings while they demanded he "bring
our boys back home." In the same period, the largest mass-circulation magazine in the country exulted in an editorial entitled "The
American Century." The mood was one of a problem definitely
solved, and of power. But the secret war had already begun.

The power was real, even if the mood was contradictory and in
some respects reckless. But power in human affairs has its own
organic characteristics. It both attracts and repels. In either case it
inspires an underlying, even subconscious fear. This effect cannot
be dissipated by protestations of peaceful intent or even by good
works. It can ultimately be truly dissipated only by a relative
change in the balance of power. The great American postwar success, the rebuilding of Europe, was not a success simply because it
demonstrated that we did not intend to use our power to infringe
on the independence of European nations; it was a success precisely because it eventually and genuinely restored to Western Europe a measure of the power, political, economic, and military,
which was almost exclusively ours in 1946. The Western European
nations feared our power then, but for historical, ideological, and
political reasons they feared that of Russia more. They were therefore, on balance, attracted to American power.

For the same reasons, the Russians were repelled by our power.
In the light of their particular ideology, it was perfectly clear to
them that with the destruction of German and Japanese power, the
United States became the principal foe of the Soviet Union and its
Communist allies throughout the world. It is of no moment that a
man trained in Western logic would distinguish at this point between a potential and an actual foe. The so-called doctrine of ultimate consequences is basic to Communist logic. Under this doctrine it is not merely legitimate, it is politic and necessary to treat
an unconverted man (or a nation) in the present as though he
already were what he is potentially capable of being in the future—
namely, an active enemy. This kind of thinking owes less to Marx
than it does to professional, universal military doctrine. The genius
of Lenin—even if it was, from the viewpoint of Western civilization, a regressive genius—was to reverse Clausewitz's famous "War
is a continuation of politics by other means," and to apply to politics, both national and international, the doctrines of war. Lenin
was perfectly well aware that this was a step backward in civilization, but he justified it in terms of the class war. He was also in
theory aware that to treat a potential enemy as an actual enemy is

ultimately to make him an active enemy, but he was blind to the full relation of this cause and effect in practice since Marx's fulminations, Russian terror, and Western error had steeled him to see his aspirations surrounded by a hostile world in which only the doctrines of war could prevail.

Thus, as the defeat of the Axis became certain, the Soviet leaders adopted—certainly not in sorrow but neither with any particular rancor; one might say almost automatically in response to the dictates of their analyses of history—the view that the power of the United States and its allies, but especially that of the United States, was hostile to them. This "new line" was by no means as hidden or obscure—and certainly not as new—as one might have thought. In June of 1945, immediately after the victory in Europe, and while preparations were just getting under way for some combined Soviet-Allied operations against Japan, I was obliged, as an American intelligence agent, to report to Washington that the Party agitators in Soviet factories had begun a "new line" emphasizing the fundamental hostility of the United States to the Soviet Union. At that moment, to avoid too quick a turn in view of the wartime alliance —never overpopularized in the Soviet Union, but nonetheless an undeniable fact—the story was that with the death of Roosevelt, the great friend and defender of the Soviet Union, the American capitalists had a malleable tool in the person of President Truman, and fears were expressed as to future American policy toward the Soviet Union. Every subsequent irritant in Soviet-American relations could thus be presented to the Soviet masses as an evidence of the predicted American hostility—or be taken by the Party leadership, as with the abrupt termination of Lend-Lease, as confirmation of the correctness of their own policy.

Besides his estimate of America as the enemy, Stalin had in mind his own projection of Soviet and Communist expansionism. In this sphere he could only forecast that U.S. policy would become actively hostile to Soviet expansion at some point; what he did not know was where that point lay. The Russians therefore set themselves two tasks: one, the probing of Western policy to see how far they could expand Communist gains without encountering applied superior power; the other, the whittling down of Western and especially American power. Not only was that power, in their eyes, too great and menacing to be endured, but its reduction coincides absolutely in time and space with the world triumph of Communism, which their ideology teaches is inevitable, however long it may be delayed.

The probing operation continues. It takes place openly—in diplomatic conferences, in summit meetings, in conflicts such as the Korean War, in crises such as Berlin and Cuba. It is the overt confrontation of power.

From the Soviet point of view, their other principal task, the attrition of American power, takes place in two ways. The first is overt. It is simply as rapid an increase in their own power as their energies can produce. They allot the minimum consistent with the maintenance of internal stability to consumer goods; they insist on a high rate of capital investment and of economic growth, all in the interests of greater economic power. Their own absolute increase in power means a relative decrease of American power. This is obviously also true of their military establishment. Their timing and publicizing of space exploits is simply a ready means of impressing the world with their own absolute increase in power, and all the better if it also demonstrates an increase relative to the United States. All of this, however, is within the confines of their own state and economy.

The second method for reducing American power takes place outside of the Soviet state. Its primary objective is to reduce American power in the rest of the world. Its secondary objective is to substitute Soviet power for American power whenever possible. The techniques of this method are many: espionage—to reduce the advantages of Western technology and military secrecy; political and psychological warfare, as in the Peace Campaign or in the struggle for dominance over the international labor movement or over newly independent states; the fomenting of civil strife—known as paramilitary operations or unconventional warfare—in areas buttressed by American power, as in Laos or southern Vietnam. These techniques all have one common denominator: they are secret operations; they avoid the open confrontation of power. They are conflict behind a curtain, so to speak, the curtain being the tacit acknowledgment of both sides that the open confrontation of war is undesirable. This conflict consists of the secret operations of the Soviet Union, its allies and partisans, and of the United States, its allies and partisans. Winston Churchill christened it the Cold War.

Churchill's phrase has popularly been taken to describe a state of mind, an attitude of nations toward each other, characterizing the years since the end of the Second World War. It is clearly more than that, being also the secret maneuvers and conflicts which are the real and predominant content of the Cold War. These secret maneuvers and conflicts—the secret war—are not the products of some mysterious black art. They are complex, but they are also an ancient, universal, and continuous part of human behavior. Athens had countless troubles with Persian- and Spartan-instigated subversive groups in its allied and tributary states, not to mention the ideologically pro-Spartan oligarchs of Athens itself; Metternich's chief of intelligence daily pieced together and read the contents of the wastebaskets provided for foreign delegations at the Congress of Vienna in 1815; from the French point of view the American Revolution was originally a secret operation against Great Britain. And so it goes in our day: Soviet agents arrested in the West, Western agents uncovered in the Communist empire; move and countermove in Germany, in Iran, in Guatemala, in Vietnam, in Laos, in Cuba—and countless other places unmentioned. The twentieth-century state, eyes on the stars, drags neolithic man on into a schizophrenic future.

The purposes of secret operations are those of state, but their substance is the relations between people. This basic fact is obscured primarily by the secrecy of these operations; it is also obscured by the existence of a professional lingo which—like all technical language—is used by professionals for greater precision and misused popularly to the confusion of the layman. I make free use herein of the term "secret operations," for example, not only because it is generally understandable, but also because it is a generic term embracing sharply different forms of secrecy: it covers a multitude of sins. These forms of secrecy which pertain to secret operations have nothing to do with the classifications of secrecy used by Government departments: Top Secret, Secret, Confidential, Restricted, etc. These latter are merely designations indicating, in general, what groups of people shall have access to the specific information so labeled. The forms of secrecy are fundamental to secret operations and pertain to the techniques by which secrecy will be established and maintained. Thus something overt can be secret, and anything covert or clandestine is—or should be—secret, but something secret is not necessarily covert or clandestine, and anything clandestine is decidedly not covert and vice versa. Anyone who has managed to work his way through that is entitled to an explanation.

In secret operations the meaning of "overt" is not only "open and visible"; more importantly, it also signifies that the person or activity is in fact what he or it is stated to be. This does not mean that secrecy is absent. The United States Navy is exactly what it says it is, the marine arm of our military establishment. But its war plans, many of its ship movements, even in peacetime, and countless other aspects of its equipment and operations are secret, that is, knowledge about them is restricted in varying degrees. More to the point, the Central Intelligence Agency, our principal arm in the secret war, has overt personnel and functions, even though virtually all of its activities are secret. The CIA is required by published statute to prepare the national intelligence estimates for the National Security Council. The personnel who do this work are overtly employed by the Agency, but the preparation and the estimates themselves are secret. Similarly, the Director of the Central Intelligence Agency and his two principal deputies are overt officials, although responsible for our secret operations.

The identity of the American CIA Director's British counterpart, on the other hand, is secret, and is withheld from all except those needing to know. The West Germans have come up with an unusual variant on this in the fact that the identity of the head of the German service, General Gehlen, is known, but only a handful of authorized persons, including but a few of the personnel of his own organization, know him by sight as such; he appears in his identity of General Gehlen only to this small group, a practice made easier by the reported fact that there is only one very old photograph of him in existence. This is not to imply that either the British or German arrangement is necessarily superior to our own; it was long ago decided that the British solution was not adaptable to our form of government and public life, and the German case is largely a fluke resulting from the chaos and confusion of the German defeat and the deliberately self-effacing personality of Gehlen himself. The desire for anonymity and the exercise of great power without public recognition are not generally characteristic of the American personality or system.

Interestingly enough, the Soviet arrangement, although differing in important respects, corresponds more closely to the American than to the British or German solutions, at least to the extent that the Committee on State Security is an overt organization and its chairman's identity is known. The French, on the other hand, tend to resolve the problem more in the British fashion. They admit, as the British do not, the existence of an overt organization—the Service de Documentation et Contre-Espionage, which is attached to the office of the Prime Minister—but they neither publish nor publicize the identity of its director. It will be seen from these arrangements that, in secret operations, while the various combinations of overt and secret reflect the different national circumstances, that which is overt is in even lesser proportion to that which is secret than the visible part of an iceberg to its underwater mass.

Of even greater importance to secret operations than the resolution of the problem of what may be overt and what must be secret is the distinction between clandestine and covert. Both are secret, but in different ways.

Let us suppose that the United States is faced with the problem of sending an agent who is a communications expert to join anti-Castro guerrilla forces in the mountains of eastern Cuba. (The illustration could quite as well concern a Soviet effort to send a similar agent to Iran, a similar British problem in Iraq, a Communist Chinese problem in Malaya, and so on around the globe.) If this agent was sent aboard a United States Navy submarine which surfaced in the dead of night off a deserted beach on the northeast coast of Cuba, where, by prearrangement, a small group of guerrillas met our man as he stepped ashore from the submarine's inflatable raft and conducted him to the safety of the mountains—this would be a clandestine operation. That is to say, its secrecy depends upon skill in utilizing natural circumstances to hide the operation, to render it invisible to the enemy. There is no effort to disguise the operation; it is secret only because it is hidden, but it is exactly what it appears to be. There is obviously a very large element of chance in any clandestine operation; a patrol passing the beach at an unforeseen time, a fishing boat coming upon the scene unexpectedly, any of a number of possible circumstances could destroy the operation's secrecy—and the operation.

A covert operation would attempt to minimize precisely this element of chance. If our communications expert posed as a foreign agronomist, complete with false identity papers, entered Cuba with Cuban Government permission, and, while on a tour of the eastern provinces, vanished one day into the mountains—this would be a covert operation. Skill is also a vital element in the secrecy of such an operation, but its most important element, and its distinguishing feature, is the use of a cover—in this case the agent's pose as a foreign agronomist. A covert operation is visible:

no effort is made to hide it from view; the major effort is to disguise it. It is not what it appears to be. In brief, the working distinction between the two forms of secrecy is that a clandestine operation is hidden but not disguised and a covert operation is disguised but not hidden. Covert operations constitute the major part of the secret war, and cover, which is discussed elsewhere at length, is probably the most important single technical element in secret operations.

Obviously neither type of operation is easy, but certainly a clandestine operation is less difficult than a covert one. By the same token, a clandestine operation is considerably more risky than a covert one. Most operations are in fact, however, a combination of clandestine and covert. To pursue our communications expert further, let us assume that, having safely landed on his beach and met the conducting party, the problem is then to reach the safety of the mountains. To travel at night would risk arousing greater suspicion —and thus greater risk of investigation—if a patrol were encountered. Accordingly, the party waits until daylight to set out, and when it does, our agent is dressed to look like a *campesino,* making his way with his companions from one village to another. At this stage he is covert, even if not perfectly so. Our foreign agronomist, on the other hand, has the advantage of his cover right up to the moment when he joins the guerrillas—caught at any point prior to this, even in making contact with the guerrillas, he has a valid cover of merely studying the soil and terrain—but once with them, and a part of their activities, he is clandestine, as are the guerrillas themselves.

The fact is that while covert operations are generally more desirable for their lessening of the risk of discovery, all covert operations invariably have some moments, however brief, when the cover does not logically hold and when they are therefore clandestine. The important point is to recognize these moments with the utmost clarity as being clandestine and to hold them to an absolute minimum, for these are the times of greatest danger. It is for these moments that the enemy is watching.

While both types of secret operations are used in war and in peace, clandestine operations are more numerous in wartime and covert operations are the common form in peacetime. The reason for this is that the consequences of discovery are generally greater in conditions of peace than in war. From the viewpoint of the individual agent, of course, the maximum consequences are the same—usually death or imprisonment, depending on the objectives and particular circumstances of the operation. But the purposes of secret operations are those of state, and for the state the consequences of discovery can be vastly different. When British aircraft during the Second World War dropped agents by parachute in German-occupied France or Poland—clandestinely—their discovery by the Germans did not affect the relations between Germany and Great Britain. An act of war, a hostile act, in wartime is but another item in the openly acknowledged contest to alter the balance of power. A clandestine act, because it involves the state, is considered a hostile act, and a hostile act in peacetime can, and usually does, disrupt in greater or lesser degree the complicated fabric of relations between states. In effect, the Soviets refused to have any further dealings with the American Administration after the U-2 affair—a consequence which was fraught with danger for the entire world.

Accordingly, states have recourse in peacetime to the greater security afforded by covert operations. Their greater security does not lie only in the fact that they minimize the risk of detection or of involvement of the state. They also benefit from a tacit agreement between states, itself the sum of long historical experience, whereby covert operations are recognized as a peacetime avenue of action which, when used, will not upset international apple carts.

The very reasons for which states undertake covert actions reinforce this tacit agreement. The reasons are various. It may be, as in espionage, that the national security requires it, and the mission can only be accomplished covertly. It may be, as in most covert political operations, that effectiveness would be nil if it were generally known that the activity had its origins in or support from a foreign government. It may also be, as in the support given to paramilitary operations, that the activity is considered necessary but is not consistent with existing friendly official relations; or, most importantly, the activity would, if undertaken overtly, risk bringing into play forces which would either defeat the mission or seriously alter the international political balance.

These reasons have, in the past, been traditionally understood between states; the covert operations which stem from them have been tacitly accepted as providing each state with the flexibility they need for self-protection. From the national point of view, at least between states of relatively equal power, the result is a sort of mutual back-scratching arrangement. From the larger point of view, the arrangement has a solid and useful foundation: it permits the pursuit of constructive, progressive policies on the overt level while preserving, on the covert level, the national safety and interest intact until more idealistic overt policies have produced concrete international results. In this light—and it is the light they read by—the Soviets fully comprehend the seeming contradiction between our own support of the UN and our support of the 1961 Cuban invasion. The rude noises Khrushchev made at the time of the Cuban invasion were in fact addressed, not to our support of that operation, but to the fact that our involvement in it was clandestine, not covert.

This politic understanding between states, it might be noted, also has a broadly beneficial effect in wartime. At a time when overt policy is necessarily harsh and publicly inflexible, covert operations provide an avenue for probing for more realistic and less costly accommodations. Thus, American covert operations centered in Switzerland during the Second World War succeeded in bringing about the German surrender in Italy contrary to Hitler's express orders, with a great saving in life and property.

This tacit agreement among governments, reached over thousands of years of experience, to let each other more or less off the hook is based, however, on the strict observance of another tradition. While a clandestine operation must, by definition, be recognized as hostile, a covert operation's patent hostility can be ignored by the victim who uncovers it only if he receives the co-operation of the author of the act. Here is the origin and sanction, even sanctification, of the established custom of silence, or at most of flat disavowal, by the responsible government when a covert operation has been uncovered.

This is one explanation—whatever others there may be—of Khrushchev's rage when, even with the talkative U-2 pilot Powers in his hands, he stated publicly his certainty that President Eisenhower was not personally responsible, only to have the President publicly avow his responsibility. For, in the professional context of the secret war and covert operations—and if nothing else Khrushchev is a professional—avowal of responsibility has a specific meaning. It is interpreted by the enemy as a threat, since it means, in the context, that the avower not only ignores established custom, but also the basis of that custom, which is the maintenance of the international political balance. The avower therefore puts himself in the position of demonstrating indifference to the international political balance; his avowal may even be taken to imply that he intends to change it by any and all means.

Even the manner of avowal also has a specific international meaning. It is not necessary to make a public statement. The use of airplanes in the American operation against the Arbenz Government in Guatemala—surely one of the most flamboyant in history —was a clear revelation of United States backing and participation. It was my understanding at the time that several CIA officials had argued vigorously against the use of airplanes—even to the point of tendering their resignations—on just these grounds, but that their arguments were overruled at Cabinet level since it was desired to make clear to the Soviets that we would not hesitate to use any means to destroy Communist bridgeheads in this hemisphere. It would seem in this latter case that the warning conveyed in this implicit avowal didn't take.

But then, covert operations are not a way to convey international warnings. Avowal of a covert operation, however implicit, is a hostile act, and it is wise never to indulge in hostile acts unless one is able and prepared to back them up. Or, as the Russians say, "If you say A, you must be prepared to say B." And, as we might say at this point, if you are going to meddle with the classic principles which govern the secret war, don't be muddled.

I have no doubt that some American muddling in these matters stems from a certain defensiveness in the face of Soviet aggression in the secret war, a kind of "We don't care if we are hostile, you were hostile first" attitude. Such an attitude can lead to a certain irresponsibility in the conduct of secret operations, and, more importantly, by alienating important foreign opinion, reduce the effectiveness of many of our operations addressed to that opinion. This plays into the hands of the Soviets and their propaganda allegations. It is true that the tacit convention which eliminates covert operations as a valid cause for war is largely based on historical practice with respect to intelligence and counterespionage operations. But the secret war today includes a great deal more than just espionage. It includes a vast range of political operations, running a gamut from simple propaganda operations, through enormous world-wide movements designed to capture the loyalties and support of peoples everywhere, to paramilitary—sometimes called unconventional or guerrilla warfare—operations in critical areas.

It is likewise true that the blame for this situation today, the spread and intensity of the secret war, rests squarely on the Soviets.

Although other Western nations were more realistic than ourselves, the United States had no permanent, peacetime, unified intelligence organization until 1946, when the Central Intelligence Group was created as a bridge between the wartime OSS and the Central Intelligence Agency which was established the following year. Even the Central Intelligence Agency was limited initially to intelligence functions. As General Marshall reportedly said when Secretary of Defense, "I don't care what the CIA does. All I want from them is twenty-four hours' notice of a Soviet attack." (The twenty-four hours is now down to fifteen minutes—or less.) The United States had no organization of any kind for the conduct of political or paramilitary operations until one was hastily assembled, within the CIA in late 1948, after the Communist *coup d'état* in Czechoslovakia. Nevertheless, it is precisely in this area of secret political and paramilitary operations that the Soviets have decided that their greatest opportunities lie. While much of American overt policy—the rebuilding of Europe, support of the United Nations, the Alliance for Progress, a world-wide chain of military alliances —is aimed at lessening the secret war, this is not enough. The Soviets have long since chosen—and give no evidence of having altered their choice—to challenge us by means of the secret war. To ignore it would be folly; to lose it could be fatal.

The secret war has, of course, both offensive and defensive aspects. The two are naturally inseparable, but all governments, as a practical matter, distinguish organizationally between the two. The offensive aspect is embraced by the term "secret operations"; the term "security" covers the defensive aspect. The principles governing the conduct of the two are identical. Nevertheless, an administrative separation between the two is universally employed: activity inside one's own country—largely, of course, defense against the enemy's operations—is defined as security, and the responsibility therefor given to security agencies; one's own operations abroad, however, are by definition offensive, and the responsibility for them is entrusted to a separate secret operations agency. In the United States the division is between the FBI—domestic security—and the CIA—foreign intelligence and operations; in Great Britain between MI-5—sometimes operating behind the cover of, but not to be confused with, Scotland Yard—and MI-6; in West Germany between the Office for the Protection of the Constitution and the Gehlen Organization; in France between the Ministry of the Interior and the SDECE. In Communist countries the administrative separation is not so rigid, but generally speaking the domestic functions are performed by the Ministry of the Interior—in the Soviet Union by the Committee on State Security, since the reorganization of the secret police following Beria's downfall—and the foreign functions by Military Intelligence.

Whatever the administrative separation may be, it is generally difficult to observe, and is in many countries a source of intense internal friction. Many offensive operations abroad, particularly political operations, must be based at home. Furthermore, both domestic and foreign intelligence services have overlapping interests in foreigners on the national territory. In the case of foreign intelligence or political operations uncovered on the home territory, there are frequently even sharply conflicting interests.

The defection some years ago of Otto John, head of West Germany's Office for the Protection of the Constitution, to East Germany was felt by many observers to have been largely a result of his defeat in a power struggle with General Gehlen over conflicting interpretations of responsibility within West Germany. During the Second World War the American FBI was even granted certain responsibilities abroad—notably in Latin America—while the OSS was to operate in active theaters of war. (While it antedated the creation of the OSS, it is a fact that the first foreign intelligence report I ever read was an FBI document reporting on a prewar high-level Nazi dinner in Berlin.) Such frictions are by no means absent from American operations. In 1949 there was a noteworthy performance in the city of Washington itself in which a continuing difference of opinion between the FBI and the CIA over the disposition to be made of a Soviet defector resulted in an open brawl between the two in a public restaurant where the Russian was dining.

Since the principles and techniques of the secret war as waged abroad and at home, offensively and defensively, are the same, however, and since my own experience has been in the offensive aspect of that conflict, this book centers almost exclusively on the secret operations conducted by nations outside their own borders. It is, indeed, the present high level of activity in this sphere, rather than the automatic reaction of increased defensive activity by domestic security agencies, which is the distinctive mark of today's secret war.

But there is nothing historically new in today's situation of aggression in secret. History is dotted with similar periods of intense secret conflict in preparation for, in conjunction with, or separate from open and conventional warfare. The only novel factor today is mutual recognition of the prohibitive cost of open, nuclear war. But this merely reinforces, granted the expansionist aims of the Soviets, their decision to proceed by means of the secret war, to apply Leninist doctrine to international relations. In brief, they accept the tacit convention concerning covert operations as applying far beyond mere espionage, and they have studied, expounded, expanded, and refined the techniques of secret operations in order to apply them to international political and social conflict. In this they have proved, so far, peculiarly adept. There is no reason, however, why the distinction should remain permanently theirs.

CHAPTER II

The Power of Secret Knowing

A distinguished Englishman, then the chief of His Britannic Majesty's secret services, once showed me, with justifiable pride, his extensive library on secret intelligence and operations. With wry amusement he chose an ancient volume, which turned out to be the journal of one of his predecessors, the secretary to Sir Francis Walsingham, who was, besides his many other duties, in charge of intelligence for Her Majesty, Queen Elizabeth the First. Opening the book at random we glanced at an entry in which this gentleman, almost four centuries before, noted: "I today went out and hired me a base fellow." He then went on to record the "base fellow's" duties, which were quite simply to inform on a particular group of his fellow subjects.

Although the officer's terminology is today archaic, something of his attitude remains with us. Those who inform in secret, those who are not what they appear to be, those who accept hospitality

in order to probe the weaknesses by which the host can be brought
to his knees, those whose true purposes are masked behind a tissue
of lies and stealth—all such people generally inspire what we take
to be a certain repugnance. In America it is usual to identify this
repugnance with morality: to feel thus is to be a moral person. The
story of the parent punishing the child who tattles instead of the
culprit is almost—but unfortunately not completely—a relished
part of American folklore. The story has often been recounted of
Henry Stimson's cold reply when, as Secretary of State, the American codebreaking operation was explained to him. "Gentlemen
don't read each other's mail," he said, pushing aside the pile of
proffered telegrams.[1]

Regretfully, I must demur from the viewpoint that this repugnance is an evidence of moral quality in the person experiencing it.
It is, in modern man, no more a sign of a moral attitude than the
apparent contempt for his hireling reflected in the phraseology of
Good Queen Bess's police chief. Resentment and dislike in both
cases, yes, but in neither case caused by anything so reassuring as
moral or social superiority. On the contrary, it is the very need for
reassurance which provokes the assumed superiority. For what the
informer or secret agent really inspires in us is fear.

Historically, in every age, in every kingdom, in every state, informers have played a key role as one of the means by which rulers
have maintained their power over the ruled. In ancient Athens
there existed an entire class of people who made their living and
were entitled to some important privileges by virtue of being informers; their existence and their privileges were a principal bone
of contention between the democratic and oligarchic factions, but
they were still used even in the periods of democratic rule. Byzan-
tium, Renaissance Italy, Stuart and Puritan England, the Japanese
Shogunate—all contained a similar class. Great as was Napoleon's
power over France at the height of his career, it was thoroughly
consolidated by an enormous network of informers established by
his redoubtable minister of police, Fouché, often described as the
founder of the modern police state but, historically speaking, far
from an innovator. As an English journal described the situation in
1887, "In the absence of 'informer' evidence, the great majority of
cases would fail for want of legal proof." Today, in the United
States of America, if you denounce your neighbor to the Treasury
for income tax evasion, you will receive a negotiable percentage of
what the Treasury collects. Every American municipal police force

in any town or city of size is dependent in large measure on informers. The FBI assiduously adds to its files, both criminal and political, by means of informers. Whether used to reinforce the police power or political power, informers are a universal prop to authority.

Culturally, the memory of the days when political power was greatly dependent upon informers lingers in our civilization. Even without the living example of the technique offered by modern Communist states, we are all instinctively fearful of the informer, the secret agent. Whether we know our history or not, our particular civilization remembers, with unspoken fear, that the informer, the man operating in secrecy, is a threat to every man's life and physical freedom. To be denounced is to run afoul of authority; to run afoul of authority is to be exposed to the cost and the caprice of justice—and justice, at its best human and imperfect, is always, to greater or lesser degree, but one aspect of the established political power.

Resentment against the informer and secret agent is not only a matter of historical memory. Any organized society is intolerant of those who set themselves apart from the prevailing norms. Any group's major rewards are reserved for those who most wholeheartedly accept and most vigorously personify the group's ideals. Psychologists, sociologists, and philosophers have abundantly remarked the similarity between the position of the artist and that of the criminal in any society. What the two have in common is the fact that they set themselves apart from society; they are by nature skeptical of its ideals, of its morals and interests; they arrogate to themselves the right to reject the established code and to live by their own. It is human nature to resent such independence, even arrogance. This resentment is the price the artist pays for the independent point of view which nourishes his art; punishment, the active expression of this resentment, is the price the criminal pays for his attempt to achieve the society's aims by asocial means.[2]

The secret agent is akin to both the artist and the criminal. His techniques are similar to those of the criminal: they are illegal or antisocial. His point of view is similar to that of the artist in that he does not accept—at least after sufficient experience he should not—the society's myths about itself. He is prone to see the society from a distance, to exploit its customs and relationships for ends which are not part of its publicly avowed ideals. While the secret agent's work gives him a valuable opportunity to see from a broader, more realistic, even if harsher perspective, he is nonetheless a man apart. We sense this, and we are disturbed by it. The fact that the secret agent in effect abuses the habits and relations of our society with the sanction, however secret, of established authority, only adds resentment to the disturbance. He is a species of legal criminal; his connection to sources of power only reinforces the underlying human reaction that he is not only a man apart, but a privileged one at that. He adopts the stance of the artist or criminal, but by a special dispensation of the powers-that-be, he is exempted from the normal risks of such behavior. This cannot help but strike us as unfair and abnormal.

The secret possessor of information produces a feeling of unease in us for an even more fundamental reason than the political history or social organization of the human race. It is simply that in any situation of human conflict information is power. Blackmail, that is, the exercise for personal advantage of the power conferred by information about another's wrongdoing, is only a crude and specialized expression of this power. The power of one man over another by virtue of superior information extends far beyond the special situation of the wrongdoer. This power is an element in every situation of human competition or conflict.

The businessman's assets are not limited to his inventory and his holdings of cash and securities; they include notably what he knows about his competitors. The responsible lawyer before entering into negotiations studies every available source for information on those whom he will be confronting. Indeed, the American business community alone generously supports a number of enterprises whose sole function is purveying information about persons and corporations. The employer telephones concerning a prospective employee: "What do you know about him?" The suitor who knows his rival's plans is thereby enabled to forestall them. The general preparing an attack must know the relative strength of the forces opposing him. It is worthy of note here that the student who steals the questions for his examination is not in fact making use of the axiom that information is power. The axiom is true of situations of competition and conflict; the student by his action shows that he has misinterpreted a situation of long-term competition with his fellow students as being a temporary one of conflict with his professor. His secret and misdirected action to uncover what is in his professor's mind is of no avail against the long-run competition of his fellow students. The principle, "Know your enemy," has a double meaning.

By and large, for information to be power it must be secret. (The qualifying "by and large" covers the instances where the opponent has not, so to speak, done his homework: he has not prepared himself for the encounter or marshaled his resources in the most efficient manner. In this case, he is by definition in an inferior position and has, in effect, abandoned the contest.) Our businessman whose assets include what he knows about his competitors also has liabilities which consist of what his competitors know about him. But what he knows they know about him is not a liability; that much he can take into account in estimating and meeting competition. What he does not know that they know about him, his resources, and his plans is precisely what they can use against him, to outwit and outmaneuver him. The rival of our suitor, knowing that his next maneuver has been given away, can alter it. If the defending general does not know that the size and state of his forces are known accurately by the enemy, and he sees no reason to reinforce or regroup them, he thereby confers value on the attacker's possession of that information. This is basic to all human competitive activity or conflict. Therefore, for a fundamental human reason also, the secret agent, the informer, provokes in us a feeling of unease. We do not know what or how much he knows.

Fundamental as these reactions may be, they are not, of course, the entire story. Other pressures tend to produce quite opposite reactions, particularly in our own times. A trace of envy of the supposed ability of the secret agent to cast aside established conventions and relationships is apparent in the fiction about private detectives and in spy thrillers. Romanticized, melodramatic, they are first cousins of the Anglo-Saxon legend of Robin Hood, the Teutonic Til Eulenspiegel, and Islam's Nasreddin.

The ideological content of the secret war today—which resembles nothing so much as the European religious wars of the Reformation and Counter Reformation—plus the enormous growth in population have brought the prestige of the state to bear on the question of informing. The theory is advanced, and supported by all the power of the state, that it is the duty of every citizen to inform. This is official doctrine even in the United States, although it is by no means clear that every American citizen has wholeheartedly accepted it. I have been, of necessity, many times approached by the FBI, or by other security agencies, about various of my fellow citizens. I have each time accepted the official view that it was my duty to speak fully; but the only times that I was ever able to do so without an underlying feeling of discomfort were when I realized that I was in a position to help someone unjustly under suspicion—a far from infrequent occurrence. Informing to the FBI is still in America a matter of individual conscience. It is not clear whether this is still so when the investigating body is a Congressional committee and the issue is the denunciation of other citizens. But the pressure of official morality is on the side of informing, and it is probably accepted by the majority of Americans at this stage.

More important, however, than either escape fiction or official morality as counterweight to an instinctive negative reaction to the secret agent is the age-old principle, "It depends whose ox is gored." This principle succeeds in polarizing and simplifying the matter, so that my agent is a hero and yours is a villain. Attitudes within the nation toward the "base fellow," the police informer, the FBI informant, the Senator's secret source in a Government department, the bank's confidential investigator, the private detective for hire, depend on to whom you talk. Discussing this subject, a former vice-chairman of the Democratic National Committee told me that his ouster from that post had come about because another faction in the party had subverted his secretary with money—so that all his confidential correspondence was betrayed. He had finally become philosophical about it, but it took years for his rage to subside. On the other hand, one of the most imperturbably jolly men I ever knew was a man who commanded a six-figure annual income because his confidential connections in the U.S. Government were such that he could inform his clients in private industry of the details of their competitors' plans and contracts.

Among nations, in the international secret war of our time, the problem is even more simplified. Here, it is the sacred cow of nationalism that decides whose ox is gored. This standard of judgment is inculcated early. Every American child exposed to American history knows the story of Nathan Hale, the Connecticut militia officer who volunteered to go behind the British lines disguised as a schoolmaster in order to provide General Washington with information about British forces on Long Island, and who was caught and hanged by the British. American children also know about John André, the British officer who, on behalf of General

Clinton in New York, secretly negotiated the agreement with Bene-
dict Arnold to deliver West Point into British hands, and who was
caught and hanged by the Americans. Concerning these two secret
agents, a leading American encyclopedia phrases the opening sen-
tences of the entries under their names as follows: "Hale, Nathan;
1755–76; American patriot in the American Revolution," and
"André, John; 1751–80: British spy in the American Revolution."
At the same time, few British children have ever heard of Nathan
Hale, and Major André is commemorated in Westminster Abbey.

The arrangement is emotionally very practical, since it allows us
to separate the conflicting elements in our ambivalent attitude toward the secret agent into "good" men and "bad" men. It is also
useful in guiding popular feeling into support for the state. Thus,
many Western observers commented unfavorably on the virulence
of the prosecutor and of the Soviet press during the Moscow trial
of Francis Gary Powers, pilot of the U-2. On the other hand, a
judge trying an accused Soviet secret agent in New York in the
summer of 1961 stated in court that "conspiracy to commit espionage is analogous to mass murder," a remark the press reported
entirely without comment.

This simplification into melodrama is avoided by the professionals of the secret war. It is neither a lack of patriotism nor of determination to win, but a simple recognition of the facts of international life, an unwillingness to underestimate their tasks, and a
desire for precision which lead them to use a different terminology
from that employed by public orators, prosecuting attorneys, and
mystery writers. Thus the words "spy" and "enemy" are not used
among professionals; they become, respectively, "agent" and "the
opposition." And there is in this certainly a tacit, even if precarious, mutual respect which is the universal mark of competing professionals. This mutual respect should not, of course, be confused
with any code of chivalry; the basic theory of this kind of conflict
begins with the premise that no holds are barred.

The possibility of isolating and identifying a class of professionals in this type of conflict is a unique feature of modern times. The
conflict itself, its techniques and maneuvers, are as old as mankind
because they are an intrinsic aspect of human relations. Before the
end of the eighteenth century, these skills were part of the attributes of every man concerned with public affairs. The famous description of Jefferson— "a gentleman . . . who can plot an
eclipse, survey a field, plan an edifice, break a horse, play the vio-

lin, dance the minuet"—could, if applied to almost all of his peers and contemporaries, have included "and conceive and execute a secret political intrigue." Benjamin Franklin and Silas Deane, among Jefferson's American contemporaries, distinguished themselves in this field. And to this day, the bribes and clandestine intrigues of Don Bernardino de Mendoza, Ambassador of Philip II of Spain to the court of Henry III of France, who—by playing on the ambitions and avarice of the Duc de Guise, the selfishness of Catherine de Médicis, and the Parisian Catholic mobs' suspicion of the Huguenots—insured that France would be so embroiled in internal strife that she could make no move either to aid the English against the assault of the Spanish Armada or to endanger the exposed Spanish flank in Flanders, remain a model of a successful combined secret intelligence and political operation. In effect, an important military victory, however temporary, was won for Spain without a single Spanish soldier ever being involved.

Ambassadors today are often expected to obtain similar results; they are enjoined, however, from using Mendoza's techniques. A division of labor in this, as in all other fields, has developed whereby only a particular group of people work with these tools. These are the professionals of the secret war. These professionals are not limited to officials and agents of the Central Intelligence Agency in the United States, of MI-6 in Great Britain, of the Service de Documentation et Contre-Espionage in France, of the Gehlen Organization in West Germany, of the State Security agencies in the Communist countries, or of their numerous counterparts in other governments around the world. The circle is larger and more flexible than that. To be sure, these official employees constitute a core—and, in our day, a bureaucratic growth—among those who may be termed professional. But beyond them anyone who at any time has had to master in action the techniques of secret operations against a stake involving his life, his freedom, or his livelihood must also be counted a professional.

Such mastery is not necessarily a matter of formal training. All governmental secret services maintain training divisions and schools, but mere exposure to their courses does not make a professional. The man must be tried. The fact that I was myself some eight years actively engaged in secret operations before I was finally dragooned into a training course does not of itself prove the point. However, the successes of the American Abolitionist underground in the mid-nineteenth century are a persuasive example, as

were the various European undergrounds organized during World
War II. In these resistance movements there were neither time nor
facilities to train the thousands of men and women who entered
into clandestine life. Some died learning, some had a natural talent,
some learned and lived—all were professionals and remain such,
whatever their later work. The experience, if genuine, and however
gained, makes a professional and marks a man. The Director-General of the French Sûreté once remarked to me apropos of some of
his own more lurid Resistance experiences that he did not believe a
man could fully understand our age unless he had spent some time
in prison. The remark is not inapplicable to secret operations.

The individuals who work inside the circle of secret operations
share one thing in common: a conscious awareness of their purpose
and function. Beyond this, however, there are great differences,
individually speaking, in degree of knowledge and in function. So
far as degree of knowledge is concerned, the scale is hierarchic:
that is, the man at the bottom of the hierarchy—in theory—knows
the least; the man at the top—again in theory—knows the most.
Information is power in this context too. The reason that this hierarchic arrangement does not work perfectly in practice is because
secret operations, while secret in their conduct and techniques,
deal with the relations among human beings and are therefore accessible or visible to the correct perception. After a certain amount
of experience has been gained, a competent agent develops this
perception; he knows in principle what secret operations are being
conducted, and he can often recognize them in fact and detail
when he himself is unconnected with them. To compensate for this,
as well as to protect information from too wide a dispersion, compartmentalization—only a bureaucracy could have invented such a
word—is standard practice in all secret services. This is simply the
organized application of the principle that an individual may know
only that which he needs to know for the performance of his own
tasks. In a secret intelligence operation, for example, the ideal—
not often achieved—is to limit any individual agent's knowledge of
the identities of other agents to one only, or, at a maximum, two.
This minimizes risk, safeguards the secrecy which makes information power, and confines broad knowledge to a relatively small
concentration of persons at the very top of the hierarchy. In this
sense, the oft-used simile which likens secret operations to an octopus is especially apt.

The tentacle of an octopus has no organ enabling it to know

what the other tentacles are doing, and yet it does not act independently. A single brain guides the movements of all the tentacles, co-ordinating them by means of nerves and muscles. The muscles of the octopus of secret operations are the ingredient of discipline in the human relations of the personnel of the operations. If this discipline—the muscle—is ineffective, obviously the operation—the tentacle—is defective. However, what constitutes effective discipline in secret operations is not the same as the military version of this quality; it is described in detail in the next chapter.

The nerves, however, must be visualized as a chain of knowing, in which the sensitivity or electric impulse which determines the function of the nerve is represented by the control of knowing. By control is not necessarily meant the limitation of knowledge; this is the function of compartmentalization. Control means simply knowing who knows what. It is important in secret operations for the reason that a man possessing certain knowledge will behave differently than if he did not possess that same knowledge; he will also have a different understanding or conception of himself and of the circumstances surrounding him.

This is obviously not true to the same extent of all kinds of knowledge, or even of the same item of knowledge in all circumstances. The knowledge of Hopi Indian lore would not particularly affect an American agent working in Poland, but his knowledge of the identity of every other American agent in Poland would be a dangerous risk for all the other agents, besides endowing him with undesirable power and possibilities of action. A more concrete example was the Allied invasion of Normandy. Everyone in the British Isles in 1944 knew there was going to be an invasion; only a specifically authorized few—the "bigoted"—knew the date or place; and even fewer knew both. And no one knew either or both without having that fact recorded in a central register—which is a more than usually formal version of control. When Hitler contemplated the invasion of the Soviet Union, the German Ambassador to Moscow was kept totally in the dark until the attack had already been launched. Knowing the Ambassador's sentiments against such an attack, Hitler and Ribbentrop well knew that he could not perform his task of allaying Soviet suspicions if he possessed the knowledge. Again control.[3]

To some extent this matter of control is one of the functions of counterespionage. However, it is also a daily ingredient in the work of anyone engaged in secret operations. It can become a passion.

One of my colleagues, directing an operation in which control was one of his principal preoccupations, gave a vivid example of how far this passion can go. An associate, coming into his office one night to work, strolled across to his window before switching on his light. Looking across the courtyard, he saw my colleague, in his office, locked in passionate embrace with his secretary. Reflecting but a moment, the observer went to his telephone and dialed the appropriate number. Regretfully relinquishing his secretary, my colleague answered his telephone, only to have the voice of the unseen observer say, "This is God speaking. Aren't you ashamed?" As my colleague later confided to a friend, he finally broke off the relationship with the girl, since all he could do when with her was worry about the fact that he didn't know who knew.

Neither discipline nor control, of course, are the object of secret operations, any more than mere motion is the object of the octopus's movements. The octopus seeks food; secret intelligence operations seek information. The information sought is by no means limited to that concerning actual or potential enemies, although that is of primary importance. Relations between states, even in an organized bloc such as the Soviet Union and its satellites, always have sufficient elements of conflict and competition so that information about each other always has value. One measure of the degree of friendliness in relations between states is the quantity and type of information they make readily available to each other. Even among the closest allies, however, there is information which is withheld—and therefore sought. If it is withheld because it would adversely affect relations, then it is of value as revealing negative elements in those relations. If it is withheld as a prerogative of sovereignty, an exercise of independence, the very reason suggests that the information is power. And in the case of a friendly but not allied state, there is always the added attraction that a mutual friend can often tell you much about your enemy— even if he is also performing the same service for your enemy with respect to you. Nevertheless, secret operations between allied friendly states are usually held to a minimum, and the greatly preponderant effort is to find out about the enemy—actual or potential.

The information sought about the enemy concerns his capabilities and his intentions. It is much easier to find out about capabilities than it is about intentions. The difference is that between poker and chess. In poker that which is hidden is the strength of the opponent. His intentions play no part in the game, which revolves around guessing or deducing his strength—his capabilities. Thus the characteristic play in poker is the bluff—the masking of capabilities. In chess on the other hand, the opponent's strength is on the board, readily visible. The game centers entirely on the opponent's intentions, and the characteristic play is the feint—the masking of intentions. In poker the player wants to know what cards his opponent holds; in chess he wants to know what moves his opponent intends to make with his visible resources. Obviously, of the two, intentions are of much greater importance, since from them flows action.

Intentions, however, are so difficult of access that a major role of diplomacy is simply to analyze intentions. Secret operations seek to reinforce the analyses of diplomacy with concrete information.

One of the constant dangers to national destiny—and to international peace—is the fact that military doctrine resorts to an extrapolation of intentions from capabilities, based on an underlying assumption that intent is always hostile. In its simplest form, this means that if a man has a gun, he intends to shoot you; *ergo,* if you find out that your neighbor has a gun, either you get a bigger gun or you move out of the neighborhood or you force him out of the neighborhood or you shoot him first. This is indeed the proper way to run an army, but far from a responsible way to guide the destinies of a whole people.[4]

Accordingly, a greater value attaches to the information concerning enemy intentions which is produced by secret operations than that concerning enemy capabilities, provided, of course, that information on capabilities is at a reasonably satisfactory level. Before and during the Second World War, one of the favorite problems of all secret operations travelers on the Trans-Siberian Railroad was whether the Soviets had built a tunnel under the Amur River at Khabarovsk, where the railroad crosses the river on a highly vulnerable bridge. The interest stemmed from the fact that if there was no tunnel, and the Japanese destroyed the bridge in the event of hostilities, then the Soviet Maritime Provinces to the south, including the port of Vladivostok, would be cut off from Soviet supplies. If there were several foreigners on the train, you could usually tell who of your fellow travelers were connected with secret operations: even if the train crossed the river at 4 in the morning, there would always be a few strollers about in the corridors, peering with bland bafflement into the murk, trying to distin-

guish a likely-looking spur track. (I reported the tunnel was built,
but I don't know to this day whether I may not have been looking
at a false entrance. The Soviets knew about all those early morning
risers too.) Nevertheless, this information, interesting as it might
potentially be, could not compare with the immediate and more
important value which attached to my report in 1945 on the
changed line taken by Communist Party agitators in the Soviet
factories, as but one indication of inimical Soviet intentions toward
the United States.

When all this information has been gathered, however, the job of
secret operations is by no means finished. Secret information is
indeed power, but it is only power in a situation of conflict or
competition. And in such a situation, power is meaningless unless
it is used, either implicitly or directly, to achieve desired goals. In
the secret war those goals are the fulfillment of national policies;
they require the adaptation of secret intelligence operations techniques to political conflict.

This adaptation encounters serious obstacles, however. Every
secret operation produces information; a purely political operation
—a youth festival, for example—also produces information and
depends for its execution upon information. On the other hand, it
is almost never that an intelligence operation is without political
effect or implication. This interrelation of information and politics,
of information as power, and the use of that power, is one of the
major problems of secret operations. Ideally, the two should be
divorced—but they cannot be. The great majority of secret intelligence operations at some point utilize an agent, or numbers of
agents, whose purpose in the operation is political: they are against
somebody or they are for something. At the same time, the purely
political agent is to information as flypaper to a fly. Furthermore,
the adaptation of secret operations techniques derived from intelligence operations to political operations is hindered—at great cost
to the political objectives—if the philosophy and techniques of information for information's sake govern. Similarly, it is out of the
question to engage in secret intelligence operations on a purely
political basis.[5]

In the 1961 Cuban affair, for example, it was impolitic—to put it
mildly—to attempt the political overthrow of Castro with Right-
wing Cuban politicians; it would likewise be inefficient to limit our
intelligence sources about Cuba to Center or Left-wing Cubans. In
the one case the political objectives are gravely jeopardized; in the

other, possible valuable information is rejected. Nevertheless, the national interest requires that we use all three. How to reconcile them? Particularly when a Left-wing politician, co-operating in a political operation, objects to the use of a Right-wing politician in an intelligence operation as implying political support for the latter —an interpretation favored and probably even expounded gratuitously by the Right-wing politico? This problem in secret operations is inevitable and eternal. No secret service has solved it perfectly yet. In the United States, unfortunately, the solution has weighed predominantly on the side of information for information's sake, to the great detriment of our political operations, our power, and our prestige. The problem will be examined in detail elsewhere.

1. According to a letter from Louis Kruh in the January 1986 issue of *Foreign Intelligence Literary Scene,* McGeorge Bundy, Stimson's biographer, replied to a query about this quotation with the statement that he "had checked the book [where the quotation first appeared] closely, and he now concluded that 'it [the use of single quotation marks around the quote in the Stimson-Bundy book] means that Colonel Stimson used that description of his thinking in his discussions with me' when we were preparing the book." In short, the quotation appears to be considerably ex post facto. A 1954 letter from Herbert Hoover on the subject says that Stimson explained that he had to denounce telegraphic intercepts "in order to preserve his relations with various embassies," and that he, President Hoover, "took no part in this matter. It was the Secretary's responsibility to conduct his department." Whatever Secretary Stimson's words at the time, he *did* close down the American "Black Chamber" in 1929.

2. This is a curious paragraph. Where it ran somewhat off the track, I think, is the point at which it began the comparison between the artist and the criminal. The original point, resentment against the informer and secret agent, is valid. Certainly there is resentment against the criminal. But it is difficult today to discern "resentment" against the artist for his independent outlook—except among those Mencken labeled the "booboisie," and the lunatic fringe who decorate some areas of our public life. The final statement gives it away: clearly, the criminal is not attempting "to achieve the society's aims"—except as the aim of amassing riches happens to coincide with a number of individual aims in the society.

3. This discussion of "control," valid as far as it goes, is at fault in omitting any mention of the social or political implications of control. It is one thing, for example, for Hitler and Ribbentrop to withhold from their Ambassador at Moscow their intent to attack the Soviet Union. It is quite

another for the Chief of Staff of the President of the United States, or the President's National Security Advisor, to withhold vital information affecting foreign policy from the Secretary of State—or, let us face it, for the White House to make a fool, if not a liar, of Adlai Stevenson before the Security Council of the United Nations with respect to the Bay of Pigs action. The health of constitutional government depends very largely on observance of democratic procedures, onerous as they frequently are in foreign relations.

4. It is only fair to quote at this point from a review of this book by a Commander Robert E. Bublitz, USN, then on duty in the Foreign Intelligence Division of the Office of Naval Intelligence, in the July 1964 *Proceedings* of the United States Naval Institute: "From a critical point of view, there are a few points with which the military reader might disagree. The assertion that 'military doctrine resorts to an extrapolation of intentions from capabilities, based on an underlying assumption that intent is always hostile . . .' might, for instance, provide the basis for a warm debate. Frequently, those with long service in the civilian branches are wont to aim an occasional indirect slap at the 'military.' Mr. Felix is no exception, but he criticizes the deficiencies of civilian policy and working-level types more directly . . ."

5. This dichotomy is as lively as ever—as those dealing with Afghanistan, El Salvador, Nicaragua, and sensitive spots in Africa and the Middle East in the Eighties certainly must be able to attest.

CHAPTER III

The Spy and His Master

In likening secret operations to an octopus, it is clear that the tentacles are made up of the chain of human relationships linking the direction of the operations to even the most remote agent. The muscles guiding each tentacle are, in turn, made up of the responsiveness, the discipline, which characterize each of the relationships in the chain. Of all these relationships—which include, of course, auxiliary services such as logistics, communications, and administration—there is one which is at the very heart of secret operations. It is the critical relationship, dictating in many cases the success or failure of the operation. It is that between what are called—in American terminology—the agent and the case officer.

It is the agent who acts and who is directly in touch with the enemy, the "opposition." The agent is exposed and visible; he operates "outside." The case officer directs the agent. He is invisible and works only "inside." The relationship between these two is the bedrock of all secret operations. Most human and organizational connections in secret operations can, in fact, be defined basically in terms of this one fundamental relationship. It is possible, for example, to visualize the entire "inside" establishment of the CIA as constituting a collective case officer and all those "working" outside as making up a collective agent. Such an image, while accurate, is meaningless, however, because it does not convey any idea of the variety, complexity, and individual elements which govern the relationship.

What is involved here is the ability of the case officer to insure that the agent's actions advance the objectives of the operation, that none of the agent's actions hinders the attainment of those objectives, and that the agent exerts his best efforts. This clearly requires domination of the agent by the case officer. The possibilities of this domination are reinforced at the outset by the fact that the case officer represents the authority which defines the objectives of the operation, and he controls the resources which make the operation possible. But woe to the case officer who relies only on these two elements to achieve his mastery. In doing so he immediately forfeits the confidence of the agent as well as his essential willingness. These two elements are implicit in the relationship, and if the relationship is properly developed in human terms, their explicit use should not be necessary, or can be kept to a minimum.

It is just here that an American weakness occurs. Time and again I have seen American case officers resort to cutting off funds to enforce discipline over an agent. One effect of this maneuver, if successful, is ultimately to reduce the agent to the status of a mere pensioner. In espionage operations this can, and often does, result in highly unreliable information; in a political operation it can be fatal. As one disgusted Cuban exile said of the CIA after the Cuban affair, "They have no idea how to work with political allies. They think in pennies."

Often this matter of funds is permitted to become an irritant in the relations between the case officer and agent simply because of American suspicion about money and fear of being victimized. Whatever may be the public impression of what the CIA does with its vast unvouchered funds, the fact of the matter is that behind every case officer is a squadron of bookkeepers and accountants, sniffing hungrily for a wrongfully diverted penny.

One highly qualified agent not many years ago worked out with the Americans a complex political operation which included considerable mailing, for which he was given a specified budget. His headquarters were in an American cover organization and, early in the operation, before he had actually received the promised funds, he had to absent himself for ten days. He told his secretary to continue the mailings, using the organization's postage meter and keeping a record of postage as obtained. In his absence a book-keeper complained of his unauthorized use of the postage meter and immediately, without any opportunity for explanation on the agent's part, the case officer was required to cancel the operation. Funds were never even granted for expenses, fairly considerable, already authorized and incurred. When the agent told me this story, almost a year later, he was still paying off the debts with which this episode had saddled him. He was not enthusiastic about working with Americans; as he put it to me, "In your system every bookkeeper is a comptroller, and every agent is required to be a bookkeeper."

Often also the American difficulty with the agent and case officer relationship is simply a reflection of the bureaucratic approach to problems and the disproportionate influence of the fetish for administration in American operations. I was once charged with the planning and direction of the American part of a combined Anglo-American operation, similar in nature to the Cuban operations, but smaller and more tentative in scope. (It also failed, with some loss of life, but at least the failure was not public.) While I was still casting about for the most qualified personnel—the area was fairly exotic, and very few Americans were at all acquainted with it—I was summoned to a conference in Washington. On entering the room I remarked an intricate organizational chart on the wall. One of my colleagues—I didn't know he was even interested in the operation—rose and then started his discourse by pointing to the chart and saying, "I have now worked this all out, and, as you will see, you need 457 bodies for this operation." He then spoke for forty minutes, without ever once even mentioning the country with which we were concerned. I confined myself to remarking that I didn't think we could find 457 "bodies" and that I would happily settle for six brains.

By way of contrast, I went to London a week later and observed the British approach to the same problem. After sitting around a table in desultory fashion for an hour or two, one Englishman finally said, "I say, why don't we get old Henry up here? He knows about this." A day or two later old Henry showed up from down in Sussex, and when the problem was put to him, finally agreed to undertake the task, although, as he said, "This will wreak havoc with the garden, you know. Just getting it into trim." He then added that he would do it only on condition that he could have six persons, whom he named, and that they be responsible solely and directly to him.[1]

Apart from the purely personal elements in the relationship, one of the principal tools in the case officer's hands for establishing and maintaining his dominance over the agent is greater knowledge. He has, after all, national resources of information behind him, and he must use them. One of the most brilliant agents I ever "ran"—as the professional saying has it—was a Rumanian Socialist who had certain definite objectives of his own. My interest in him had to do with his usefulness in the international Socialist and labor movements; his consuming interest, however, was anticolonialism. His very brilliance made him difficult to control, and his initiative in pursuing numerous of his own objectives could have involved me in activities which I had no intention or authority to support. I achieved a certain balance in our relationship, however, by dint, not only of heavy reading of dossiers, but also by talking at every opportunity with people who had known him in his early life, long before we became associated. In this manner I accumulated quite a store of information about him, which he did not suspect. Occasionally, when reminiscing, he would discuss some incident in his early political life. At these times I would invariably also adopt an air of reminiscence—not of knowingness—and exhibit as detailed a knowledge as possible of the time and persons of whom he spoke, usually capping it off by some misinterpretation of his own role in a particular event which would require him to explain, to excuse, or to deny. The point was made. When, therefore, in order to present me with a *fait accompli*, he embarked on some delicate negotiations which he knew very well I did not desire, and about which I heard

only by the sheerest accident, no lecture or confrontation was necessary. Over a drink I brought the conversation around to the
objective he was pursuing, and then merely remarked that the negotiations which he had undertaken were bound to result in failure.
He never knew how I knew; it was sufficient that I did. He made
no excuses, but tacitly accepted the seeming—but actually dubious
—fact that he could not get around me. Accordingly, he brought
the subject out in the open, argued its merits, and ended by acced-
ing, even if reluctantly, to the point of view I was required to
express. Every case officer must have a bit of Stephen Potter's
Oneupman in him—but it is best to be able to back up a ploy.

Obviously the case officer's authority, at least vis-à-vis the agent,
must be unassailable. This means ideally that the agent's contacts
with the organization should be limited to the case officer only.
This is usually possible in espionage operations, but in political
operations it is much more difficult. In many American political
operations the agents—even if they are political allies they are still,
in the terminology of secret operations, agents—are often in touch
with several persons in the CIA, as well as with appropriate policy
officials in the State Department. The possibilities of end-runs in
such a situation are endless. Whatever may have been his other
difficulties, in this respect one can only sympathize with the position of Richard Bissell, the CIA deputy director in charge of the
1961 Cuban operation, and his aides, when it is realized that the
members of the Cuban Revolutionary Council had simultaneous
access to Adolf Berle, Jr., in the State Department and Arthur
Schlesinger, Jr., in the White House. In a quite different type of
operation, I once had the ground cut out from under me very
effectively by just this kind of multiplicity of contacts. Following
an exploratory conversation with a prospective agent, the agent
was dissatisfied at the conditions I posed, under instructions, for an
agreement, and called several days later at the State Department.
He mentioned my conversation to an official there, who quickly
replied, "Mr. Felix's conversation with you was unauthorized."
Whether the official merely intended to rebuke his caller for mentioning something the official could not properly admit to knowing,
and did so clumsily, or whether he intended to sabotage the operation, I never found out; I had no choice but to quit the operation.

However imperative the need for the case officer to dominate the
relationship with the agent, there are major and intrinsic obstacles
to his doing so. For one thing, the relationship is not that between

employer and employee, particularly in political operations, nor is it the military one between superior and subordinate. In its theoretically ideal form the case officer would be master and the agent servant. The case officer would define the objectives, and the agent would obey unquestioningly, his skill completely—and successfully —at the disposition of the case officer. Obviously, no human relationship attains such barren simplicity. The military system is an attempt to approach such a relationship, but every new officer in a military service soon learns that it is not sufficient merely to give an order for leadership to be real and effective. How much more so is that true in secret operations, which exist in an unrecognized sphere, a sort of tacitly unobserved shadow world which is nonetheless starkly real, and in which the generally accepted constraints and values of conventional relationships do not apply. And how even more true is it in the case officer-agent relationship, in which the unavoidable fact is that it is the agent who acts. To this extent every agent is a free agent. The case officer can neither be present at the action, partake of it, nor supervise it on the spot. A man thus dependent upon another is not in an intrinsically good position to dominate their relationship.

This basic problem is intensified by the fact that communications between the case officer and agent are frequently highly tenuous: there may be long intervals between meetings, or communication may consist of no more than occasional radio signals. In a great many cases even where liaison is more immediate than by radio, personal contact between case officer and agent is rare or nonexistent. Where it is nonexistent, contact is maintained by "cutouts."

A cut-out is a person, also an agent, who acts as intermediary between the case officer and his agent. Cut-outs serve one or both of two valuable functions. They permit oral contact between a case officer and an agent when actual physical meeting would be excessively dangerous and written communication undesirable. They are also used in situations where it is desired that the agent not know the true identity or even appearance of the case officer or principal agent. It not infrequently happens that even the cut-out does not know the true identity of either agent or case officer. In one case in my own experience I was saved great embarrassment by the fact that the agent had no knowledge of the true identity of either myself—as case officer—or of the cut-out. Some months after giving him some money and a mission—via the cut-out—this agent defected to the Soviets. Thanks to the cut-out device, all he could inform the Soviets was that a man he knew only as "Mike" gave him money and instructions on behalf of a man named "Ray" whom he had never seen. No great loss.

When conditions permit, the cut-out may be a device such as a "drop," a person or place by means of which written communications can be safely exchanged without personal contact. Drops are an opportunity for real ingenuity: a classic device involves sending a theater ticket to the agent; his neighbor, sometimes the case officer, more usually a cut-out, then exchanges documents with him in the darkened theater, often without a word passing between them.

Where personal contact is dangerous or impolitic but nonetheless imperative, resort is had to the "safe house." The safe house is a place where personal contact can be made under circumstances and precautions which minimize risk. Brothels were at one time traditionally favored as safe houses; nowadays, however, they are professionally regarded as booby traps, the inmates usually having been corrupted by the police into becoming informers.

A further difficulty in the relationship stems from the recruiting process. The fact is that as often as not the initiative comes from the agent. He proposes a course of action which he is, or claims to be, equipped to carry out. In effect, he is offering a special skill. This gives him some bargaining power; he can negotiate, even if only within small limits. In the operation in Hungary which is described in Part II of this book, the entire escape chain worked through one agent who proposed to me its organization—at a time when he could well guess that I must have been casting about for such a mechanism. He could accordingly negotiate with me the conditions under which we would work together; my sole initial card in playing out our relationship was my ability to turn down his proposition—certainly not in my own interests. The agent's ability, in the case of his own initiative, to bargain, rather than defer to commands, rests on his uniqueness, real or alleged.

If, on the other hand, the initiative comes from the case officer, who has presumably made a choice of the best available and possible person for the mission, the agent's uniqueness is immediately conceded and underscored. He has even more leverage than the agent who takes the initiative. If the case officer permits himself to feel uneasy about these basic facts, if he handles them awkwardly in an attempt to suppress them, the relationship can be overburdened with duplicity from the outset. In place of the confidence which should characterize it, both case officer and agent are in danger of behaving like a pair of irascible spouses, each trying to impress the other with his greater indispensability to the relationship—to the detriment of its true purposes.

There are ways, of course, of overcoming some of these initial advantages of the agent. American practice has achieved a certain sophistication over the years in this respect. Faced with a specific task, the CIA will usually make a considerable effort to determine who is the best qualified man. They will then study the man's chain of friendships, and more often than not it is possible to reach one of the man's friends in such a manner that, if he does not do the recruiting himself, at least the official who does so approaches the prospective agent with the benefit of the friendship. Another tactic is to overwhelm the prospective agent with rank; an approach by a "high official" is not only flattering to the vanity, but is an implicit mark of confidence.

Unfortunately, American practice may be well conceived but often falls down badly in the execution—in this as in so many related fields where what matters is not so much what you do but how you do it. A friend told me he had finally refused to arrange any more contacts for the CIA because, in too many cases, having been importuned by the agency to speak on their behalf to some important friend, the CIA either never followed through or spoke once with the man and left him awaiting a further word which never came. Another friend, whom we shall call Frank, recounted to me his own experiences in this regard. He had worked in the CIA for several years and had left—in a far from satisfied frame of mind. Nevertheless, about three years later he was approached and asked to act as agent in an operation which would have meant completely altering some urgent and, to him, vitally important plans. He explained his difficulty but said that he would be willing to undertake the operation anyway in view of the importance they seemed to attach to his participation, adding only that he must know definitely about it within two weeks. He heard nothing further, ever. But about two years later he was at a cocktail party in Washington, talking with a Cabinet officer, when Allen Dulles, Director of the CIA, walked up. The Cabinet officer turned to Mr. Dulles and said, "Allen, you know Frank, don't you?" Mr. Dulles responded heartily. "Why, of course I do," he said. "I've been trying to get Frank back into our work for the past five years." As

Frank, later explaining to me his stupefaction, said, "I guess the explanation is simply that it's a very big organization." He added moodily, "At least, I hope it's no worse than that."

A further basic difficulty in the case officer-agent relationship is the question of objectives. The case officer has usually received his objectives from above; they are expressions of national policy or interest. As such, they are also subject to change. The agent, on the other hand, has generally defined his own objectives; his service is for the purpose of accomplishing certain aims which are of personal merit to him, and his objectives are less flexible. An agent is chosen for a particular operation because of his abilities to achieve the case officer's objectives. But it is a rare occasion when the purposes of the agent who possesses the necessary abilities are identical with those of the case officer. Some coincidence there may well be, but in that case the case officer has to reflect carefully on whether the agent's purposes other than those which coincide with his own might not be the source of conflict at a future crucial moment. A community of interest may also exist, but the very phrase requires that the case officer weigh the possibility of achieving his objective against the fact that in a community of interest specific objectives and means must usually be negotiated. Negotiation there must be, and most often is, but it is never without some cost to the case officer's ability to dominate the relationship and the operation. What the wise case officer seeks is an agreed reconciliation of purposes.

To accomplish this, however, he must know as much as possible about the agent and all of the agent's aims, but people do not often go about openly proclaiming all of their purposes—particularly not if they understand them clearly themselves. Nevertheless, the motives of agents—and, it should be added, of case officers as well—fall into identifiable categories. The most accurate assessment and fullest understanding of which of these motives or combinations of several of them moves the agent must supplement the case officer's greater knowledge of the field of operations and detailed knowledge of the agent's history and talents, in order for him to establish and maintain maximum control of the agent. In ascending order of desirability and dependability, these categories of motives are money, compulsion, personal gain, ambition, political support, and duty.

The agent who operates only for money certainly exists; cities like Vienna, Beirut, Hong Kong, Zurich, trading places of information and centers of maneuver for both sides in the secret war, are full of men attempting to glean a living from selling their services, without regard for nationality, as agents. Obviously, however, the provider of secret services for money is all too prone to the temptation to overstate his accomplishments, if not deliberately to falsify them, both in advance of any arrangement and in practice. More importantly, he must always be assumed to be available to the highest bidder; and it is always obligatory to assume that the highest bidder will be the opposition. In periods of great confusion and violent transition, such as existed in Europe immediately following the Second World War, agents operating for money are frequently able to make a success of their work. Networks are disrupted, former relationships are altered, patterns of movement and communication are in chaos; in such circumstances a secret service, for lack of anything better, will buy an agent. Likewise, in cases of very limited actions requiring special skills or local knowledge—a guide in the mountains or jungles, a clandestine boat trip, a difficult border crossing, a particular document sought from the confidential files of a bank—a hired agent may be used. But generally a competent secret service avoids, as much as possible, the agent working for money. It is worth noting that there has seldom been a Western trial of a Soviet agent which revealed anything more than relatively trifling sums to have been involved. It is not that the Soviets are penurious in these matters; they simply observe the classic principle that a hired agent is the least desirable.[2]

Compulsion to force an individual to act as a secret agent takes many forms and is not infrequent. Blackmail is one form of such compulsion, and it is a favorite Soviet technique. It is by no means limited to sexual matters. But it is a regrettable fact—accurately understood and utilized by the Soviets—that Americans, and to a lesser extent the English, are particularly subject to blackmail in this sphere, profusely decorated as it is by a rich welter of complexes among so many Anglo-Saxons. However, at least one of my American colleagues in time past gave the right answer when confronted with the problem. Shown a series of highly compromising photographs of himself with a lady not his wife, he was threatened with transmission of the photographs to his wife and—notable Soviet deduction from American sociology—to his mother and father. His answer was brief. "Superb photography," he cried. "I'll take a dozen copies." He at least understood that if you're going to go out, it may as well be laughing; the tears are for later. In his case, interestingly enough, they weren't; neither he nor his family ever heard of the matter again.

In the period immediately following the Second World War the Soviets were able to recruit a number of agents in Europe among former fascists or collaborators, by means of either threats of revelation or promises of immunity from prosecution—depending on the individual circumstances and the extent of Communist power in the given country. Another favorite Soviet device is the holding of hostages, usually family, in order to compel service as an agent. One of the strange elements in Soviet behavior in this connection is the fact that almost uniformly they hold to promises made about members of a family held as hostages—release from imprisonment, special privileges, or even release from Soviet territory—although they are notorious for not honoring promises to the victim of compulsion himself.

It is also a fact that compulsion is not limited to the Soviets. In many Western European countries it is made perfectly clear to resident foreigners, particularly refugees in difficulties, that the necessary permits and facilities for work and residence are dependent upon their reporting regularly and fully to the intelligence authorities. And American officials are far from immune to the temptations which are offered by the possibility of having a hold over a man. Nevertheless, it stands to reason that the recruitment of an agent by compulsion is a very limited technique. An agent moved only by fear of punishment is certainly lacking in initiative —perhaps one reason the Soviets favor the technique—and is in no frame of mind to exploit his own skills or possibilities to the fullest. The most important limitation on such an agent is his lack of reliability: hidden betrayal is a constant possibility, even when the hold over the agent still exists, and it is pretty much of a certainty when the hold is relinquished. It is also fairly certain that if the agent is uncovered by the opposition he will co-operate fully with them.

The agent who is moved by prospects of personal gain is a more subtle and sophisticated variant of the agent who seeks only money. He is similar to the latter in that personal enrichment is his ultimate goal. He is dissimilar, however, in that his scope is wider since he knows and acts on the principle that secret information is power. His intent is to turn that power to personal profit. It is extremely rare that an operator of this type is so crude as to hope to extract profit from the blackmailing possibilities which secret operations may give him. He usually counts on his participation in a secret operation either to give him access to information otherwise unobtainable or to put him in a geographical location or social position, any or all of which he can turn to good account. The good account is usually expressed in money, but it may also be influence or position or merely opportunities. His intent is seldom to profit from the operation itself; on the contrary, he generally renders reasonably good service up to a point. His personal gain comes more or less as a sideline to the operation, a calculated windfall, a sort of fringe benefit. The limitations of such an agent in terms of control and dependability are obvious: since the fringe benefit—never acknowledged by him to be paramount—is to him the important part of the arrangement, his participation in the operation has an element of falsity which, if not recognized and compensated for by the case officer, can lead to serious errors. Furthermore, his mobility is affected, since he is in fact tied to objectives which are not those of the operation; most importantly, the extent of his reliability—though not necessarily his loyalty—is questionable for the same reason.

At first glance ambition seems like a strange motive to associate with secret operations. It is not readily clear what ambition can be satisfied by work in a field hidden from the public gaze and without philosophical or aesthetic rewards. It nevertheless does play a valid role, largely because of developments in the past twenty years. Prior to the Second World War the secret war was limited in scope and intensity. Its professionals were men who performed valuable services for their governments, but their influence was by and large limited. A particularly capable official might be respected and his counsel sought on a variety of problems, but in general the professional of secret operations remained a technician playing no role in the process of decision. Today, all over the world, on both sides of the Iron Curtain, that has changed. The real power which is now wielded by the upper echelons of secret operations is no less considerable for being unadvertised to the public.

In Communist countries the men who control the secret operations apparatus are high Party functionaries and participate in major decisions. It is noteworthy that as time goes on more and more of these men achieve their high Party rank via advancement in the secret operations apparatus and not the reverse. Secret operations have tended to become a career, an accepted path to governmental power. The infamous Gabor Peter, Chief of the Hungarian State

Security Authority, the AVO, and master of a reign of terror engulfing tens of thousands of victims, was a major power in the
Hungarian Government until his fall; he had spent his whole adult
life in the Soviet secret operations apparatus; only ten years before
his fall from power he had been a Soviet line-crosser, that is, an
agent maintaining continuous clandestine liaison between case officers in Soviet-controlled territory and Communist agents in en-
emy-controlled territory. The ultimate achievement of power is by
no means limited to the control of secret operations themselves.
Two British former secret operations officials with whom I collaborated in postwar operations are now increasingly influential Members of Parliament. One of President Kennedy's ambassadorial ap-
pointments was a man who made his mark in Washington through
some years of outstanding work in the CIA. No one familiar with
Washington in the decade of the Fifties discounts the heavy weight
of the CIA complex in the important American foreign-policy decisions of the period. No one familiar with the realities of what C.
Wright Mills has styled "the power elite," or what Richard Rovere
has more lightly but as penetratingly dubbed "The American Establishment," discounts the pressures and influence the CIA can
bring to bear in the private sectors of the American scene. In the
United States the possibilities are formally recognized in a system
whereby "outside" agents are brought into "inside" posts in the
CIA Washington hierarchy, and vice versa, all the while advancing
in their careers.

Ambition, therefore, has become a real motive for entering into
secret operations. It is obviously a reliable motive for an agent—or
for a case officer. Its drawback is that of all bureaucracies: the
desire for advancement tends to cloud the judgment, impair initiative, and stifle the willingness to risk controversy in favor of con-
formity and the path of least resistance.

Political support is a highly reliable but varied and complex
motive. It transcends limitations of nationality and is a prime
mover in the secret war. For it to constitute a motive, however,
there must be a political conviction, consciously and independently
arrived at. This makes it differ markedly from patriotism—although patriotism may be an element in arriving at a political
conviction. The agent or case officer moved by patriotism is not
acting on the basis of an independent political conviction. He is a
product of the system in which he has been raised; he accepts, in
greater or lesser part, and without doubt or challenge, the tenets of

that system; and he is prepared to act on them. A man moved by the desire to give or obtain political support, on the other hand, is acting on the basis of a political conviction he has arrived at personally and independently; his objective is political, but defined by himself.

In 1961 the British discovered that a Foreign Office official, formerly British Consul in Seoul at the time of the North Korean invasion of South Korea, had for ten years been acting as a Soviet agent. His motive was solely political support, arising from his conviction, arrived at while interned in North Korea, that the Soviet system deserved to win. But an outright defector is far from being the sole example of an agent so moved. It was an earnest—but unfulfilled—hope of the dissident French Army generals and colonels in Algeria, long before the attempted putsch of April 1961, to enter into working relations with the American CIA. Their motive was to gain secret American political support, and indeed they tried hard to press their viewpoint that any solution of the Algerian problem other than their own was dangerous to the interests of the United States as well as to those of France. But even the judges at the trial of General Challe and his collaborators publicly recognized that these were patriotic Frenchmen.

For the secret services of all the great powers, the most frequent opportunities for the establishment of effective espionage nets in a foreign country come from citizens of that country who seek in exchange support for their particular domestic political objectives. Most of the agents in a network I directed in Hungary immediately following the Second World War were moved solely by their hope that they could thus help to bring about effective American support against the Hungarian Communists and their Soviet backers.

But political support as a motive does not necessarily mean full collaboration. On the contrary, a case officer using agents whose motive is political support must have the clearest possible understanding of precisely what is being offered and demanded. The Polish anti-Communist emigration, for example, is composed of a variety of political groups holding widely divergent views on Polish domestic affairs. Some consider American support detrimental to their own Polish interests and therefore withhold co-operation in American secret operations. Others take an opposing view, but in differing degrees. Not even those most eager for American support, however, will collaborate in any American enterprise which involves so much as a tacit acceptance of American policy toward certain German problems, in particular that of the Polish-German boundary. On this point, all Polish exile groups are one with the Warsaw Communists in insisting on full recognition of the Oder-Neisse frontier—a problem in which the United States, by its public position in favor of postponing this question for decision in a peace treaty, appears to all Poles to be supporting in fact the West German claim for boundary revision.[3]

Notwithstanding such limitations and complexities, which result in a certain independence in the agent, an agent whose motive is political support is among the most dependable. He is often the most competent as well, since the process of personally defining his own objectives produces both self-reliance and clearheadedness. Such motivation is particularly valuable for an agent operating in his own country's secret service; he then has what the Soviets term —and lay great stress upon—political consciousness.

In the international conflicts of our times nationalism is the great wellspring of a sense of duty. As a motive for an agent, a sense of duty ranks high. It insures his reliability, and it eliminates any necessity for bargaining about objectives. Since the fulfillment of a sense of duty provides its own rewards, the agent thus moved is devoid of any falsity in his position; anonymity, lifelong if necessary, is acceptable. The sense of duty is the single great advantage of military intelligence services. In the period prior to the Second World War the American intelligence organization was limited to the Army and Navy and a few officers in the Foreign Service. These men are by and large unknown and unsung today; in almost all cases their devotion to secret operations meant a sacrifice of their careers as military, naval, or diplomatic officers—the concept of the "well-rounded" officer as being the only one meriting the posts of highest responsibility is no new invention. But these officers nonetheless performed highly valuable services for the country, and the fulfillment of their sense of duty in doing so left them, with few exceptions, personally content. An agent moved solely by a sense of duty suffers only one potential impairment. Since he accepts unquestioningly the objectives he is to serve, it is possible, and does happen, that he has no genuine understanding of these objectives. To this extent he is sometimes lacking in imagination in technique and in the fullest and best comprehension of the circumstances in which he finds himself.[4]

Nobody enters into the world of secret operations as a lark. The demands are too rigorous, the issues too weighty and complex, for a mere adventurer. Some men in secret operations have indeed a strong sense of adventure; some relish the feeling of being privy to secrets; some experience personal satisfaction at being thus able to operate outside the framework of normal order and society—but these are attributes of the life, and as reasons for adopting it they are insufficient. Some men and women even become involved in secret operations unconsciously, so to speak; a chain of circumstances ensnares them without a clear or definite realization or decision on their part. But sooner or later understanding of the nature of their work comes to them. At this point, if they go on, it is with awareness, and it is in response to the motives described above.

It is rare, however, that an agent—or case officer—is moved by only one of these motives. Such purity of motive does not correspond to the complexity of most human beings. When it does occur, it is usually for special reasons, generally of short duration, and often results in fanaticism—not a desirable quality in a field where coolheadedness and breadth of view are prime qualities. In the vast majority of cases motives are mixed, and if properly understood by the case officer the mixture can contribute to the usefulness of the agent. The value of one highly useful American agent in Latin America, for example, for years depended upon his ability to move freely among the very wealthy. The fact was that he was a social snob, addicted to a form and level of living for which he would otherwise have needed vast personal resources which he did not have. His functioning as an agent was, therefore, to some extent an example of the agent working for personal gain, in this case the connections and standard of living which his cover required. However, he had also a strong sense of duty—perhaps it compensated him for what would otherwise have been a parasitic existence —and his reliability was therefore not at all in question. Similarly, his very interest in the kind of life he led contributed to his usefulness and success in his circumstances, to an extent that could probably not have been matched by an agent moved by duty alone.

In the matter of mixed motives the Soviets do not hesitate even to attempt seemingly impossible mixtures, as, for example, the effort to inculcate, in a prospective agent whose basic motive would be compulsion, some motive of political support. In 1945 the Soviets promised safe-conducts to sixteen leaders of the non-Communist Polish Resistance for purposes of negotiation, but when the men arrived they were arrested, taken to Lubianka Prison in Mos-

cow, and ultimately tried for alleged anti-Soviet activities. Before
the ultimate decision was made to stage trials, however, there were
the usual long interrogations. Zgygniew Stypulkowski, one of the
sixteen, shows in the following extract from his account of his
interrogation the mixture of motives suggested by his interrogator
(italics are mine):

The [interrogator] had, in my opinion, in the first stage of
investigation, three tasks. The first was to get from me all the
details of my life, and of the life of my family; to judge my
intelligence and find out my weaknesses, my ambitions and my
will-power. The second task he had to perform was to put into
my mind the idea that the most important task for me was to
defend myself; to be free at any price—*that was my duty for
myself and also for my family and for my country. My country,
he said, badly needed my support, my work.* Finally he had to
destroy my mental balance by throwing me constantly from optimism to deep despair. . . . *He expressed regrets about my
family, but he insisted on knowing where my son was.* I said I did
not know. *He tried to convince me that it was my duty as a good
father to find him,* and that he would help me. . . . At 4 a.m.
one day . . . we talked about books . . . he tried to soothe
me, and succeeded. . . . Then he took my arm, looked in my
eyes and said, "I am sorry for you. I regret very much that you
are in such a bad state, and sitting here in this Lubianka Prison.
But I am very happy to be able to tell you that my Government
is not interested in having your head or in putting you in one of
the labor camps in Siberia. *On the contrary, we need you because
Russia's historical task is to rule over Europe.*"

Pretty crude, one might say. In Mr. Stypulkowski's case the
method definitely didn't work—he is today a distinguished Polish
exile leader. It has nevertheless worked in an astounding number of
cases.

The agent's motives are not only important in establishing and
maintaining the case officer-agent relationship; they also play a role
in terminating that relationship, a process and problem referred to
in American parlance as—the word never failed to strike me as
unnecessarily macabre— "disposal." There is a popular belief that
once a secret agent, always a secret agent. This is not true. There
are always men who are called upon from time to time for special

services—the CIA maintains a regular, formal list of such personnel, whose clearances are always kept up to date—but there are equally those whose usefulness is ended with a particular operation. This sometimes poses an economic problem for the agent; it always at least poses a security question for the case officer. In estimating the degree of risk involved in disposing of an agent his motives and personality will obviously play a role. As importantly, however, this is another one of those questions where it matters more how you do it than what you do. In brief, insight and tact are of the essence. This is especially true of political operations, where the consequences of termination may seem to an agent to involve vital questions of policy as well as the purely personal question of his living. However, even in these cases, most people don't mind a "No," but much depends upon how it is put. About the worst way to put it is not to put it at all.

As in the matter of recruitment, bureaucracy impedes American practice in this sphere as well. Often arrangements are canceled without notice or explanation, as in the case of the man who fell afoul of the postage meter and the bookkeeper. Even less justifiable is the tendency, all too often indulged, to frame an agent, or publicly to besmirch his reputation, as a means of disposing of him. A ludicrous case of this sort occurred some years ago when an American agent who was also the beneficiary of one of the great American fortunes was charged with diverting funds to purchase an automobile for himself—an unprovable assertion in the particular circumstances of his work and ridiculous on its face—and was hastily dismissed in disgrace. As a colleague remarked at the time, "At least the Russians wait until a man defects to our side before they falsely accuse him of embezzlement." Slander and smear are too often used by the CIA in these matters, and all too many American agents have left its service dangerously embittered.

While these techniques of "disposal" may be the expected responses of moral people who, when faced with an amoral problem, cannot understand the category and therefore behave immorally, this is no justification for ineptitude. And not all of the ineptitude is accompanied by immorality. One of the most violent and influential critics of the CIA in print in the United States today is a man who worked for almost three years for the Agency on highly important matters. The case officer handling him—himself a senior official—had great difficulty doing so, and finally decided to abandon the operation. Instead of talking it over with the agent, he sent a minor functionary to inform him brusquely that he was fired. The official—and the CIA—have paid needlessly and many times over in the years since in blood-inked editorials and in jeopardy to the security of some of their operations. None of this excuses the agent's petulance—but the responsibility to dispose of him smoothly was not his; it was the case officer's.

Sir Francis Walsingham's secretary oversimplified things considerably; there is much more to it than simply going out and hiring "a base fellow."

1. This seems to have become a popular story. Phillip Knightley's *The Second Oldest Profession* (New York: W. W. Norton, 1987) states, pages 286–287: "Early in 1956 CIA officers in London remember listening in dismay as an SIS representative outlined a plan to engineer a coup in Syria. . . . Following yet another meeting, this time in London, the CIA officers reported to Washington: 'After sitting around a table in a desultory fashion for an hour or two, one Englishman finally said, "I say, why don't we get old Henry up here. He knows about this." A day or two later old Henry finally showed up from down in Sussex and agreed to undertake the task, although as he said, "This will wreak havoc with the garden, you know. Just getting it into trim." ' " Knightley (whose 1968 *The Sunday Times* Insight team book on Kim Philby spoke of "Christopher Felix") footnotes the source of this story as "Unsigned article, *New Statesman,* 7 July 1978." The meeting was not in 1956, did not concern the Middle East, and the remarks were not "reported to Washington."

2. The 1986 trials in the United States of the Walker ring—Soviet agents in the U.S. Navy—revealed more sizable sums at stake (the prosecution charged receipt by the principal of some $1 million over a number of years, and of sums around $350,000 for subordinate members of the network over shorter periods). Perhaps this should be modified to say that, although generally penurious taskmasters, the Soviets are willing to accommodate greed if the circumstances give cause for confidence (i.e., the agent's hopes for pay are combined with sufficiently professional performance), and, obviously, the results are worth the cost.

3. This has been overtaken by events. West Germany's *Ostpolitik* brought the first Western concession to the Russian-dictated Polish western border (agreed to at Potsdam by the British and Americans under the impression, according to Churchill's memoirs, that the Neisse River mentioned was the eastern, not the western, branch of the river, whereas the Russians intended, and got, the western branch). The 1976 Helsinki Accords on Security and Cooperation in Europe, with the United States as a signatory, confirmed those borders (and acted, in effect, as the peace treaty

the United States sought). But later events have shown that all this has given neither Russians nor Poles contentment in Poland.

4. Much of this is still true, but as November 1986 showed, concerning dealings with Iran in the White House itself, the United States is not at all immune to the confusion arising from varying interpretations of the obligations of "duty." The duty of an officer of the American Government (including the Armed Forces) is to the Constitution. But once into the body of that document, and under the influence of the American mystique of the Presidency, many an officer will identify the President—the Commander in Chief—with the Constitution. The tradition (for the private citizen and the Executive Branch) has been that you do not refuse a request of the President. But this is custom, not law.

CHAPTER IV

The Art of Cover—I

As open warfare depends upon weapons, so does the secret war depend upon cover. Weapons are not in themselves the purpose of war, but they shield the soldier and enable him to advance to his objective—or they protect his retreat. Cover shields the secret agent from his opposition. It puts him into position to accomplish his mission. Ideally, it should also protect the mission against at least the worst consequences of the agent's being uncovered. Dealing as it does with human beings, their relations to each other, with what they feel and impressions, their insights and their actions, cover is an art.

During the Second World War an Englishman whom we shall call Geoffrey was living in Tangier. As a mildly eccentric bachelor whose small private income enabled him to indulge his liking for the climate, the good life, and a certain sense of the exotic, Geoffrey had already spent some years there. In peacetime, he was no different from the majority of other members of the Tangier British community. In other words, his cover for his work as a British intelligence agent—which he was—made sense precisely because he didn't stand out.

The outbreak of war changed that. In fact, the problem became exactly the reverse. For Geoffrey to continue and to cultivate those Axis contacts which were desired, he now had to have a cover which would isolate him from his fellow Britishers. It had to be one which would explain his continued presence in Tangier and would make him acceptable to his German, Italian, and Spanish sources. It would certainly not be sufficient for him merely to pose as a pro-Axis Englishman; it is the fate of turncoats, usually unforeseen by them, to be regarded with double suspicion by their new-found friends. There is always a counterespionage official somewhere who continues to suspect that even the most sincere defector is a double agent.

Something was needed which would lend authenticity to Geoffrey's banal—in the eyes of covert operations professionals—protestations of pro-Axis sentiments. Like most Englishmen of his class Geoffrey had had various scrapes in his past and was given to occasional hell-raising of sorts. It was decided to play up this aspect of Geoffrey; in fact, to put on the act of the Englishman going native, running to seed in his exile—a sort of Somerset Maugham China Seas character in a North African setting. But it had to be authentic; Geoffrey had to live his cover, as the professional saying has it.

He did so. He went from women to men, from alcohol to drugs, and from bad to worse. Geoffrey perfectly fitted the Nazi preconceptions of the errant, degenerate Englishman. He was not simply isolated from his compatriots. He lived in a sea of their opprobrium. In London his superiors had an easy check on his progress simply by reference to the number and the violence of denunciations of Geoffrey by Britishers—some themselves agents, but unwitting. But Geoffrey successfully accomplished his mission. He never once gave away his cover. Even after it was all over he didn't give it away. And it killed him. It wasn't just the drugs and alcohol; the hatred and contempt of people one likes can easily be physically unbearable.

Not all cover is as dramatic, or as damaging, as Geoffrey's. But all good cover owes its success to the element which made Geoffrey's so effective: it reaches into the mind of the opponent, thinks as he would think, and then creates a combination of fact and fancy, of actual arrangements and contrived impressions, which the opposing mind is prepared to believe. In all human conflict the stronger man is he who can think as his enemy thinks—can read his mind, as we say—and the victor is he who seizes the advantage this gives him. Hannibal at Cannae, Nelson on the Nile, Togo at Tsushima, Bradley in Normandy—all demonstrated and then exploited this ability in its most dramatic form. Its value is as true in covert operations as in commercial competition, in secret as in open warfare. Good cover cannot be created without this ability. The competent agent knows that, in this sense, good cover is an intimate relationship between deceiver and deceived. And in the strangely altered world of covert operations, in which real and unreal change places hourly, the deceived are necessarily both friend and foe.

Cover takes an infinite variety of forms. Certainly the commonest—and widely used by people outside of covert operations, including bankers, ambassadors, and lovers—is the large cocktail party or diplomatic reception. At these affairs, meetings and conversations which would be for one reason or another undesirable if deliberately arranged elsewhere can take place seemingly casually —under the cover of the cocktail party.

The budget of the United States Government is itself a cover Buried in it is the budget of the Central Intelligence Agency, whose funds are nowhere publicly recorded but are instead scattered about through the appropriations of the rest of the Government in a manner that is reportedly proof against even the closest scrutiny. In other words, the Central Intelligence Agency receives its appropriations under the cover of the Federal Budget.

Cover may be no more than a story. The cover story is most frequently used to explain the visible evidences of a clandestine operation or to provide an explanation when an operation encounters difficulties. The U-2 flights, for example, operated—at least on their own bases—under cover of meteorological research. When the Soviets protested what turned out to be Powers's violation of their frontiers, a previously prepared cover story was given out by the NASA, stating that these were meteorological research flights and that on this occasion the pilot reported having difficulty with his oxygen equipment while on a triangular flight course within Turkey, one leg of which brought him close to the Soviet border. The story went on to state that it was therefore assumed that the pilot lost consciousness and, while unconscious, inadvertently crossed the Soviet border.

The failure of this cover story illustrates—among other things—several points about cover stories in general: they should not be too precise or too detailed, and they should not be forthcoming too quickly or all at once.

When Bulganin and Khrushchev paid their official visit to Great Britain aboard a Soviet heavy cruiser, there was great Western interest in the ship itself. In the midst of the visit the Russians protested that the ship had been attacked in Portsmouth Harbor by a frogman. Whatever was the true mission of Commander Crabbe, the British Admiralty's underwater expert, it was clear from the Soviet protest at the time, and from the Commander's disappearance, that the Russians had caught him. British official announcements on the subject were quite some time in coming. When they came, they came piecemeal. First there was an announcement about the mysterious disappearance of a man who had registered at a Portsmouth hotel. It was some time before a further announcement gave his name. Then a newspaper reporter uncovered the fact that he had arrived in Portsmouth with underwater diving equipment. To this there was an official announcement, eventually, that investigation showed Commander Crabbe occasionally did some research on underwater work for the Admiralty, under contract. This was followed, later, by a denial that Commander Crabbe had been on official business when he visited Portsmouth, and that was the last officially spoken on the subject. Throughout all these statements there was an air of vagueness, implying alternatively that Commander Crabbe didn't exist or that he was such a tremendous enthusiast for underwater diving that it was highly probable he had gone to Portsmouth on his own for several days of his favorite sport.

To be too precise in a cover story qualitatively increases the chances of repudiation of the story; to be too detailed increases those chances quantitatively. To speak out too fast is to show your hand before you know all you can about what your opponent is holding in his; and to tell all in one bleat eliminates your chances to improvise as the situation develops. The proof of this British pudding lay in the fact that the Soviet visit went on to its planned completion, and, following their single protest, the Russians dropped the matter.

It is typical of the peculiar combination of drama and irony characterizing covert operations that, at the same time that Commander Crabbe was being discovered by the Russian watch aboard the *Sverdlovsk* in Portsmouth Harbor,[1] a Soviet espionage ring was functioning smoothly ashore in the British Underwater Detection Establishment at Portland. The principal agents were a couple who conducted their operations under the cover of a bookshop; they were well and favorably known in the neighborhood where they lived. They were uncovered and arrested only years later, in 1961. And when this finally occurred there was considerable doubt as to their true nationality and identity. Their personal cover of false identities and Canadian citizenship held up even for a time after their arrest, until American authorities came forward with a positive identification of them as American citizens with past records of Communist activity in the United States.

This couple, the Cohens—alias Kroger—lived in a quiet residential section in a house in which was found, after their arrest, a radio transmitter and other clandestine equipment. In fact, the only proof of their involvement in espionage was radio signals from the house to the Moscow area. They themselves never received documents from the sub-agents working at the Portland Naval Base. These were transmitted to the Cohens by a cut-out who was in due course brought under British security surveillance. Even after arrest, however, the Cohens produced a cover story. It was that they had lent their house several times in their absence—as in fact they had—to friends, among them the cut-out, and they denied knowledge of the hidden equipment or of those friends' activities, or indeed any responsibility for them.

The effectiveness of the Cohens' cover story was of a very high order. It endured for a considerable time by professional standards, and even continued to confuse the investigators after the couple's activities had been revealed. (The Cohens' true identity was not uncovered until about a month after their arrest; the true identity and nationality of the cut-out—a Soviet citizen—was not actually announced until some ten months after his arrest.) Furthermore, it was not a defect in the cover which destroyed the operation; it was the matter of those radio signals. The camouflage and detection of radio signals is a separate, highly technical aspect of covert operations. Furthermore, the effectiveness of the final cover story, given after their arrest, is not to be measured by the fact that the court, in convicting and sentencing them for espionage, rejected it. Its effectiveness is more properly measured by the extent to which

other agents and activities of their group were protected by the
story and its accompanying delays and confusion. And who knows
who and what these other agents and activities were? Moscow
does; London and Washington do not. Who can properly estimate
the true extent of the defeat represented by the arrest of the Cohens? Only Moscow can. This is good cover at work.

Cover is not created by recourse to a theatrical supply house.
Disguise is rarely feasible. Exceptions always exist, of course, and
the outstanding one in my experience is a non-mustachioed British
general who periodically operates disguised as a woman. As he
once said to me, "Not flashily attractive, you understand, but not
motherly either. Just chic, don't you know."

In covert operations, including cover itself, that which is false is
called notional. The nonexistent intelligence network and false reports created for his superiors in London by the hero of Graham
Greene's *Our Man in Havana* were notional—and are a far from
rare occurrence in espionage. An entire U.S. operation was once
financed by a notional oil millionaire, for whom a life history and
personality, complete with foibles and eccentricities—including his
adamant refusal to see persons whom he was aiding financially—
had to be created.

That which is true is called legitimate. (This word has been
extended into a somewhat dubious phrase used by CIA insiders to
describe someone not in the business, as "Oh, he's legitimate.")[2]

The best cover is that which contains the least notional and the
maximum possible legitimate material. Probably one of the most
dramatically successful covert operations of modern times was the
Soviet espionage ring in prewar Manchuria and Japan headed by
Richard Sorge, who operated as a German journalist. Everything
about Sorge's cover was legitimate; its sole notional feature was his
explanation of his whereabouts in the years when he had actually
been living and training in the Soviet Union. He set something of a
record in the realm of cover by successfully maintaining his without a single respite for nine years. In his case, as in the Cohens', his
arrest was not due to the breakdown of his cover, but to his radio
transmissions to the Soviet Union.

Aside from the mission itself and the circumstances in which it
is to be accomplished, the most important items in creating cover
are the history, talents, and personality of the agent himself. An
agent without journalistic background cannot use journalistic

cover. The saying, "Do not send a boy to do a man's job," has a literal meaning in the art of cover.

During the Occupation of Germany, we sent a man there whose cover was a job in one of the numerous Occupation Government offices. More than that, however, it was essential to his mission that he appear to be a low-level, obscure employee, although he was in fact a high-level covert operations official with considerable authority (and is today a high official of the U.S. Government in a quite "legitimate" field). We wanted no attention drawn to him which would interest Soviet agents in his activities or which would make it difficult for our own agents to contact him quietly. In brief, we had left him his true identity, but we had given him a notional personality. As it turned out, his notional personality was inescapably in conflict with his true personality and talents. He hadn't been in Germany more than a few months when our mistake became obvious. Driving about in a large red convertible, he was soon immersed in every American group activity up and down the Rhine. He was president of the American Ski Club, he was a trustee of the American Church, his wife was president of the American Women's Club, his office was one of the liveliest in Germany, and his house was overrun with people gaily planning charity bazaars and Hallowe'en dances. We wanted a self-effacing, invisible man; we got a prominent community leader. The mistake could probably have been avoided if we had attached more importance to the fact that he had been president of the student body at his university.

Perfect cover is an ideal, rarely achieved in practice. Necessity imposes something less than perfection, and so it is sometimes necessary to resort to such a dangerous device as a notional identity. Notional identities obviously depend upon the histrionic ability of the agent and his capacity to believe, think, eat, sleep, and live his false identity. The famous Sorge, although operating under his own identity, nonetheless possessed this capacity to a high degree. A heavy drinker, he one night ran his motorcycle into the wall of the American Embassy in Tokyo. Taken to a hospital, he emerged from a coma some days later, but was delirious for several more days. Not once, even in his delirium, did he ever say anything which could arouse the slightest suspicion—a fact respectfully noted in his report by the Japanese official who finally tracked him down.

In the world in which we now live, notional identity also de-

pends upon the forger. All covert services of the great powers
maintain special offices for the forgery of documents and seals of
all kinds. (This is one reason the U.S. Department of State gets
very upset when American tourists lose their passports.) Immediately after the Second World War, before the U.S. had adequate
facilities for forgery, American operations depended heavily upon
private enterprise in this field. I had a man in Rome who for $500
would deliver a Venezuelan passport which he proudly said was
"valid anywhere, Signor—except Venezuela." I also had a Hungarian refugee in Salzburg who, when he finally received his visa to
the U.S., with which I had been able to give him some help, gratefully delivered to me his entire remaining stock, which included
identity documents and border guard seals for every country in
Eastern Europe except Poland and the Soviet Union itself. Unfortunately, my Salzburg friend was not available when I once had to
move an agent through the Soviet Zone of Austria. It fell to me to
forge the name and date on an expired Soviet pass—the forgery
was nothing compared to the problem of erasure.

Cover cannot always be created quickly in a desirable form. It is
often necessary to resort to the process known as building cover,
which is nothing more than engaging in actions which will increase
the plausibility of the cover. I once sent a man wandering aimlessly
about Europe for eight months looking for just the right place to
live, so that his final choice—a particular house in a particular city
—would not seem prearranged.

Cover is not a durable commodity. By its very nature some people have to be privy to the secret—to them cover is revealed, meaning disclosed under authorization—and obviously the more people
who know, the greater danger of the cover being blown—meaning
discovered or unauthorizedly disclosed. (It is this fact which causes
cover to be described as light or deep; obviously, the fewer persons
to whom the cover is revealed, the deeper the cover.) The fundamental rule in all cover arrangements is that if cover is endangered,
the operation is suspended until cover can be rebuilt or new cover
developed. I once lost five urgent weeks obeying this rule.

Assigned temporarily to a foreign capital, my work necessitated
my presence in one office, but my cover required my presence in
another. This was solved by revealing the cover to one secretary in
the cover office, who was supposed to take all my calls, state that I
was out, and then give me the message where I was really working.
When the inevitable happened and the secretary fell ill, her tempo-

rary replacement took a call for me with the cheery remark, "Oh, he doesn't work here. He just comes in and picks up his mail occasionally." As the caller was a Belgian diplomat, it was decided to suspend the operation temporarily and rebuild the cover by the simple expedient of having me spend a suitable time in the cover office. So I spent five empty weeks there, lunching twice during the period with the Belgian diplomat and making sure that on both occasions he came to the office to pick me up.

At that I fared better than a colleague in neutral Turkey during the Second World War. A former journalist, he was working for General Donovan's organization in its formative days, when it was still the Office of the Coordinator of Information. My colleague showed up in Istanbul as a journalist. His second morning there, he came down to breakfast at his hotel to find the Turkish police awaiting him. They simply sat him down in a corner of the lobby and asked, "What is your connection with General Donovan?" After giving him plenty of time to protest that he was a journalist, had previously been in Turkey as a journalist, as they well knew, and had no connection with General Donovan, the police quietly handed him a long telegram. It was addressed to my colleague and was composed entirely of five-letter code groups, except for the signature which succinctly read, "Donovan, Coordinator of Information." Within an hour he was on the train to the Syrian border, with plenty of time to visualize a new secretary in Washington, eager to please, obeying quite literally the order to "get that off to him in Istanbul right away."

The Turks can scarcely be blamed for being alert, even nervous. Only six months before, the British Minister to Bulgaria had arrived at the same hotel, with his entire staff, following the rupture of British-Bulgarian diplomatic relations. When the British diplomatic baggage was all finally assembled in the lobby, at least one part of it—to the mortification of one Britisher a bit negligent about technicalities—exploded and wrecked the place. It had only just been repaired when my colleague came to town.

On occasion, even blowing cover can be—don't anyone lose the thread here—part of cover. I once encountered an Englishman in Greece during the Civil War whom I had good reason to suspect was a covert agent—and he the same of me. He mentioned that he was working in a bank, and when I politely asked which one, he left in confusion. He came back to the same bar the next day—it's true what they say about some bars—and glancing at a piece of paper, said proudly, "About that bank. It's the Royal Corinthian Island and Specie Bank." (Or some such obvious concoction.) An intramural joke, of course—provided we were working to the same end. But if his mission was also to uncover and report on our activities, his cover could logically include partially blowing it to us to inspire our confidence. This kind of non-elevating thinking is necessary in the part of cover, but it is a poor agent who shows he is engaged in it. People do get suspicious, particularly of suspicion.

1. In March 1963, Mr. Larry Cott, of Honolulu, Hawaii, kindly corrected me—in what he politely called "minor errors," which "someone could use to try to challenge your overall accuracy"—as follows: "In the Commander Crabbe [other authors spell this Crabb] incident you have Bulganin and Khrushchev arriving aboard the cruiser *Sverdlovsk.* If memory serves, B & K came in the cruiser *Ordzhonikidze,* and she was the ship involved in the underwater incident. *Sverdlovsk* visited England, but that was in June 1953 at Spithead, Southampton, for the naval review following the Queen's Coronation. *Sverdlovsk* aroused considerable interest because she steamed into harbor, backed down at her assigned berth, put over her chain to the buoy and secured from mooring in something like eleven minutes. It was an impressive display of seamanship." Both Mr. Cott and I indulged in another error: the proper name of *Sverdlovsk* was *Sverdlov.*

2. I assume the jargon in this as in other respects has probably changed in the past twenty-five years.

CHAPTER V

The Art of Cover—II

The lone agent, operating under a personal cover, à la E. Phillips Oppenheim, is certainly not extinct, but he is fast becoming an anachronism. In a world of organization men, the best cover for an agent is to be an organization man. The adventurous explorer has been converted into an executive of a large travel agency; the writer in quest of stories and color has been replaced by the administrative director of a large private educational mission abroad; the independently wealthy expatriate with friends in high places everywhere has become the vice-president of a great corporation; and—alas!—Mata Hari works from 9 to 5 as a research assistant on the staff of a mass-circulation magazine.

This melancholy development is known as organizational cover. At the very outset of developing organizational cover a vital decision must be made. This is whether or not the use of the organization as cover will be revealed to one or more responsible officers of the organization itself. General practice is to try to sanction the arrangement wherever possible. This is a practical matter, since an agent bound by the full-time work requirements of an American company is pretty well hamstrung in his ability to do anything else. It also is preventive medicine against possible future embarrassment, of a type I know from experience.

After a particularly grueling two-year stint, I arranged to take a brief respite in the form of an overt and "legitimate" six months' job in an eminently "legitimate" Government office in Europe. My chief took an instant dislike to me since, as I eventually discovered, he suspected that I was there to engage in skulduggery beyond his control, and most likely to report on him. With patient effort and some show of frankness I finally began to ease his suspicions, and life became a little more restful. At this moment, unfortunately, my successor in my previous operation ran into some trouble which he felt warranted a message to me. In it came, addressed to me via my chief, but in a code which he could not break. The temperature in his office as he handed me the telegram made me think I was picking up my mail in the deep freeze. I apologized, went to my office, deciphered the message, composed a reply including the request that I be left alone, enciphered it, and then returned to the deep freeze to ask that he transmit the reply. I explained what had happened, without going into detail, reassured him as best I could, guaranteed it wouldn't happen again, and finally felt that he was mollified. Even more unfortunately, my restful life had softened my brain so that, while I deciphered well enough, I had forgotten how to encipher. My message was unreadable at the other end. Back came another message, by the same channels as the first. Protesting my innocence, I knew what George Washington would feel like if, returning to life and remembering that he hadn't chopped down the cherry tree, he had to read American history books. As I was innocent nothing was lost but my brief respite. However, much could be lost by an agent at a crucial point in his operations whose unwelcome true status was uncovered by his superiors in the organization. And their feeling of having been tricked would be fairly sure to make his true status unwelcome.

Most organizations take a co-operative and responsible view of these activities. However, there are some which, either because of the nature of their work or their vulnerability to charges of providing organizational cover or simply because they do not agree with covert operations in principle, will not sanction such arrangements.

The Russians have serious problems of their own in this field. Since almost all activity in the Soviet Union, and certainly all Soviet foreign activity, is organized and directed by the state, no Soviet agency can provide plausible organizational cover. Consequently, they most often use foreign organizations, obviously without sanction. It is this which explains their inability to resist the temptation offered by the UN as cover for some of their agents.

Cover is by no means confined to the problems of individual agents or of espionage operations, or to the concoction of stories to explain mishaps. More effort is probably expended today—at least by the Soviet Union and the United States—on cover organizations than on single agent cover. Cover organizations—let the reader beware—are not to be confused with organizational cover.

In contrast to organizational cover, which uses legitimate agencies for cover purposes, cover organizations exist solely for the purpose of providing cover. They are an enabling and protective device, usually for large-scale operations. Their great advantage lies in the fact that, once established, no further cover for the individual agents who make up the organization is necessary. In fact, a great many people who need not even know that they are functioning as agents can be brought into an operation. The purpose is simply to set in motion, under ostensibly independent auspices, activities for which the government does not wish to avow responsibility. It is not, therefore, the activities themselves which are covered, but only the link between them and the government.

Cover organizations are usually an expensive matter. Furthermore, they are, for the most part, suited only to political or paramilitary operations and not to espionage. Consequently, they are usually reserved for activities which are direct expressions of a government's foreign policy. They are infinitely more complicated than the Israeli Government's feeble attempt in 1960 to disguise a nuclear energy establishment by the simple statement that it was a textile plant.

Cover organizations are no new device. Americans can reflect on the historical fact that American independence is in large measure due to French ingenuity and success with one cover organization. In 1777 Louis XVI was persuaded by his ministers that it should be French policy to support the fight of the American colonists for independence from Great Britain. The French Government, however, was not yet prepared to put such a policy into effect openly. While Lafayette and scores of other young French officers, inspired by libertarian sentiments, volunteered for service with the Continental Army, this was by no means the type of significant aid that was needed or that the French Government contemplated.

The answer was found in the person of Pierre Auguste Caron de Beaumarchais, poet and playwright, author of *Figaro* and a man well known for his espousal of the ideas of the Enlightenment. Beaumarchais, a wealthy man, was granted letters patent to found a private trading firm in Paris, under the name of Hortalez and Company. This firm promptly entered exclusively and actively into the promotion of North American trade. It was well equipped for the purpose by the presence among the principals of Silas Deane— whose qualifications, besides being an American, were that he was an agent of the Continental Congress. The doors of the French Treasury and of the French arsenals were quietly opened to Hortalez and Company, and the firm forwarded on to America vast and decisive quantities of arms, munitions, textiles—and money. Among many other things, these supplies included nine-tenths of the arms and munitions used by the Americans at the Battle of Saratoga. (It is sad to be obliged to add that Beaumarchais, who was himself out of pocket for considerable expenses, was eventually forced to protracted litigation to recover these sums. The case was only solved in 1835, when the American Congress finally reimbursed his heirs.)

The range of cover organizations is vast. They embrace activities in every corner of the globe—save for that cold exception to the Cold War, Antarctica. They exist in all fields of international life: political movements, youth organizations, religious groups, the arts, publishing, education, labor, professional societies of all kinds, banks, foundations, and friendship societies. Some are very large organizations, playing a genuine role in their particular fields. Others are merely support agencies, usually for funding purposes; people everywhere are interested in money, where it comes from and how much, to the extent that the transmission and provision of funds is one of the most difficult aspects of covert operations. Some are, by now, long-established, permanent features of the international scene. Others come into existence for a specific, limited purpose and are disbanded when their function is accomplished.

Some are highly successful in their maintenance of cover and indistinguishable from genuine institutions; others carry with them an aura of falsity. One significant feature of the present situation is that this aura of falsity does not affect the value of the organization; even the opposition accepts the legend of the cover since it accords with their interests. One very large American cover organization, in existence for some years now, is well known by everyone in its field to be a Government operation, even though it cannot be proved. Nevertheless, on the Western side this is accepted and the cover honored because it serves a useful co-ordinating function, and it is accepted on the Soviet side because it is recognized as a major Western gambit, for the abandonment of which a price will have to be paid—the problem on both sides is how much.

A general acceptance of transparency in cover organizations is a fair indication of international tension and of a situation of crisis. During the Greek Civil War I journeyed to Lake Prespa, a large body of water in the middle of which the Greek, Albanian, and Yugoslav borders intersect. At that particular moment in history the Yugoslavs were still aiding the Greek Communists, as were the Albanians, but the Yugoslavs and Albanians were on bad terms due to the Tito-Stalin rupture, and the Greeks, except for the Communists, were obviously hostile to both the Yugoslavs and the Albanians. In addition, there was considerable intrigue among the Greek Communist rebels, as pro-Yugoslav and pro-Cominform agents sought to sway them in that dispute.

By day the lake was an idyl of mountain beauty. The still waters lay undisturbed, and the mountains rose blue and brown in the hazy sunlight. Nothing moved. But when darkness fell, hell broke loose.

From the north shore of the lake the put-put of a Yugoslav boat heading for Greece or Albania could be heard; and then from the western Albanian shore more boats would put out; and finally, traffic of all factions would embark from the Greek southern shore.

A machine gun would open up; rifle fire crackled all around the lake and on the waters. Tracers would tell the direction of fire, but not who was firing at whom. An occasional flare would give just enough light to distinguish a boat, but nothing about its occupants. A respite meant everybody was landing successfully, but it would be followed by even more vigorous boating and shooting. Lake Prespa was the Grand Central Station of secret agent movements of Southeastern Europe. The trouble was that all the commuters were armed and had nervous trigger fingers.

Into this muddle of peace and war the British covert services had sent a mission to check on the traffic and perhaps do a little commuting of their own. For some obscure reason of propriety, London had decided to cover the mission as being a British Consulate at a town near, but not on, the lake. For me to proceed further on my journey it was necessary for me to have my passport stamped by the Consulate. I waited one entire day and never saw a soul. On the second day, late in the afternoon, the "Consular" staff came in to replenish their ammunition. Roaring up in a jeep, as fine a "Consular" group of fighting men as I have ever seen entered the Consulate, armed to the teeth. When I explained my need, the "Consul" looked blank. "Jarvis," he called out, "where's that blasted Consulate seal? I saw it a couple of weeks ago." Jarvis, chewing on some tinned beef, went to a corner piled high with heavy wooden cases. "In with the Sten ammo, I think," he muttered.

When I had my passport duly stamped, and had brushed Jarvis's corned beef out of it, I congratulated the "Consul" on his cover. "Hah!" he said. "We haven't got time for that in this show. They'd have done better to make this a branch Naval Attaché's office and send us a gunboat—with searchlights." With that, he and his "Consular" staff were off to the lake for a night's work. The "Consul" was right. The secret war had become a shooting war, and nobody really cared about his cover. Nevertheless, this indifference to cover can only be indulged in by the West in times and areas of gravest crisis. It is one of the seeming inequities of the secret war today that, in general, world public opinion does not permit such transparency in Western political cover organizations while it is often indifferent to such transparency in Soviet political cover arrangements.

To many this indifference to the unmasking of Soviet political cover, this seeming inequity in judging Soviet and American actions, is an affront. At best they regard it as the mark of deceived or misguided minds, or Communist dupes. To be sure, this is sometimes the case. But I personally believe, on the basis of not inconsiderable experience, that this is a very defeatist view of our situation. If it is true that, for example, the millions of supporters of the Communist Peace Campaign were all, or even a majority, Communist dupes, or that everyone who agitates against nuclear testing or nuclear warfare is a Communist dupe, then we may as well throw in the towel throughout the rest of the world. The dupes have us badly outnumbered.

But I do not believe that is the case. The Peace Campaign was launched initially, in 1948, as a Soviet cover organization aimed at reinforcing Soviet policy concerning Western defense. The U.S. Government reacted with statement after statement showing conclusively that this was a Soviet initiative, in support of Soviet foreign policy. The technique didn't work. The Campaign succeeded beyond the Russians' fondest hopes, even to the extent that years later, when they intervened in Hungary, they had to pay a high price in loss of prestige with the very people they had won in the Campaign. In brief, people were indifferent to the unmasking of the Peace Campaign as a Soviet initiative. I do not believe it was because they were dupes; I believe it was because people—in this specific issue—liked what was offered. In large areas of the world the mere word "Communist" did not—and does not today—automatically close people's minds to the subject matter. The fundamental question is, what is being offered? And because we failed to understand this, we were outmaneuvered on this occasion.[1]

Very well, it will be said, but then why are we, the Americans, required at the same time to be so careful about our cover? To my mind, the answer is a double one. For the first part, it is simply that if we come up with as good an idea as the Peace Campaign we won't have to worry too much about our cover. The second part is what I believe to be the fact that more people than we realize judge the Soviet Union and the West, particularly the United States, on our own estimates of ourselves. The Soviets do not pretend to a distinction between public and private initiative in foreign affairs. People accept this and ask only, what is being offered? But the West claims there are, or should be, large areas of private initiative, including foreign relations in the broadest sense, in a well-ordered society. People assume we practice what we preach. More sophisticated opinion, aware of our problems and needs, realizes we cannot always, in this period of conflict, do so. Naïve opinion censures us for the unmasking of our cover; more sophisticated opinion merely expects our cover arrangements, by and large, to hold up. In short, we are not being unfairly penalized in the secret war; we are merely paying a price for what we say we believe in.

It is possible that political cover organizations are more numerous today on the Western than on the Soviet side. This is not to be taken as an indication of greater skulduggery on our part. On the contrary, the proliferation of such organizations in the West is a measure of the intensity of the secret war and of Soviet aggression. It is, encouragingly, a barometer of our response in that conflict.

Some observers hold that, from the point of view of international relations, the Soviet Government, and its imitators, are a cover for the Russian Communist Party—whose name, Vsesoyuznaya Kommunisticheskaya Partiya (Bolshevikov), All-Union Communist Party (of Bolsheviks), contains nothing except the language to label it as Russian. From the viewpoint of cover experts, the purpose of this cover is not secrecy; it is to obtain international privileges, immunities, and powers to which a political party has never before been entitled. In other words, it launches on the international scene, as the equal of governments, what was a domestic political party. Political parties are instruments for advancing particular viewpoints on the organization of society. A government which is merely a cover for a political party is, in its international relations, moved to interfere in its neighbors' forms of organization of their societies. This is the ideological war.[2]

In nations with more than a single political party, it is only the duly elected government which can act nationally and internationally. Consequently, the rallying of democratic public opinion to action short of war is a difficult process. It can really be accomplished today, on the necessary scale, only by government. Furthermore, in a world of acute tension, private organizations cannot be permitted to undertake international actions which affect the relations between states and the balance of power. Such actions must be reserved to governments. However, many such actions, particularly political, would lose their effectiveness internationally if it was known that the action was sponsored and directed by a foreign government. Or the action might, if undertaken overtly by the government, risk bringing into play opposing forces which would either defeat the action or seriously alter the international political balance. For the West, the answer to this dilemma is the cover organization. It is a means for organizing and utilizing valuable but diverse public opinion in the common national or international interest.

Once this problem is understood, the necessity and usefulness to the West of the cover organization becomes clear. It can also be seen that the West is better equipped in this game, by reason of its greater variety of views and interests, than the Soviet Union. However, this is not necessarily comforting news, for whatever their problems with organizational cover and with cover organization, the Russians suffer no impairment of their ability to exploit another important and common variety of cover for political operations—the front organization.

The difference between cover and front organizations is the subject of some argument among professionals. Cover experts agree that differences exist, but they are often blurred in practice. Many organizations contain features of both, and some cover organizations grow into fronts, and vice versa. Briefly, however, a front organization goes a step or two beyond a cover organization in complexity. Whereas a cover organization exists to mask government involvement in an activity, a front organization hides not only the government involvement, but also the true purpose of that involvement.

Let us suppose that it was suddenly reported from Antarctica that penguins can talk—Penguinese, an ancient Romance languáge —and have certain plans of their own for the continent. A delegation of Penguins would be seated in the UN, and the powers interested in Antarctica would agree that, pending further discussion and negotiation with the Penguins, the present treaty renouncing national territorial claims on Antarctica would continue to be honored.

The first thing that would happen would be the simultaneous establishment of (1) a Soviet-Penguin Friendship Society— Antarctic Branch headed by four Penguin Communists secretly trained at the Soviet South Polar station at Mirny; (2) the Royal Society of Penguin Lovers—Honorary President, Lady Florabella Ffinch-Hyde, noted linguist and bird-watcher; (3) The Penguin Educational and Development Corporation—a private, nonprofit New York corporation headed by a retired Admiral who commanded the last four expeditions to Antarctica; and (4) La Société Française pour la Diffusion de la Culture parmi les Oiseaux Parlants—Monsieur le Président, Guy Pamplemousse, former Socialist Governor-General of Indochina and myna bird collector. All cover organizations.

When interest in Antarctica was at its height, the cover organizations were stumbling over each other's missions to the Penguins, and a summit conference had agreed to keep the Cold War out of Antarctica, a Uruguayan named Schmidt would suddenly issue a call for the founding of an International Union of Antarctic Veterans (IUAV)—purposes: pensions for Antarctic veterans, the exchange of reminiscences among Antarctic veterans, and the provision to the public of factually objective information about Antarctica. The organization would be formed, and at its first Annual Congress, held in Tahiti, the Union would send greetings to its Penguin friends, call on the UN to demand pensions for the membership, and authorize the publication in Greek, Tamil, Swahili, and Guarani of fourteen booklets on life in Antarctica. At the second Annual Congress, held in Accra, Ghana, Schmidt, by now permanent Secretary-General, would point out that no pensions had yet been granted, but that the booklets had sold like hotcakes, and he therefore proposed to distribute a dividend to the membership. Proposal warmly accepted, and Schmidt's suggested resolution on keeping the Cold War out of Antarctica passed unanimously. Fifty-eight additional booklets authorized, this time Urdu, Tibetan, and Gaelic being added to the list of languages.

At the third Annual Congress, held in an oasis in Baluchistan, Schmidt would deliver a ringing speech about pensions, noting that the membership was pretty seedily dressed this time—except for the members from the Soviet Union and the People's Democracies. Sitting down without comment on how the year's booklets had gone, or any mention of a dividend, he would be succeeded as speaker by a Norwegian whaler who had only learned to read the year before by setting type on the booklets. Consequently, he would read his address in broadly accented Swahili, to the gratification of various African members. Translation would show that it was a fiery resolution condemning United States imperialism in Antarctica. Before the resolution could be brought to a vote, Schmidt would deliver a report on the year's activities, showing booklet sales at an all-time high, and announce a dividend, payable at the close of the Congress. The resolution, strengthened from the floor, would then pass by a large majority—and be headline news all over the world the next day. A Penguinese edition of *Pravda,* carrying the resolution on page 1, would be distributed free by the Soviet-Penguin Friendship Society in Antarctica.

Only *The New York Times* would report—besides the resolution on page 4—the interesting information, on page 97, that the American membership, and most of the British and French members, had walked out of the Union, and borrowing carfare home, had established the Free International Union of Veterans of the Antarctic (FIUVA), with headquarters in Arkansas. It would also carry the new organization's announcement that investigation showed that Schmidt, although a Uruguayan, had a Swiss grandmother who had been Lenin's laundress in Zurich in 1912. Furthermore, except for eight library sales and three private purchases of the Greek editions, all of the booklets, to the tune of 1,480,000 copies, had been purchased by SOVEX-IMPORT and used as fill in the Aswan High Dam. FIUVA's announcement would also charge that IUAV was a Soviet front organization. They would be right.

This story—which, except for the Penguins, is by no means as ridiculous as it sounds—illustrates an important difference between cover organizations and front organizations. In a cover organization most of the responsible personnel are aware of the true nature of the organization—of the link to government which is being hidden. In a front organization there may be relatively few of the leading personnel who know; their link to government is hidden— frequently by personal cover—and their true mission is carried out behind the front of the organization's ordinary functions, and behind the front provided by the unwitting personnel.

To some persons all of this has an unsettling ring to it. I know of directors of cover organizations who have resigned on learning officially that they were serving a government-financed and directed group, even though, on accepting appointment, they heartily approved the organization's aims and activities. With all due respect for the scruples and principles which have moved such people, I personally believe that their viewpoint is outmoded by events and by urgent needs. I myself join in their longing and nostalgia for the private initiative, independence, and spontaneity of the nineteenth-century ideal. But, after all, that same ideal, in allegedly more halcyon days, encompassed the Panamanian Revolution, which produced both Panama and the Panama Canal, and for which the United States Congress ultimately paid an indemnity of $8,000,000 to Colombia, the Revolution having been

managed by the New York law firm of Sullivan and Cromwell
under a fee from the U.S. Government—then without a CIA.

We live in a period of sharp conflict in which, for the moment,
the driving forces are two great centers of power. Both powers
proclaim their desire to avoid open conflict of the kind which
would call into play the ultimate weapons; but they also for the
moment feel obliged to continue steps to maintain or gain overt
military advantage. Steps of this sort such as nuclear testing are
bad enough, but they are hostile only implicitly and by indirection.
A step such as the Soviets' 1962 attempt to station their missiles in
Cuba, however, was an act of overt, direct hostility; it could barely
be dignified as even clandestine, and that only to the point of a
rashness which suddenly faced humanity with destruction. It is
this kind of direct and overtly hostile confrontation of the powers,
whether in Cuba, Berlin, or elsewhere, which covert operations—
competently conducted, of course—are historically designed to
avoid. To this extent—and in more than one sense—we might all
pray for more and better cover.[3]

1. I have seen no evidence in the past twenty-five years suggesting that
this is not still the case.

2. The late Dr. Graham Stuart, Professor of Political Science and International Relations at Stanford (under whom I had studied in the late
1930's), wrote me in 1963 that he felt this paragraph embodied the crux of
the problem of the Soviet Union and the international community. He did
not (nor did I in the paragraph) mention China. China too has a government that is merely a cover for a political party, and while the Chinese have
in the past interfered widely abroad (cf. Zanzibar, 1964), their effectiveness
seems limited by their vast domestic problems. With increased economic
development and strength the Chinese may, of course, assume as trouble-
some an international role as the Russians have played for six decades now.
Nevertheless, and notwithstanding Professor Stuart, I feel that something
should be added to the formulation here. The fact is that there are one-
party governments that are not internationally disruptive, or not seriously
so. What is missing in the formulation, therefore, is the combination of one-
party government with messianic zeal and nationalistic expansionism. The
Russia of the Tsars had an abundance of the latter two characteristics (cf.
"The Third Rome"), which contributed to more than two centuries of
territorial conquest. That territorial expansion only became international
disruptiveness on a worldwide scale, however, when the ingredient of the
Bolshevik Party's seizure of the Russian Government was *added* to the
preexisting recipe of messianic impulse and hegemonic ambitions.

3. There seems to have been a sea change in this respect since the 1960's. The Cubans, as surrogates for the Russians, acted openly in Angola from 1975 on, as did the Russians themselves in Afghanistan in 1979 and subsequently. The response of the United States in both Angola and Afghanistan, frequently debated openly in the Congress, cannot be qualified as covert, any more than can the Reagan Administration's open embrace of the Nicaraguan "contras." Sometimes this kind of flouting of good sense on both sides is deliberate: the justification is the desire "to send a signal" to the other side. A properly designed covert "signal" is, of course, just as effective as open bellicosity (assuming that the "signal" is intended for the other side, and not just to enhance domestic appearances).

CHAPTER VI

The Open-faced American

While cover is an art it is also an American weakness. The weakness is both conscious and unconscious. Its conscious aspect is summed up in the reaction of a young and able Harvard graduate whom I had employed for a covert operation in the Mediterranean area. His cover was to be a minor starting clerkship in a shipping firm. When this had been explained to him, he responded, in tones of shocked protest, "But you've got to give a man a cover he can be proud of!"

The unconscious aspect is typified in the experience of a New York corporation executive with whom I was once discussing these problems. A cultivated and elegant man, he was once a guest in a London club. He repaired his first afternoon to the steam room, where he found himself alone and, except for wisps of steam, completely without "cover." He was, he thought, indistinguishable from any Britisher in a steam bath. A club member, a total stranger, entered and, sitting down next to my friend, said, without preliminaries of any kind, "I say, so nice to have an American here."

In the conscious department we must recognize the influence of the Horatio Alger legend and its modern-day Organization Man version. Success is not its sole component; success must also be visible, even conspicuous. The American dream can be a serious handicap to the American agent. Most Americans in the CIA view their work as a career. Its ultimate rewards for them are certainly not financial; but they are matters of recognition, of advancement in the hierarchy, and of power and influence as a high Government official. Very few men are willing to spend long years under cover outside of the Government; the few who do so are remarkable.

I refrain from any estimate of the number of Americans who might be willing to undertake an assignment similar to that of Rudolf Ivanovich Abel, a Colonel in the Red Army who, having succeeded in entering clandestinely into the United States, operated a very successful Soviet spy ring in New York. Separated from his wife and children in the Soviet Union, he for years lived obscurely in New York making an ostensible living at various small odd jobs. And when finally apprehended, he denied all and took his sentence stoically. (His exchange in 1962 for Powers was not his doing, but that of his American lawyer.)

I referred to the question of how many Americans might be *willing* to undertake an assignment like Colonel Abel's. There is also the problem of how many Americans might be *capable* of undertaking such an assignment. In the unconscious department it is a sad fact that all too often American agents look and act like American agents.

Any big-city dweller by his twenty-fifth year—and often earlier —can instinctively spot a plainclothes policeman or a detective. Connoisseurs of that subject can even distinguish between city detectives and private detectives. Similarly, in the world of intelligence, FBI agents—that is, career FBI men who have been through the FBI Academy, as distinct from subagents who only work outside the Bureau—stand out just about like pink carnations in a vase of red roses. Perhaps the widespread comments on their heavy preference for gabardine have now led the Bureau's agents to change into less uniform garb. But experience tells me no one has been able to do anything about their expressionless faces and their transparent reticence. They are of a mold—not unlike the comic strip's Dick Tracy, who any fan knows only laughs once a year and can keep his counsel for as long as five years at a time, no matter how baffled his Chief becomes.

Unfortunately, the same is all too often true of American agents abroad, even if for less obvious reasons. As a nation we may still be maturing, but by now the American has become a readily identifiable physical type abroad. It is not only his appearance; there are such things as gait, manner, and, above all, accent which weigh heavily. Then there are intangibles such as psychological reactions, the approach to facts and situations, the content of idle conversation, daily habits. I myself have passed as an Englishman—but in not very discerning company, obviously never in England, and only by denying indignantly that I was English and claiming proudly that I was a Welshman.

This is about the maximum available to most American agents. There is an obvious logical exception which strangely often fails in practice. These are first- or second-generation Americans. Their principal and most obvious asset is language—the Achilles heel of countless American officials and agents abroad. Apart from the language, however, two things count against them. The first is that the emigrant from a smaller country is easily traceable and even recognizable in his native land—and suspicion, at least on the part of the official authorities, attaches quickly to him. Elsewhere than his native land his situation is better, but, in these days of rapid communications and countless dossiers, his cover story frequently has as many difficulties to overcome as that of a native-born American. An Eastern European exile, for example, who fled Communist persecution in his native land may encounter a sympathetic reception in India or parts of Southeast Asia, but the way is open for the local security or counterespionage authorities to find out much about him from his original country.

All this applies mostly to first-generation Americans. Second-generation Americans suffer some of these handicaps, plus a special one. Sociologists have long remarked the features of American society which produce a desire on the part of second-generation Americans to be more American than the Founding Fathers. This is a goal, represented usually in terms of material gain and community standing, that they will not surrender lightly—indeed cannot, without serious internal conflict, surrender at all.

Notwithstanding these difficulties, the principal exceptions to

American agent cover weaknesses are first- or second-generation Americans. One of the most astute and effective American agents I know—political, not espionage—came to this country as a child from Russia. (In fact, in one of CIA's rare gestures of gratitude, he was awarded a medal and citation. Called to Washington, he was summoned to the Director's office, where Allen Dulles read the citation, bestowed the medal upon him, talked warmly with him for a period, and then, at the conclusion of the ceremony and interview, took back the medal and citation for safekeeping in the vaults. Still and all, it was a nice gesture.) It must be admitted, however, that this agent's accomplishments are more distinguished by virtue of his ability to deal with a very touchy, temperamental, and diverse group of people in difficult circumstances rather than by any particular mastery of unusual cover problems.

All this should not be taken as indicating that the American problem with agent cover is simply that Americans cannot pass as foreigners. It is more subtle and complex than that. From the cover point of view, there is nothing wrong in giving an American agent abroad an American cover; in fact, as implied above, it is the only practical course. But to be an American abroad in itself presupposes—for foreigners—certain things, all of them the result of the modern impression held by foreigners of Americans—whether justified or not. One is the American pride in remaining conspicuously, even aggressively American.

This is expressed in more than PX's and American cars. It is implicit in the American prejudice against "expatriates," a prejudice remarked by knowledgeable foreigners and not held, for example, by Dutchmen or Swiss or Norwegians or Chinese or Japanese toward their own compatriots abroad. In 1958 an American general stationed in Orléans, France, issued a public statement to the effect that he wanted no American in his command who had been abroad longer than four years as he felt they could no longer be good Americans after such an extended exposure to foreign influences. He then suited action to word by departing for the United States shortly thereafter, at the end of his own four years—but not before he had backed down from the ensuing hue and cry by explaining that he had meant that his personnel lost touch with the latest American technical developments. Whether the general meant that or not, I was once told by a high Presidential adviser, who disagreed with my views, "That's the trouble with you Americans who live abroad so long. You become un-Am—" He had the grace to pause and amend his sentence, if not his thought. "You have to adapt too much to the circumstances you live in," he concluded. Foreigners know that, in American eyes, the American has to have a good reason for living abroad.

Related to this is the American view that life abroad, even in the world's most civilized countries, is a physical, psychological, and cultural hardship. This view, known to foreigners not only from their reading, but also from the complaints, clannishness, and attitude of superiority of all too many Americans, reinforces the general belief that an American abroad must have an especially good reason for being there. Lastly, the well-known American addiction to material success, status, and recognition further presupposes a compelling reason for residence outside the United States.

Occasionally the interrelation of what the American is, what the foreigner thinks he is, and what the American thinks the foreigner ideally ought to think he is produces some unexpected results. It was, for example, and still is widely assumed by professionals that a certain bank in a European city is a Soviet cover organization. As U.S. operations in Europe grew in complexity, and their financing became a real problem, it was at one point decided to follow the Russian lead and to take over a certain old-established but relatively inactive bank in a large American city, revise its charter, and establish a branch in Europe. Apart from the fact that the new board of directors was almost too distinguished to be believable, the operation failed because the man chosen to lay the groundwork in a peculiar way overdid his cover.

The local government was not, at that time, issuing charters for new banks; it was necessary to purchase the charter of an existing bank. As it happened, I knew of a small bank that was willing, for a reasonable sum, to sell its charter, subject, as required, to the Finance Ministry's approval. Unfortunately, the emissary from America talked too much. Instead of saying merely that his principals in America wanted to enter banking to make money, he talked incessantly and widely about how local interest rates were usurious. It was his principals' intention, he said in noble, ringing tones, to introduce modern banking practices, to put credit within reach of everyone, for the ultimate benefit of the entire local economy. While he was delivering these sentiments, of course, his hearers, many of them bankers, hastened to the Ministry to protest strongly in advance against the approval of any charter for such disruptive elements. (As a colleague of mine remarked at the time, "A good example of all cover and no agent.")

The conscious and unconscious elements in the American character and personality have led, at least in the domain of agent cover, to two defects. One is excessive use of Government cover abroad; the other is a certain transparency in private cover arrangements.

The use of Government installations abroad as cover is not necessarily a defect in itself; it is a matter of proportion. The proportion applies both to the number of covert operations officials in relation to the number of legitimate officials, and to the number of covert personnel under Government cover in relation to the total covert personnel in any area. Too many covert officials masquerading as legitimate Government officials increases enormously the risks of embarrassment; it also undermines the reputation and effectiveness of the legitimate officials. In addition, it subjects the CIA to a charge which in its own interest, and that of all American covert operations, it ought to avoid: that of exercising a disproportionate influence over United States policy. And finally, too many covert officials working under Government cover, in relation to the total number of covert personnel, produces too great a uniformity of point of view in intelligence reporting and diminishes the scope and effectiveness of covert political operations.

The general situation was described clearly by Thayer Waldo, an American reporter, who wrote in the *San Francisco Chronicle* concerning the Cuban operation:

This reporter spent the first half of last year [1960] in Cuba. At that time, with the U.S. Embassy still in operation and fully staffed, eight of its personnel were CIA agents, three worked for the FBI, and each of the Armed Services had from one to five operatives assigned to intelligence work.

No special effort was required to learn these facts or to identify the individuals so engaged. Within thirty days of arrival in Havana, their names and agency affiliations were made known to me, without solicitation, by other correspondents or Embassy employees.

The latter included one CIA man who volunteered the identities of all three persons accredited to the FBI; and a Cuban receptionist, outspokenly pro-Castro, who ticked off the names of six CIA agents—with entire accuracy, a later check confirmed.

In addition to Embassy staffers, the CIA had a number of operatives (I knew fourteen, but am satisfied there were more) among the large colony of resident U.S. businessmen. One of these, a roofing and installation contractor, had lived in Cuba from the age of six, except for service with the Army during World War II—as a master sergeant in G-2, military intelligence. Predictably, that known background made the man a prime target for observation by Castro's people when U.S.-Cuban relations began to deteriorate seriously. He was shadowed day and night, his every contact reported. Yet the CIA made him its chief civilian agent in Havana.

The American dilemma which all of this reflects can be handled in three ways. The first is by the classical rule of covert operations: if cover is blown or even seriously endangered, suspend the operations until cover has been rebuilt or a new cover developed. The second way is simply to ignore the problem, hoping to get by. The third way is to rely heavily upon agents of foreign nationality. The third way, which has, of necessity, been widely used in American operations, poses problems other than cover—chiefly political—which are discussed elsewhere. In describing cover as an American weakness I had in mind chiefly our heavy preference for the second solution over the first. It is a root cause of our troubles.

In the course of the 1961 Cuban operation, a recruiting office for the anti-Castro forces was established in New York. In due time, the press uncovered this center. At the appearance of the very first article on the subject, the recruiting office was closed. Correct procedure—even if the reason was the proximity of the United Nations rather than a breach of cover. At the same time, however, stories began to fill the newspapers of the training and preliminary operations taking place in Florida, Guatemala, and elsewhere around the Caribbean. The operations continued unchecked. To complain later that the American press was unpatriotic or irresponsible in publishing these stories is unworthy petulance.

This lesson was brought home to me succinctly, if painfully. I was once in immediate charge of an operation similar to, but considerably smaller than, the Cuban operation. To my chagrin, I picked up a leading American newspaper one morning to find that one of the better-known American foreign correspondents had the entire story, with shattering accuracy, starting on page 1. When I saw him shortly thereafter I gave him the usual bureaucratic reproach for irresponsible journalism. His answer was quick. "Look, friend," he said, "that story didn't come to me from any confidential briefing. If I could put it together so could the Russians and a lot of other people. Take it as a measure of how well your arrangements are working." I found the logic irrefutable.

Knowledge of the projected Cuban operation was by no means confined to American reporters. Was Castro's Foreign Minister, Dr. Rau, also unpatriotic when he presented these same stories before the United Nations? Can anyone believe that Dr. Rau's sole source was American newspapers? That Castro sympathizers and foreign correspondents of all nationalities didn't know what was going on, once the cover wore thin? The responsible party in this situation was not the American editor; it was the American official who, knowing that cover exists to mask connections and activities from the press just as much as from anyone else, and that the cover on this operation had been blown, decided to go ahead anyway. In other words, he consciously chose the second solution over the classical rule.

To state that an official was responsible is not necessarily tantamount to saying that he was wrong. For a variety of reasons I personally believe the decision in the 1961 Cuban operation was gravely wrong. But this does not vitiate the principle that, in any given situation, the ultimate authority, recognizing that perfect cover is an unattainable ideal, can weigh the risks and decide, without being either arrogant or irresponsible, to ignore the classical rule.

The U-2 case illustrates the point—plus a few specific weaknesses.

Faced with the implications of our cover difficulties, the Government made a concerted study in 1954 to find new ways of meeting our needs for intelligence about the Soviet Union. The U-2 was one result of this study. Its primary appeal was, of course, the unquestionable veracity and reliability of the information it could produce.

So far as the basing of the planes and the transmission of the collected information for processing were concerned, the operation used American and allied airbases as cover, plus a cover story that the planes were engaged in meteorological research. The flights over the Soviet Union were, however, clandestine rather than covert. There was no conceivable story which could cover the presence of the airplane 1,000 miles from the nearest Soviet border nor, with the photographic and monitoring equipment aboard, explain the role of the pilot as being other than what it was. If there was any cover for the flights themselves, it lay in the technical performance of the aircraft—its ability to fly above the range of Soviet anti-aircraft weapons and at a speed which guaranteed it could outdistance any pursuers.

This protection, however, was subject to two risks: one, mechanical failure; and two, Soviet development of weapons which could intercept the aircraft. It is still not clear which of these eventualities materialized. In any event, the decision was made that the potential results justified the risks. General Eisenhower has stated that the operation was justified on exactly these grounds, namely, that the advantages outweighed the risks. The four-year history of the operation certainly seems to support this decision. So far so good.

However, responsible cover for the operation would not be limited to these considerations. It would also of necessity have to embrace the steps to be taken in the event of an interception of the aircraft. Clearly this had been taken into account in the U-2 operation. How well it was taken into account is another matter.

When Powers's flight was overdue, the cover story was issued. Its announcement by the National Aeronautics and Space Administration was authoritative reinforcement for the story that these were meteorological research flights. The story itself, of a flight over a triangular course within Turkey, with one leg approaching the Soviet border, of a message at about this point from the pilot reporting difficulties with his oxygen equipment, and the suggestion that the pilot must have lost consciousness and inadvertently crossed into the Soviet Union while in this condition, was adequate. The accompanying bellicose assertion that the Russians must have outrageously destroyed the airplane was gratuitous and politically inept. It was not, however, the fundamental defect of the cover story.

The defect was simply that, at the very least, for the story to be at all plausible, the airplane had to be totally destroyed. And for it to be a fully valid cover story not only would the airplane have to have been destroyed; the pilot would also have to be dead. Even with only the wreckage of the aircraft, the Russians—as was shown—could make a mockery of the cover story. But with only the wreckage, public opinion would be inclined to believe that the Russians were lying in their charges of deliberate overflights for reconnaissance purposes, and the issue would ultimately have been obscured in dispute. With the pilot alive, however, the possibility of clouding the issue was materially lessened. Powers could certainly not have hoped to pass as anything except an American pilot. But if he himself had maintained the same cover story as that given out by the NASA, it is possible, though not certain in the face of the evidence the plane wreckage provided, that the issue could have been kept sufficiently in doubt so that Soviet ability to exploit the incident would be kept to a minimum. This is what might be called the last-ditch function of cover.

But Powers talked. (According to CIA announcement in March of 1962, at the time of Powers's appearance before the U.S. Senate Armed Services Committee, this was in keeping with his instructions.) Naturally, the same people who thought all signers of the Peace Appeal were Communist dupes alleged that Powers was a Soviet agent. This again is a defeatist view which clouds the true problem. Personally, I wonder about the role of the American Dream in this case. From Powers's public statements in Moscow and from his published letters to his wife, it appears that his chief motive in his work was to save the money to buy a house.

There is evidence that the role of both plane and pilot had been thought about in advance. The Russians claimed that the U-2 was equipped with a button which, when pressed, would totally destroy the aircraft and the pilot, and that Powers had been told only that it would destroy the plane after the mechanism had first ejected him. This is open to conjecture, in view of Powers's statement that the destruction switch was designed to eject him first, and that, prevented by gravity from reaching it, he was only able to eject himself but not to destroy the plane. If the Russian version is true —which we will never know—the question whether or not Powers knew the true function of the button is immaterial. If Powers knew, then the cover for the operation ultimately depended upon his suicide. If he did not know, it depended, in effect, upon his murder. It is axiomatic among covert professionals that a cover which depends for its success upon the suicide of the agent is not reliable. It is only slightly less accepted that a cover which depends for its success upon the murder of the agent, even by mechanical means, is also not reliable. Victims have a way of behaving unpredictably and thereby unconsciously outwitting even mechanical devices.

But regardless of advance provisions for plane and pilot, we come back here to a fundamental weakness of American cover practice. The cover for the U-2 operation was good as far as it went. My own view is that the cover did not go far enough. It could have gone farther, far enough to preserve the reputation and prestige of the United States Government, not to mention the stature and capacity for maneuver of the American President, but only by one means. That sole means was the story the agent himself would give to his captors. The CIA public statement on the case does not mention whether Powers was told of what the NASA cover story would be in the event of disaster. The point is far from academic. If Powers's instructions were as stated by the Senate Armed Services Committee ("pilots should . . . adopt a cooperative attitude toward their captors [and] are perfectly free to tell the full truth about their mission . . .") the question arises of why the detailed and belligerent NASA cover story was originally issued when Powers was missing.

Our problems and weaknesses with cover do not stop with the difficulties of adapting the American personality to this work or with a recurring slipshod tendency in our arrangements. The basic weakness is a heavy preference for the alternative of hoping to get by over the well-founded rule of pausing when cover is endangered. It is tantamount to downgrading cover as an element in covert operations, which is, in turn, like playing baseball without a bat. One of our fondest national legends is that if you want success enough, success will come. But in covert operations, even more than in open war, it is vital to plan for both success and failure. Cover is the realm where this is done.

On April 15, 1961, three B-26 bombers—a type of plane then still in Castro's Air Force—raided military targets in Cuba, mostly airfields around Havana. The planes then flew to Florida where, upon landing, one of the pilots was permitted to see the press. He gave out a laboriously detailed account of how he and his companions, who he said were all officers in the Cuban Air Force, had planned to defect from Castro for months. Fearing detection of their plans, the group had taken to their planes that morning, he said, and, as a final gesture of resistance, had bombed military targets on their way to exile in the United States. This was the cover story—for, as a quick count of his Air Force told Castro, the bombers had come from outside Cuba.

The bombing had a twofold purpose: militarily it was supposed to cripple Castro's Air Force in preparation for the invasion, planned for forty-eight hours later; politically, it was supposed to create the impression before Cuban and world opinion—including American—of a mounting opposition to Castro inside Cuba. The military success of the operation did not depend in any way on the cover story. Its political success, on the other hand, was totally dependent upon the cover story. As anticipated, the press—particularly the American newspapers—gave a big play to the cover story. Castro's denial that any of his Air Force had defected was thrown into doubt. The impression was created of strife, potent opposition, and turmoil in Castro's Cuba. So far so good. In the hue and cry the basic defect was barely visible.

But it was there, all the same. It was simply that there was a definite time limit on this initial success. That limit was the day when a foreign correspondent left Cuba and reported the truth. For world opinion, that day would occur when any reputable correspondent filed his story supporting Castro's denial; but the effectiveness of this eventuality, at least for American opinion, could—unfortunately all too easily—be sharply limited by denunciation, and the limit put off until an American correspondent returned with the true story—as later happened.

Those responsible for this operation could not but be fully aware of this time limit. They were also aware that the invasion was scheduled for forty-eight hours later. Since the blowing of this cover story would seriously compromise the U.S. Government's reputation and integrity—not the least with the American press itself—there had to be an assumption that the cover would hold beyond the obvious limit. There were only two possibilities which would have produced such a result. One was that the invasion would succeed, in which case the true story would have been suppressed or overlooked or even condoned in the aura of success. The other was that the invasion would be partially successful and the story forgotten in the drama of civil war. It is impossible to know which of these alternatives weighed most heavily; most probably both weighed equally in deluding the authors of this scheme that it was usable. The fact that certain Americans in New York were approached—by American officials—prior to the Cuban invasion and offered jobs as advisers to a new Cuban Government-to-be suggests that not much distinction was being made between total and partial success. And in making a judgment about cover it doesn't matter. For any operation which relies on success for the preservation of its cover, or presupposes that success will obliterate the fact of blown cover, is not a covert operation. It is not even clandestine. It is a gamble.

American weaknesses with cover will not be solved by looking for scapegoats. The problem is more complex than the individual responsibility of some official and more profound than the organizational chart or allotted powers of some government agency. It is compounded of three main elements.

One is, as was suggested by the Powers case, the psychological limitations on Americans acting as agents.

Another is a certain slipshod quality at the professional level, which is not so much a lack of thoroughness as it is the hope to get by. In the summer of 1960 two young Americans, traveling ostensibly as students gathering materials for treatises, were arrested by the Russians in the Ukraine on charges of espionage. (It is worth noting that each denounced the other and that they were forthwith released and expelled from the Soviet Union.) They were traveling, they said, on grants from the Northcraft Educational Fund, of Baltimore, Maryland. An American reporter, hoping that the Fund itself would be able to refute the Russian charge, uncovered the fact that no such organization existed in Baltimore or anywhere else. In this case, a minor expenditure for a one-room office and a telephone listing would have saved the U.S. Government considerable embarrassment.

The other main element in our difficulties stems from the highest levels of Government. At these levels decisions are made on whether or not to proceed with those operations which engage the world-wide power and position of the United States. No one who has observed this decision-making process can be other than sympathetic to those who carry the burden. But it is my impression that where those decisions have led to difficulty or even disaster, it is because at this level there was too little understanding of the nature and importance of cover. A certain desperation governs such decisions; there is a feeling that political and power considerations outweigh cover. When, for example, the overthrow of the Arbenz regime in Guatemala was decided upon in 1954, and the highest levels of Government insisted, over the vigorous protests of CIA professionals, on the use of aircraft in the operation, no serious observer—and there were millions in Latin America—believed that Colonel Castillo Armas just happened to be the owner of a number of American bombers. The question can properly be asked whether we would not have had more Latin American support in the Castro problem if we had not been so flamboyant in Guatemala. Cover certainly does not outweigh fundamental considerations of politics and power; but in covert operations it is an integral part of the international political results of those operations.[1]

Whatever may be the shortcomings of the open-faced American in this work, they are never ameliorated by Americans either overconfident of or desperate for success.

1. A remarkably classic example of the flow of consequences from this relationship is provided by the Reagan Administration's operations in and with Iran. There was abundant secrecy (a good deal where it should not have been), some rather successful clandestinity, and covers so ill-conceived and flimsy as to leave, in the sad end, only two alternative views of the President of the United States: either a rash and clumsy schemer, or a cheery dreamer unaware of the realities about him.

CHAPTER VII

Intelligence

On a single November day in 1961 the European Edition of the New York *Herald Tribune,* containing not even four pages of general news, carried four stories concerning espionage. A former German staff sergeant in the Waffen SS and his wife, arrested while traveling in the Soviet Union as tourists, pleaded guilty before a military court in Kiev to charges of espionage in the Soviet Union on behalf of the United States. In Cairo two members of a French official mission to Egypt, arrested six days earlier, appeared on television to confess to charges of espionage against the United Arab Republic on behalf of the French Government—the confessions amounting to admissions of "routine political and economic reports" sent to the French Foreign Ministry and including a report of the possibility of an Israeli attack on the U.A.R. In Washington and Bonn the United States State Department released a 21-page document analyzing Communist espionage activity in Berlin and Germany, including the case of an American woman Armed Forces employee who had been, under the guise of a romance with an ostensible American citizen whom she met at the American Embassy Club in Bonn, the victim of a fairly crude Soviet attempt in East Berlin to blackmail her into passing secret documents to the Soviets. And finally, in probably the day's most plaintive note, Prime Minister Nehru of India told his Parliament that "international spies" outnumbered the normal population of the Himalayan border town of Kalimpong. "Every important country has espionage agents functioning there," he said, with what one can only imagine, in the absence of further details, must have been a catch in his throat.

A fairly representative daily selection. The Russians accuse the Americans, incidentally dragging in the West German problem; the Americans accuse the Russians, mixing in the East German problem for good measure; the Arabs accuse the French, sideswiping the Israelis in the process; and neutral Nehru, without being specific, accuses everybody, thus by implication correcting the day's omissions of mention of Britain and China. Without judging the merits or validity of these particular cases, and leaving aside their self-righteous exploitation by prosecutors and propagandists, the question can fairly be asked as to what all this activity is about. Assuming, justifiably, that the number of espionage agents caught is at any given moment only an infinitesimal fraction of the total operating, what are these thousands upon thousands of people looking for? The answer is: secret intelligence.

The official American definition of intelligence is "evaluated information." The evaluation simultaneously concerns both the credibility of the information itself—a process involving a check against information already in hand and an educated guess as to the new information—and the reliability of the source. The two cannot be totally divorced from each other. Obviously, a report that the Moroccans are mobilizing 30,000 men for an attack on the

Spanish territories bordering Morocco is one thing if it comes from a taxi driver in Casablanca and quite another thing if it comes from the official in charge of mobilization in the Moroccan Ministry of National Defense. All other things being equal, the official source will be evaluated as of high reliability, and—in the present state of affairs—the information being credible, the report will be considered valuable intelligence on which some action may be based. If, however, the taxi driver's report is supplemented by, say, forty similar reports from merchants, including army suppliers, from families whose sons have allegedly been among those thus conscripted, and from a variety of citizens throughout Morocco, then the information takes on the status of a widespread rumor. In this case, the problem becomes that of assessing the credibility of the information itself: Was the rumor deliberately circulated, and if so, by whom and why? Is it a reflection of a state of alarm among the Moroccan populace? Is it an implied threat to the Spanish by the Moroccan Government to hasten negotiations? Did the Spanish spread the rumor to provide a justification for some action they plan? Or is it simply a genuine Moroccan action which could not in the circumstances be kept secret? While the lone taxi driver's report would warrant no action whatsoever, the widespread rumor would require action to provide answers to this whole series of questions—would require action, that is, of an intelligence service whose government felt it had an active interest in Moroccan-Spanish affairs.[1]

The matter of the authoritativeness of the source can never be ignored, but it is sometimes overdone in the light of the credibility of the information. In the summer of 1945, the Soviet passenger-freighter *Balkhash,* of 15,000 tons, and bound for Vladivostok, was proceeding at night through the Straits of La Perouse from the Sea of Okhotsk to the Sea of Japan. As the Soviets were not yet at war with Japan, the ship's lights were blazing and the large red Soviet flags painted on the hull, together with the letters "U.S.S.R," were floodlit. Sometime around midnight the *Balkhash* was torpedoed and sank in a very few minutes, with some loss of life. The survivors were rescued by Japanese fishing vessels and coastal craft during the night and the following morning. Several weeks later I forwarded to Washington a report concerned not with the fact of the sinking, but with the reaction of Soviet citizens to the sinking of a Soviet ship by an *American* submarine—which was withal remarkably philosophical—since it was accepted by Soviet maritime authorities that, in the then state of the Japanese Navy, the submarine could only have been American. The result for me was a peremptory query from my superiors as to the basis for my assumption that the submarine in question was American. When I replied that I was reporting a Soviet reaction to a Soviet assumption, based on logical deduction, that the submarine must be American, I was coldly reminded that I was reporting mere rumor without labeling it as such, and thereby casting doubt on the reliability of my reports. (Much later, in Washington, I got to the bottom of this one: my chief acknowledged that it had in fact been an American submarine, but added, "You didn't think we were going to admit it to you, did you?" Nevertheless, I took the reprimand so to heart at the time that when, several months later, a reliable Soviet source informed me, twenty-four hours in advance of Moscow's declaration of war, that the Soviet Union was already at war with Japan—which I reported with all haste—but then six hours later, fearing trouble for himself, denied his earlier information, I canceled my original message, only to awaken the next morning to Moscow's announcement.)

The question of what is authoritative and what is not is also relative. A highly authoritative source may convey eminently credible information, but the question must always be asked—most particularly in the case of highly authoritative sources—"Why?" The danger of planted information—a complex subject covered in the next chapter—is always present. To this extent, a stolen document is often intelligence superior to a gratuitously conveyed secret from whatever source, since it obviates the risk of deliberately misleading information. The "why" does not apply only to the danger of planted information, however. It must also be asked of the source whose bona fides are beyond question. The danger here is of an intelligence headquarters believing what it wants to believe—a failing that has affected almost all the world's secret services and governments at one time or another. The outstanding recent example was, unfortunately, provided by the American Government in the 1961 Cuban affair. There was neither malice nor an effort to mislead in the reports of anti-Castro Cubans—nor in those of American agents in Cuba tied to American commercial interests undergoing expropriation—that an invasion of Cuba by anti-Castro exiles would result in an uprising of the Cuban people against Castro. This was their natural, human, logical bias, reflecting hopes which touched the very core of their beings. The fault was not in the bias of those so reporting; it is a rare man who in their circumstances would have done otherwise. The fault lay with those who, in evaluating these reports, gave them too much weight. They did not accept fully the logical answer to the "why" of these reports—perhaps because the answer countered their own hopes; they discounted more dispassionate, even if unpopular, reports of observers such as Claiborne Pell, a politician with considerable experience at the working level in foreign affairs, who, while still Senator-elect from Rhode Island, visited Cuba privately and quietly, and reported that hopes for an anti-Castro uprising were, at worst, wishful thinking and, at best, premature.

The problem of the bias of the evaluators is one that is unavoidable in intelligence; it extends even to information of fullest credibility from the most reliable sources. There was a story circulating just after the Suez invasion of 1956 which I have never verified, but which, even if only apocryphal, is still plausible. According to this story, a Secretary of the American Embassy in Israel—no secret agent by any means—stumbled onto the fact of the forthcoming Franco-British-Israeli action against Egypt by the simple expedient of an accidental but friendly conversation with some French Air Force pilots who were in Israel with their Mystère jet fighters to aid the Israelis. It was alleged that the Secretary's report of this information was not only suppressed, but he himself was reprimanded. The story could well apply to any country. After all, the German High Command in World War II had at least three reliable reports stating the date and place for the Allied invasion of Normandy, but they chose to believe in a later date and, even after the landings had taken place, that the real Allied assault would take place in the Pas de Calais. And Alexander Foote, in his remarkable account of his World War II experiences as a Soviet secret agent in Switzerland, has pointed out how Red Army intelligence, suspicious of what appeared to be too great ease and rapidity, month after month rejected his network's greatest achievement of almost daily detailed reports of battle order and plans straight from the Headquarters of the Wehrmacht, the German Navy, and the Air Force, in favor of banal reports from a man who was in fact a German agent.

Bias in evaluation can never be fully overcome in an intelligence service and, more importantly, in supreme government councils; it cannot even be tempered by shuffling and reshuffling the organizational charts; and it can only be compounded by creating evalu-

ators to evaluate the evaluators. Within the intelligence establish
ment, the only effective safeguard lies in the individual competenc
and qualities of its members. Doctrinaire partisans, superpatriots
men of provincial outlook, bureaucratic climbers—all are, in thi
field, dangers to the national safety, however comfortably they ma
accord with the popular temper or ethos or with the preconcep
tions of legislators and of the Administration in office. Perspective
perspicacity, worldliness, a soundly philosophical outlook, th
knowledge and sense of human history—these are the individua
qualities which minimize error in the interpretation and evaluatio
of information. (Contrary to the tenets of the majority of America
administrators, intellectual brilliance—even if eccentric, trouble
some to the organizational charts, or occasionally shining throug
a bottle of whisky—is also a valuable asset. A sense of humor, o
the other hand, may be of no particular national interest, but is a
essential prop to the sanity of those who work in intelligence.
Professional excellence inside the intelligence establishment is bu
half the story; to be effective as a safeguard it must be comple
mented by international political sagacity in the nation's foreig
affairs leadership.

The definition of intelligence as "evaluated information" doe
not, unfortunately, touch upon the most important element which
confers value on intelligence—and which also explains the tru
objective of all secret agents. The objective is secret intelligence, a
stated above, but the emphasis is on the vital element contained i
the word "secret."

The need for intelligence is an effect, not a cause. It is the resul
of situations of human conflict or competition which, between na
tions, run the gamut from the inescapable frictions and rivalrie
among allies, through the wary maneuvers of potential enemie
and the covert clashes of the secret war, to open hostilities. What
ever the degree, the essence of the situation is human conflict. I
any such situation, as we have seen previously, the most potent an
useful information about an opponent is that which he does no
know you possess.

Thus the meaning of "secret" in the phrase "secret intelligence'
is precise and specific. It does *not* mean that the opposition doe
not possess the same information. By definition, since the informa
tion came from them, they do. What is secret, what is unknown to
the opposition, is the fact of your possession of the information
The contrast between Pearl Harbor and the subsequent Battle o

Midway is an obvious example. American possession of the Japanese codes prior to Pearl Harbor yielded only the information that a carrier task force was on the high seas operating under radio silence—with the results known to history. The Japanese had to consider the contingency that the Americans had broken their codes, but the very fact of their victory at Pearl Harbor was, to them, important evidence that we had not succeeded in doing so. Accordingly, Japanese radio traffic prior to the Midway battle, only six months after Pearl Harbor, revealed not only the whereabouts and destinations of two Japanese striking forces, but also (correctly interpreted) showed that the northernmost of the two fleets had a principally diversionary purpose. Admiral Nimitz was thus enabled to concentrate his defending forces at the point of maximum danger—with the resultant decisive U.S. victory at Midway. Needless to say, only one ill-advised public statement by a member of the commissions investigating the Pearl Harbor debacle, or by any of the principals in the disaster, to all of whom our possession of the Japanese codes was known, would have sufficed to make the Midway victory impossible.[2]

This is not to deny either the existence or value of non-secret intelligence, i.e., intelligence which the opposition either knows or must assume you possess. In fact, the great bulk of intelligence is obtained overtly from a vast range of sources. The study and analysis of publications, broadcasts, statistics, diplomatic and military reports yield an enormous amount of basic information. (Such research and analysis is the overt function, in the United States, of the intelligence branches of the State Department, the Defense Intelligence Agency, the armed forces, the Atomic Energy Commission, and the CIA.) Furthermore, a great many of the new scientific intelligence operations, such as communications analysis and nuclear explosion detection, are overtly acknowledged; only the scientific devices or techniques are secret. (In the detection of nuclear explosions, even the end result is made public, since, in this almost unique case, the national power is reinforced and not weakened by demonstrating knowledge of enemy actions.) The remainder of intelligence—including that universal governmental prop, the routine surveillance of cables, telegrams, and mail—is secret intelligence, i.e., intelligence which the opposition assumes you do not possess. Such intelligence is, at a guess, quantitatively no more than 20 per cent at maximum of the total intelligence available to a major government. Yet, whether political, military, economic, or scientific, it is intelligence of the highest value.

It is this very precise meaning of the word "secret" in "secret intelligence" which dictates some of the fundamental characteristics and techniques of secret intelligence operations. It is, for example, the basis of a perpetual misunderstanding between the public, the press, and legislatures—particularly the American—on the one hand, and the executive branch of government, including the intelligence services, on the other. This is the misunderstanding which arises when a secret agent is caught. In such cases, it is fundamental secret intelligence practice on the part of the capturing government never to reveal publicly what it was precisely that the agent had obtained. (This is why the legal indictments of captured secret agents are always couched in broad, vague terms, and the evidence made public generally limited to proving the activities of the accused without specific reference to information he obtained. Such trials frequently cause almost as many headaches to the intelligence authorities—particularly in America, where the statutes and precedents in such cases are of fairly recent origin—as capturing the agent in the first place.) It is at this point that an article usually appears somewhere pointing out that the Russians—or the appropriate nationality—already know what the agent knew, so what is the Government being so tight-lipped about? If the Russians know it, why can't we? Even an editor so personally experienced in secret intelligence operations as the Englishman Malcolm Muggeridge recently expressed pique on this subject. "Secrets which are known to have leaked, far from being written off, are guarded with particular ferocity," he wrote in the *New Statesman,* and added, in evident exasperation, "The most wonderfully complicated locks are put on the stable door after the horse is gone."

If it is remembered that the secrecy which is at stake is not whether or not you know something, or even whether the enemy also knows the same thing, but the more complicated fact of knowing whether the enemy knows you know it, the reason becomes apparent. It is simply that any public discussion of the information obtained by a captured agent risks conferring validity, for the enemy's benefit, on that information. In effect, you risk evaluating the information for the enemy. The public statement, "The Government is embarrassed that the recently apprehended enemy agent discovered the location of our 27 secret missile bases," or "The Prosecution demands the death penalty, the accused having stolen and transmitted to the enemy the Army's war plans," obviously confirms to the enemy that what he has is of prime value. Silence, on the other hand, downgrades the information in the enemy's possession. He is left to follow the course of the public trial, while wrestling with several vital and unanswerable questions: How much of what our agent transmitted to us do they really know was transmitted? The plans for the East Coast antimissile defense system, for example? Will they change them, knowing we know them, or do they not suspect we do, and therefore will leave them as they are? And what about that purported summary of a meeting of the National Security Council? Their silence certainly gives us nothing concrete with which to evaluate that report —which we were doubtful about anyway. And so on. Silence may not undo all serious damage, but it is the only way to minimize it. (Silence also has a positive aspect. For years following the surrender of Japan, American authorities refused any official mention of the case of Richard Sorge, Soviet agent who operated in Japan until his arrest in 1943, for the reason that the ramifications and techniques of that network were of great value in uncovering other and subsequent Soviet operations—a fact dependent in large measure on the Soviets not knowing how much we had learned from the Japanese archives.)

Similarly, the concept of secrecy as hiding from the enemy your possession of information, more than the information itself, dictates, in the reverse case, the practice of secret agents in the field and the preparations they must always make for the eventuality of capture. The cardinal principle in secret intelligence operations is the observance of priorities of expendability in the event of compromise, discovery, or arrest. The first and easiest thing to dispose of in case of danger is money and property. (One of the many reasons why secret intelligence is an expensive business.) The very next thing is the individual agent himself. While it is obviously incumbent on every agent, as a matter of primary personal and professional interest, to observe meticulously all possible security precautions concerning himself, it is a bald fact that, when the choice must be made, the national interest dictates that the agent himself has a high priority of expendability.

After the agent himself come the "lines of communication." This phrase can be taken to include a clandestine radio transmitter or codes, but it more usually refers to the human connections, the prearranged relationships and contacts in the field and running back to the headquarters, which make up a secret intelligence network. The lines of communication are the entire conspiratorial apparatus which links all the individual agents together to form a functioning network, ranging from the "place of conspiracy"—a predetermined time and place of meeting between agents who have lost contact—to the methods of transmission of intelligence to headquarters. (It can easily be seen that, faced with the choice between the loss of a single agent and the compromise or destruction of an entire network, the single agent is the more readily expendable. There are, of course, sub-priorities here: the loss of a cut-out who knows no true identities is much less serious than the arrest of the principal agent. But the point is that without "lines of communication" there is no secret intelligence network; there is only a useless number of unconnected, unco-ordinated, and unresponsive individuals.)

The least expendable asset is information already transmitted to headquarters, or anything which will provide a clue to that information. It is the agent's ultimate duty, in the event of danger, to insure, by any and all means, that the knowledge of information already transmitted does not, either directly or indirectly, become available to the opposition. (There is obviously a time limit to this necessity, but it depends entirely on the merits of each individual case and is not a matter which a single agent is usually equipped to judge.) It is bad enough to lose a functioning intelligence network to the enemy; it is a double or triple loss also to have all the operation's previous work wiped out at a single blow—for if the enemy knows what information you already possess, it is, by definition, no longer secret intelligence. This point is all too infrequently understood even by secret agents themselves. They are often under the illusion that, in the event of danger, they burn their papers or swallow scraps containing cipher keys or make other such heroic gestures to hide proof of their illegal activity or to protect the government they are serving. These are desirable objectives, certainly, but they are very much secondary to the fundamental necessity to preserve the secrecy and hence value of secret intelligence already obtained.

The matter of codes illustrates the point clearly. The secret breaking of a code is a major disaster (or triumph); the opposition's possession of the code, being unknown or unsuspected by the user, is secret intelligence of exceptionally high value. However, this eventuality is not and cannot be the responsibility of the agent, provided he observes all necessary precautions in the use of his codes. The fundamental utility and security of codes is the function of the headquarters' cryptographic staff. But mere compromise of a code—that is, any set of circumstances which leaves unresolved the question of whether or not the opposition benefited from those circumstances to obtain or to break the code—can be almost as damaging. (There is no practical difference so far as countermeasures are concerned between knowing the opposition has obtained the code and the obligation rationally to assume they have it. Once, at the outset of a mission traveling across Communist territory, my pockets were picked and my wallet stolen in, of all places, a circus. Besides money and personal documents, the wallet contained—I am ashamed to say—a scrap of paper on which was written an unidentified random phrase which happened to be the key to my double transposition code. It was highly likely that I was merely the victim of a hungry and light-fingered citizen; I nevertheless had to assume that the security police were light-fingered, if not hungry, and that any cryptographer, looking at my quite innocent scrap of paper, would have no choice but to try it out as the key to a double transposition code. Even though I could remember the phrase, I still completed the rest of the mission in silence —which did nothing for the timeliness of the information I was seeking and for which my base was waiting.)

The possession by the opposition of a code has effects both forward and backward in time. If you do not know your code is broken, the opposition has the entire backlog of the network's efforts, plus the ability to monitor the entire operation into the future. If, however, you know the opposition has the code, or are obliged to assume they have it, their advantage over future operations can immediately be canceled either by substitution of another code or silence until an alternative code is obtained. But nothing can repair the damage done to the intelligence already transmitted: it simply ceases to be intelligence. For this reason a secret agent has no better ally than a good memory and no more dangerous enemy than a nice, orderly, complete set of files.

Finally, and most importantly, this precise definition of secrecy in the phrase "secret intelligence" means that intelligence, to be secret, must be obtained in such a way that the opposition does not know what is being obtained. The steps the agent takes to mask his activity are merely elementary security; his main concern must be to keep the enemy from knowing what he knows, rather than the

mere fact that he knows something. This is one reason a micro-
filmed document—obtained without anyone's knowledge—is more
durable intelligence and superior to information obtained, no matter how secretly, from a secret, even if genuine, sympathizer in the
enemy camp. But since such uncompromised opportunities for obtaining information are extremely rare, the standard procedure in
all intelligence services is to seek wherever possible to establish
lines of communication in such a way that persons providing information do not know its ultimate destination. More than one potential purveyor of secret information—even for the highest motives—
has been bewildered to find his sincere advances rebuffed by the
very services he hopes to assist. The rebuff arises, however, only
partly from possible suspicion of his motives. An additional reason
for rejection of his offer is the fact that to accept it puts him in the
position of knowing the identity of the end-users of the information; this knowledge on his part increases the risk of the enemy
being able to invalidate all previous information passed by him if
they uncover his activities. In brief, if you know the recipient, you
can sometimes deduce what information he has received.

Similarly, it is this distinction between the act of obtaining secret
intelligence and the sure knowledge of what is being obtained
which explains in part the international tolerance of military at-
tachés. While a part of this tolerance is due to the "I'll accept your
legitimate spies if you'll accept mine" theory, it is also just as
firmly based on the conviction of the receiving government that it
can control—that is, know—what information an attaché is obtaining. In most countries this is done by discreet surveillance. In
the Soviet Union and its satellites, however, the surveillance is
done with the heaviest and most obvious possible hand—not only
as a control measure, but also as a forthright obstruction to any
activity at all by the diplomat or attaché being so conspicuously
and ubiquitously "tailed."

It may seem superfluous, even banal, to point out that the information sought in secret intelligence operations is originally in the
possession of foreign nationals. In brief, the sources of secret intelligence are, by definition, foreign. However, this pedestrian but
fundamental fact has important consequences for the conduct of
such operations. Foremost among these is the constant necessity to
gain and hold the co-operation of foreign nationals who have the
essential access to the desired information—even if such a foreign
source is hostile. There are secret intelligence operations which do

not involve foreigners; I suppose the U-2 operation could be counted as one, although even here the co-operation of foreign governments was required for the basing of the airplanes. Nevertheless, the overwhelming majority of operations depends heavily upon foreigners for their ability to produce anything of real value. The complex of Soviet operations designed to obtain information about nuclear weapons would have been impossible without the co-operation of American and British personnel.

The vital question of whether a foreign source is willing, whether he knows and understands what he is doing, is one on which a clear and precise decision must be taken at the very outset of any operation. It is here that a most accurate assessment of the foreigner's motives, capabilities, and general emotional and intellectual posture must be brought into play. A man thoroughly disaffected with the regime under which he lives may regard services to a foreign intelligence service as fulfilling a higher duty to his own nation. If such a feeling is genuine, his knowledge of what he is doing it for may be an essential part of his co-operation, even if it does constitute an added risk to the security of the operation and the secrecy of the information he provides. Here the Soviets have a valuable asset in the ideological loyalty of foreign Communists to the Soviet state. However, they also suffer compensating liabilities. The facts of life under Soviet power provide plenty of disaffection which can be exploited by others for secret intelligence purposes. This is patently true of the satellite countries; but even in the Soviet Union itself, with its rigid safeguards, its xenophobia, and its security mania, there is exploitable disaffection. (This is not to lend the slightest credibility to the fantastic Soviet charge that Lavrenty Beria, Stalin's long-time secret police head, was an American agent. Even Trotsky, hounded and persecuted—and ultimately murdered—by Stalin, would have balked at any kind of co-operation with capitalist intelligence services. However, in my own experiences with the Russians I found a sufficient, even though always limited, number of useful Soviet sources, although I admit that to do so I became a temporary expert in fence-climbing, back-alley skulking, and general dodging. I never recall without a twitching of my nostrils one source whom I always met in a particularly filthy and foul-smelling public toilet. For a long time I hoped that my superiors would someday comment that "This information stinks," thereby giving me an opportunity for a witty and pungent rejoinder, but my chance never came.

An intelligence service cannot, however, limit itself to using disaffection on the part of foreign nationals for its sources of information. Furthermore, if at all possible, it is desirable—and sometimes necessary—that the foreign source not understand clearly what he is doing or for whom. The most desirable such situation is one in which the source does not know that he is in fact providing information to a foreign intelligence network. This ideal was achieved by Richard Sorge—the Soviet agent of German nationality working in Japan during the Second World War—who achieved the position of Press Attaché of the German Embassy in Tokyo. The Embassy staff naturally were under the impression that they were talking with a loyal Nazi colleague, and many—though not all—of Sorge's Japanese sources believed they were working with a German ally. A variant of this situation consists in the source knowing that he is providing information, while laboring under a carefully sown misapprehension as to who is really benefiting thereby. Let us take the hypothetical case of an Iraqi Government functionary who is profoundly disturbed by a flirtation between the dictator, General Kassem, and the local Communist Party. He may genuinely fear the possibility of eventual Soviet domination of Iraq and the danger of ultimate loss of the Kurdish territories in the north. At the same time, the Israeli Government, in the interests of elemental survival, must have all information possible about their Arab neighbors. The Iraqi official, as a patriot and as a good Arab, would never consider for one minute aiding the Israelis. But, in his concern, he would consider entering into a working relationship with the Americans, who would constitute, in his mind, the logical counterweight to Soviet influence in Iraq. The simple solution to this problem is that the Israeli agent who recruits this official poses as an American agent. It is sad to have to relate that this technique enjoyed, at least during the Fifties, a certain vogue in many parts of the world, with the Americans as the favorite substitution. We were not without our faults during that agitated decade, but not all the faults ascribed to us were really ours.

An even more frequent variant is the situation in which the source knows for whom he is working, but is necessarily and deliberately misled as to his true purpose. Shortly after the Second World War American intelligence entered into a working relationship—reasonably productive for a period—with a monarchist group in an Eastern European country. These people were under the impression that this was a co-operative arrangement in which the Americans were supporting their political aim of restoration of the monarchy—which was definitely not U.S. policy. Nonetheless, American support for the group even included a clandestine radio over which political messages were broadcast to the population. The group's operations inside the country also produced considerable intelligence, which they gladly turned over to the Americans as a by-product of what they regarded as a political collaboration. It was, of course, the intelligence which was the true and sole interest of the Americans. Needless to say, bitterness and recriminations filled the air the day American support ceased—even though its termination was alleged to be based on the political and realistic grounds that the cause was hopeless. (While I personally believe that this particular operation went too far, my opinion is based on specific political grounds. It is irrelevant to apply a moral or an "American" standard here; the same story could be told of the intelligence services of any of the major powers. Even more pertinent is the fact that sincerity of purpose or nobility of motive does not exempt those who enter into the life of conspiracy from the rules and risks of that life.)

From this frequent necessity to disguise motive, purpose, and even identity flows one of the major and identifying characteristics of secret intelligence operations—the existence of a potential or actual element of falsity, marked specifically by duplicity and deceit, in the basic case officer-agent relationship.

Contrary to general belief, the major difficulty in secret intelligence operations is not the actual laying hands on "the loot," so to speak (or, as French gangster argot mysteriously has it, *"le grisbi"*). As often as not the moment of acquisition of information, whether it be in written or spoken form, is a mere mechanical detail or a matter of wit and patience. It is generally a phase of relative calm, a lull, so to speak, sandwiched between the two principal difficulties besetting the gathering of secret intelligence. In a well-conceived and skillfully executed operation the information which is sought should be obtained almost automatically—as the result of prior successful solution of these two major problems.

Of these problems the most difficult is chronologically the first. It is that of placing the agent in a position and a role whereby the information comes to him with a minimum of risk and as a natural by-product of his position. This is, of course, a major function of cover, and here, as usual, one aims for perfection and seldom achieves it. It is one thing, for example, to be Cicero, the valet of

the British Ambassador to Turkey during World War II who was
an agent of the Germans and whose position enabled him
clandestinely to rifle the contents of the Ambassador's safe while
the latter slept. An eminently successful operation. But how different and better a thing to have been the Soviet agent Sorge in Japan,
with automatic and unquestioned access to both German and Japanese information sanctioned by his role as a German official—and
flavored, perhaps even improved, by his affair with the wife of the
German Ambassador.

It is in this matter of maneuvering one's agent into position that
skill, judgment, ingenuity, and keen understanding of other peoples
are called for in the highest degree. The classic method is "penetration," meaning, in its historic form, the placing of the agent within
the structure from which it is desired to obtain intelligence. Obviously the flow of defectors back and forth between East and West
in the secret war affords numerous opportunities for such direct
penetration. Precisely because this is so obvious, however, it is a
difficult technique, risky, and not usually productive. Barring unusually suspicious circumstances, such as exist at the outset of or
immediately following a war, for example, the technique of direct
penetration generally requires time, and plenty of it, for success.
Clearly, if you want to put an agent into the Central Committee of
the Soviet Communist Party, you are going to have to wait a long
time while he fights his way up the ladder of the Communist hierarchy. (There is a recurrent story, for which I have no means of
vouching, that the Poles did in fact achieve this with Stalin's prewar Politburo.) Furthermore, while you await your agent's maneu-
vering into the desired position, you risk his ultimate success if you
use him. This difficulty has led to the technique of the "sleeper"
agent, whose tasks are defined in advance to fit a certain eventuality; meanwhile, no matter what the period of time, he is not used.
A notable example of the "sleeper" agent was the innkeeper whom
the Germans introduced into the British Naval Base of Scapa Flow
not long after the First World War. He didn't stir during all the
years until the outbreak of the Second World War; he was then able
to provide the information which permitted a Nazi submarine to
sneak into Scapa Flow early in the war, torpedo the aircraft carrier
Ark Royal, and escape untouched.[3]

Security measures being what they are in our times, direct penetration poses extreme difficulties. Accordingly, a favorite—can one
say popular?—technique, and far from a new one, is that of indi-

rect penetration, also known as subversion. The advantage of subversion is that it avoids the complications of choice of agent and the preparations and delay which are part of direct penetration, since it utilizes someone who is already in position to obtain the desired intelligence. In subversion the problem is not that of tailoring the agent to the task, it is that of tailoring the method of recruitment to the character, disposition, and motives of a selected potential agent. The continuous Soviet efforts to blackmail U.S. Government employees into their service is but one form, albeit crude, of subversion. A more refined form was evidenced in the case of the British diplomat who was persuaded, as a result of reflection during a period of internment in North Korea during the Korean War, that "the Soviet system deserved to win."

Another alternative to direct penetration is to have someone else in a more advantageous position do the work for you. In secret intelligence operations this means, as a practical matter, working relationships with other intelligence services. The intelligence services of many smaller nations do not, by the simple fact of nationality difference and because of lesser prominence as leaders in the secret war, suffer the disadvantages of the great powers. Furthermore, they often hold unique assets, as witness the very large Polish population in France or the Greek populations in Bulgaria, Rumania, and the Soviet Union. The result is a constant and vigorous competition among all the great powers for strictly exclusive working relationships with the services of lesser powers, which relationships most often turn into a control of the lesser service. Thus the immediate postwar period saw a lively scramble by all the great powers for exclusive dominance over the intelligence services of the smaller nations. There was, of course, no doubt anywhere that the services of the Eastern European states, with the exception of Yugoslavia, were not merely controlled by, but were to all practical purposes integral parts of Soviet intelligence.

The other major problem in secret intelligence operations is chronologically the second, but involves more danger than the first. This is the problem of how to get the information, once obtained, back to the headquarters. The most significant secret intelligence in the hands of an agent who cannot transmit it to the sole place where it can be used is, of course, valueless. But this is no easy trick. The comparison drawn above between the case of Cicero, the German agent who was the British Ambassador to Turkey's valet, and that of Sorge, the Soviet agent in the German

Embassy in Tokyo, pointed out that, in the light of the classic criteria, Sorge was much better positioned than Cicero. Yet Cicero was never caught, whereas Sorge was arrested and executed by the Japanese. The difference lay in the means of transmission of information. Cicero passed his information to the Germans in a series of clandestine meetings in Istanbul and Ankara, and by means of letter drops; Sorge relied on a clandestine radio transmitter.

Here is the source of another salient characteristic of secret intelligence operations. No matter how covert an operation may be, no matter how carefully devised and skillfully executed the cover, the precise moment of transmitting the information is, in almost all cases, clandestine. It is thus the moment of greatest danger in such operations. The great majority of secret intelligence agents who are caught are apprehended at the moment of passing information. (In the Portland Royal Naval Base case the arrest of part of the network took place at the moment of passing documents; the other members of the network were apprehended as a result of monitoring and then locating the source of clandestine radio signals to Moscow—both being the actual moments of passing information.) The reason for this is not because security services hope to improve the chances of prosecution by evidence obtained *in flagrante delicto;* it is quite simply that, being clandestine—there is no cover which can adequately explain the illegal transmission of documents or information to unauthorized persons, whether it be hand-to-hand, by letter, or by radio—this action is the most vulnerable in the entire operation and is often the only moment when agents can be caught. Secret inks, letter drops, and an everchanging series of devices, including the constant development of techniques to obstruct the location of clandestine radio transmitters—all are part of the continuous effort to transform this vulnerable moment from clandestine to covert, or to minimize the clandestine risk. However, defense techniques are also constantly being devised, improved, and revised, so that the problem remains a major one. For this reason—and because, as stated earlier, a clandestine act is internationally interpreted as a hostile act—such risky methods as illegal radio transmissions are generally kept to a minimum in peacetime. The prevailing solution to the problem the world over in peacetime is usually a series of cut-outs and letter drops by which the information ultimately comes into the hands of agents having diplomatic immunity and is then forwarded on in an embassy's regular diplomatic mail or telegraph traffic.

From the viewpoint of the over-all national interest, there is another characteristic of secret intelligence operations which weighs heavily, above all in the balance and outcome of the present East-West secret war. It is that the need for intelligence cuts across all political lines. We have already noted that, for intelligence to have the needed quality, variety, reliability, and breadth of coverage, it cannot be limited to sources chosen solely for their political ideology or compatibility with one's own political aims. West Germany's Gehlen Organization is a case in point.

General Gehlen held high responsibilities for German intelligence on the Eastern Front during the war. With the collapse of Germany in 1945, Gehlen salvaged the records of his extensive networks throughout Eastern Europe and the accumulation of years of intelligence about the Soviet Union, the Red Army, and its leadership. All this mass of material Gehlen hid in various places in West Germany. He also gathered a group of his best subordinates and instructed them to go into secure hiding. He then did the same, waiting a sufficient time until it became clear to the American Army that what they lacked most of all was any real and detailed knowledge of the Red Army which faced them across a long border and with which they were constantly being called upon to negotiate and solve an infinite variety of problems—from the regulation of Allied communications with Berlin to the repression of Peasant Party leaders in Bulgaria. When, in due course, General Gehlen emerged from hiding and presented himself to the Americans, an agreement was reached which permitted the Gehlen Organization to function as a unit, under the command and direction of Gehlen himself, even though at the outset for the sole benefit of the United States Army. In the temper and climate of postwar Europe and in the light of Allied political aims, such an agreement was politically indefensible; indeed, Gehlen had succeeded where all the rest of the German political and military hierarchy had failed, namely, to persuade the Western allies, or at least a part of them, to co-operative action against the Soviets. From the viewpoint, however, of the national security of the United States, of its armies in Europe, as well as of the security of Western Europe itself, the agreement was not only justifiable but essential. (This arrangement, it might be added, was as weak consommé compared to the witches' broth of Soviet collaboration with the Germans in wartime in the apprehending and execution of the Polish Underground connected to the Polish Government-in-Exile in London.)

Here arises the crucial conflict between the requirements of secret intelligence operations and the aims and methods of political warfare. This conflict never ceases. It goes beyond the question posed in an earlier chapter of how to reconcile, as an example, the need for full and reliable intelligence about Cuba with the political aim of assisting anti-Castro but also anti-Batista Cubans in their action to free Cuba from Soviet influence. For the consequences of this conflict will still continue to appear even after a policy decision, designed to regulate or compromise the conflicting interests, has been made at the highest level.

At one point in the postwar period, for example, a political operation was undertaken in the West which had as one of its objectives the creation of political unity among the Albanians in Western countries—a sizable number in proportion to the million-and-a-half population of Albania itself—excluding, quite naturally, pro-Communist Albanians and those with records of collaboration with the Italian or German occupations of the country. So far so good. But as it happens, by the simple facts of geography, a goodly number of Albanian exiles, including some of the most capable leadership, resides in Italy. It was perhaps understandable that the Italians should take a position strongly in favor of the inclusion, in any unified group, of the Albanians who had in the past loyally served Italian interests in Albania, and it was equally understandable that such a course would prejudice the potentialities of any such group in Albania itself. What complicated the operation throughout was that American intelligence, as distinct from American political agents, tended—naturally enough—to regard the advantages of close relations with the Italian intelligence services as outweighing the objectives of the political operation, and were therefore inclined to favor the Italian point of view in purely political matters. Needless to say, the Greeks, working through the British, had similar objectives—equally repugnant to the Albanians of Albania, who are quite aware that the Greeks regard most of Albania as a Greek province called Northern Epirus. (This particular soufflé rose to new heights when Marshal Tito of Yugoslavia—feuding then as now with the Albanians—announced the formation of an Albanian Committee in the Kossovo region of Yugoslavia, where there live some 500,000 more Albanians.)

It could be argued, of course, that this type of conflict could be resolved by more vigorous action with allies and more rigorously enforced policy decisions within a government. The argument has some merit, but only to a small degree, for the conflict is inescapable. For one thing, the Western world is organized as an alliance, not a train of cowed satellites. For another, even with their supreme word within their empire, the Soviets have the same troubles: one of the all-time feats of political tightrope-walking and agitated duplicity was performed by a high Soviet official who once found himself caught on a festive occasion between the East Germans on the one hand and the Poles on the other, with both demanding contradictory assurances about the Polish-East German border.

At the level of secret operations, the Soviets themselves recognize the perpetual conflict between intelligence requirements and political action, and rigorously separate the two insofar as that is possible. (Local Communist Parties may provide a recruiting base for Soviet intelligence, but it is only in rare cases of need that active Communist Party members will be found to be functioning as integral parts of an intelligence network.) This separation is in fact only for convenience and security at the lowest working levels; above that level in the Soviet hierarchy, as everywhere else, the decision must be taken in favor of either political objectives or intelligence interests when, as inevitably happens, the two conflict.

The American Government has experimented back and forth between separation of these two principal branches of secret operations—which is wasteful, expensive, and often produces worse collisions of interest in the field than at headquarters—and integration of the two branches—which fails to safeguard the legitimate interests of either—and a series of compromises between the two. Here again the best solution is in the last analysis dependent upon the breadth of view and the ingenuity of the men who must make it work.

1. The fact that today Polisario or Polisario/Algeria must be substituted for Spain in the equation does not eliminate the equation.

2. A number of studies and memoirs, too lengthy to catalogue here, which have appeared since this was written suggest that this brief summary of a complex subject is oversimplified, and that the principal emphasis should probably be put on what I only inserted in parentheses; i.e., "correctly interpreted."

3. The same reader in Hawaii who corrected me on the Russian cruiser in Portsmouth Harbor (see the notes to Chapter IV above) also pointed out that the aircraft carrier torpedoed at Scapa Flow in 1939 was not the *Ark*

Royal but the *Royal Oak*. The late Ladislas Farago, who served in the U.S. Navy under Admiral Zacharias in World War II, asserted (in his book, *Burn After Reading*) that no such German spy (whether an innkeeper or a watchmaker, as he has also been described) existed at Scapa Flow, and I believe it is now generally accepted that he was myth, not fact. Some "sleepers," however, *are* fact.

CHAPTER VIII

CE versus Security, and Other Devilry

Counterespionage, usually called simply by its initials CE, is a widely misunderstood branch of secret operations. Its purpose is not to apprehend enemy agents—that is an aim of the security forces. It is the word "counter" which causes the trouble, since it is generally interpreted to mean "against": a defensive operation against the enemy's intelligence operations. Quite to the contrary, CE is an offensive operation, a means of obtaining intelligence about the opposition by using—or, more usually, attempting to use the opposition's operations. CE is a form of secret intelligence operation, but it is a form so esoteric, so complex and important as to stand by itself.

The flavor of CE operations was caught to hilarious perfection by Peter Ustinov in his *Romanoff and Juliet*. In the play Ustinov, as the Prime Minister of a small, neutral nation squeezed between the giants of East and West, calls on the American Ambassador and learns that the Americans know about a secret Soviet maneuver in the contest to dominate his country. After a bit of reflection the Prime Minister—crossing the stage—calls on the Soviet Ambassador. After some preliminaries he says to the Soviet Ambassador, "They know." The Soviet Ambassador replies calmly, "We know they know." Back to the American Ambassador goes Ustinov. "They know you know," he says conspiratorially. The American Ambassador smiles confidently. "We know they know we know," he answers. Ustinov returns to the Soviet Ambassador. "They know you know they know," he says. To this the Soviet Ambassador replies, triumphantly, "We know they know we know they know." Once again the Prime Minister calls on the American Ambassador. "They know you know they know you know," he says, weary and curious at the same time. The American Ambassador repeats it after him, counting on his fingers. "WHAT?" he suddenly cries in horror.

The ultimate goal of all CE operations is to penetrate the opposition's own secret operations apparatus: to become, obviously without the opposition's knowledge, an integral and functioning part of their calculations and operations. CE thus differs from other general secret intelligence in having a single, specialized target.

The superior interest of this target—the opposition's secret operations—over most others in intelligence is marked. A successful penetration of an opponent's secret operations organization puts you at the very heart of his actions and intentions toward you. You share his mind and thinking to an intimate—and reliable—degree impossible in any other secret operation. This means that so far as intelligence is concerned, you know what he knows. You have thereby annulled, in one stroke, the value to him of his secret intelligence about you; you have neutralized the power of his secret knowing. Even more importantly, through your knowledge of his intelligence interests and of his political operations, as revealed in his policy papers and instructions, you are in possession of the most reliable possible indications of his intentions. Most importantly, you are in a position to control his actions, since you can, by tailoring intelligence for him to your purposes, by influencing his evaluation, mislead him as to his decisions and consequent actions.

The above, of course, describes the ideal. The actual practice of CE moves along for the most part at a level of compromise well below such total success—although it is the ideal which forever animates both theory and practice.[1] The kind of total success which is the ideal of CE is more or less ruled out by the facts of human conflict and organization. Even if it were true, for example, as has been alleged, that Admiral Canaris, chief of the World War II German Abwehr, was in fact a British agent, this still did not prevent various Abwehr subordinates from achieving a number of genuine and striking successes in their operations against the Allies. And even between friendly or allied secret operations organizations there are distinct and specific limits to the degree and substance of co-operation—in other words, to the easiest kind of penetration and control. Secret services may sit on the same bed together; they may even turn back the covers part way; but they never actually get into the bed. Even at a partial level of fulfillment, however, CE operations (unlike the demi-vierge) can be enormously effective.

Penetration is the technique par excellence of CE operations. But much of their complexity arises from the fact that effective and successful penetration is not limited to the single possibility of introducing one's own agent into the enemy's operations. The same effect can be achieved in many substitute ways and most often is, if for no other reason than the imposing difficulties and length of time which are the usual prospect for planting an agent in another service.

The commonest substitute for planting one's own agent is the "turning" of an enemy agent. Turning an agent, that is to say, convincing a man working in another cause that he should change sides and continue active in the conflict, with all the added risks involved, is clearly a psychological operation of immense complexity. As if this were not enough, the operation has the inherent weakness that what can be done once may perhaps be done twice. In a recent British case of this sort, on which the British Government has understandably refused all comment, all the pitfalls were demonstrated. A British agent, working in Germany against the Soviets, was approached by the Soviets to serve them. He agreed to do so—which made him a double agent, i.e., an agent who is working on two sides, but to the knowledge of only one, each side believing he is working exclusively in their behalf. Then, however, as a part of his operations on behalf of the Soviets, he informed the British of the Soviet approach to him and agreed to act as a double agent on behalf of the British. The British were thus led to believe that he was also acting as an agent of the Soviets but was really serving Britain. In fact, however, the man was a triple agent: from the British point of view he was a British agent who had falsely agreed to work for the Soviets—a standard penetration double agent, unturned from his original loyalty. But from the Soviet point of view he was a British agent who had agreed to do his real work for the Soviets and then had, in a second, false turning, honored his first turning. The latter was the truth of the case, as eventually the British discovered. So long as the man was a double agent—turned once, but falsely, as the British thought—he was valuable to the British; but his value to the Soviets rested on the fact that he was really a triple agent—a man turned twice, in this case once genuinely and once falsely. In brief, once turned makes a double agent; twice turned makes a triple agent, and so on. The decisive question is precisely which turns are genuine and which are false. This is but one of the problems which makes CE an extraordinarily complex affair; the determination of which turns are genuine and which false is a painstaking exercise in the control of information, of who knows what when, that requires constant alertness and a simultaneous grasp of both large perspective and detail. It is obviously an intellectual exercise of almost mathematical complexity.

The problem is further complicated by the existence of another kind of multiple agent, that is the triple—or even quadruple—agent working for three, four, or more different services. This type of multiple agent is generally a lone operator working for his own profit, and the question of turning is not as important with him. I once knew of a Viennese hotel porter who was working simultaneously for—and being paid by—the American, British, Soviet and French services, and who also—without pay—did his duty as an Austrian citizen. This kind of agent is usually something of a freak, however, and appears as a phenomenon only under very special circumstances, such as existed in Vienna at the end of World War II with four powers in occupation of the city. It is a dangerous gambit—even though my porter friend still is a leading fixture in Vienna—and is not of the same quality of professional interest, because of its patent unreliability, as the agent genuinely turned as between two conflicting services.

It is not unnatural that men who specialize in affairs of such complexity should regard themselves somewhat as the Cabots of the intelligence world, speaking only to God. CE practitioners do in fact believe, with some justification, that CE is the queen of all secret operations. This view is based on the undeniable fact that, for the mere conduct of their daily work, CE men must of necessity know more than anyone else, not only about enemy operations, but also about the operations of their own service as well. It is this greater and broader knowledge which leads CE specialists to the belief—often, but far from always, mistaken—that they can and do control all other secret operations. In the sense of control of knowledge as used in Chapter II—knowing who knows what—the control is real; in the sense of direction of operations, the control is real only in proportion to the lack of alertness of their colleagues, allies, or enemies.

CE's spread of knowledge extends also to all relations with any other services. CE men do not conduct the relations with other services, generally speaking. But they must be fully informed about the extent and substance of them. If, for example, it is decided, as a policy matter, to consult with the French services or to act jointly with them in a certain operation, it is of utmost importance that the CE men know the substance of the contacts with the French. The fact of French possession of a particular item of information may mean nothing to a political agent working with them; to a CE officer, however, it may well constitute decisive proof of enemy penetration of the French services or of secret French actions of particular interest to us.

This ubiquity of CE interest and activity can sometimes be a bit jolting. I once conducted a political and highly secret operation in an area in which it was decided, for political reasons, to exclude a neighboring but friendly service from both participation and knowledge. The first step in the operation involved the passage of a boat, at night, through waters adjacent to this friendly country, and the discharge, in a nearby hostile area, of several infiltration agents. My agents reported success, and I went about my business fairly calmly. Fairly calmly, that is, until one of my CE colleagues called on me and read to me, at great length, the report—alarmingly accurate—of the passage of the boat, its passengers, their destination, their equipment, and, unkindest cut of all, a somewhat detached professional critique of the operation. My operation had been penetrated by the friendly but excluded country; their service, at the same time, was penetrated by our own CE man—with the result that I had quite a bird's-eye view of my own operation.

Such information can be highly useful and even reassuring, however. I was once obliged to engage in some very ticklish and difficult negotiations with a political group thoroughly under the domination of the local intelligence service. For weeks on end we met daily and pursued our talks. In the evenings members of the group with whom I was negotiating would report to the local intelligence service. During the night our own agents in the local service, the result of penetrations and turnings by our CE officers, would report what my fellow conferees had commented and what their reactions and plans were as a result of my day's work. In the early morning this information was passed to me by our CE agents. I thus entered each day's talks with a quite accurate and highly useful idea of what faced me across the table.

It is perhaps understandable that the ideal of all CE operations is a form of penetration in which the intervening factor of an agent is removed. This occurs when an enemy network is captured—intact and in its entirety. Such cases are rare and are most often the result of a lucky accident—but this doesn't stop CE men from forever trying to achieve it. The most notable example in recent history of such an operation was the German Operation North Pole in World War II. Early in the war the Abwehr arrested two Dutch underground agents infiltrated from England at the moment of their arrival in the Netherlands, but after they had already given the signal of safe arrival. The Germans were lucky in that these two agents were the first of a projected series; they had as yet no connections in the Netherlands who could relay the word to England of a mishap. The agents were secretly imprisoned and no mention made even in German Army reports of their capture. Then by a combination of information found on the captured agents, of deductions from radio signals intelligence, of threats to the prisoners, and—unusual for the Abwehr—of the ability to think as the enemy would think, the Abwehr succeeded in entering into contact by radio with the agents' British headquarters and passing themselves off as being the agents.

For two years the Germans were able to maintain this tour de force, organizing in conjunction with Dutch-British headquarters in England ever new secret forays into the Netherlands of additional agents—all of whom were met on the beach or on the landing grounds by the Abwehr and imprisoned. The falsification was so perfect that on various occasions the Abwehr itself—acting as the Dutch underground—sent out "escaped" Allied prisoners to Spain through the channels indicated by London; the Abwehr even once blew up—over the understandably irate protests of the local German commander—several German barges in Rotterdam in order to prove to the British how well the "underground" in the Netherlands was working. The entire operation was a rare achievement, but to CE men it excites that admiration which only the professional ideal can arouse.

Men dedicated to a profession are susceptible to seeing them-

selves in terms of fulfilling exactly the image of the profession
Intelligence officers are no exception. Malcolm Muggeridge, writing in the *New Statesman,* said on this subject,

> The identity of "C" (head of the British services) was also
> disclosed, along with other unpublished information about
> MI-6, in an article in the New York *Herald Tribune* by Stewart
> Alsop. I asked Alsop subsequently whether his disclosures had
> any repercussions. He said there had been some rumblings in
> Anglo-American intelligence circles, but that Menzies himself
> had been appeased by the epithet "legendary" which Alsop had,
> with sagacious forethought, applied to him. "Legendary" was
> precisely what, in my experience, all Intelligence Brass wanted
> to be.

I have only one clue as to what this image might be in the case of
CE officers. It came during a visit to France. I called on a high
French CE officer, bearing, among other things, friendly greetings
to him from an American CE colleague. On seeing the Frenchman
I was instantly struck by his extraordinary physical resemblance to
the American officer. The same long, thin face, elegantly pointed
chin, aquiline nose, sensuous but disciplined mouth, sunken
cheeks, deep-set eyes illuminated by a kind of controlled fire, thick
black hair surmounting an aristocratic forehead. I immediately
conveyed the greetings of Mr. X. The Frenchman acknowledged
them with just a trace of a smile, but with an air of respect. "Ah,
oui," he said. "Monsieur X." A moment's reflection, then—grace-
fully, even appreciatively—*"Un homme macabre."*

It can be seen that CE operations are offensive operations which
depend for their existence as well as success on constant, if controlled, contact with the enemy. Security, on the other hand, is a
defensive operation which seeks to destroy the enemy's operations
and to cut off all contact with him as dangerous. Here lies one of
the classic conflicts of secret operations. With the discovery of an
opposition network, security will pause only long enough to seek to
uncover all members of the network and will then call for its oblit-
eration. CE will insist on exploring the possibility of exploiting the
network, of—as the phrase has it— "playing it back" to the enemy.
I remember discussing an American operation which had been
penetrated by several foreign services, including the Soviets, with a
security officer and then with a CE official. Referring to the opera-

ion's headquarters, the security man said, "Good Lord, stay away
'rom that place. It's a catastrophe. There are more foreign agents
n there than our own people that we can count on." As he spoke,
his genuine worry was evident. The CE man, on the other hand,
spoke calmly, almost wistfully. "Quite a sponge that place. We've
picked up a lot of interesting threads there," he said.

As with the conflict between political and intelligence objectives
—and techniques—there is no master solution for that between CE
and security. Each case must be handled on its merits. Since there
is no impartial authority which can decide these cases in the event
of disagreement, however, and as there is often no time for such
bureaucratic procedures, it is often found that CE and security are
in practice working at cross purposes, even though in the same
field and on the initial basis of much the same information.

Counterintelligence is generally used as a synonym for counterespionage. Despite the sanction given it by the U.S. Army's
Counter-Intelligence Corps, the term is a misnomer. It suggests, in
its strictest sense, an impossible kind of exchange of volleys, in
which the lethal bullets are bits of evaluated information. There is,
nevertheless, a secret operation which could conceivably be described as counterintelligence—although it is not. This is the deliberate planting of information with the enemy or the undertaking of
an act or series of acts which will create a desired impression upon
him.

When the purpose of such an operation is to test the opposition's
reaction to a given piece of information, whether true or false, it is
a simple intelligence operation. It is the intelligence equivalent of a
military probe or of a political trial balloon.

When the same operation is undertaken with the purpose of
tracing the course and ultimate destination of the planted information, it is a CE operation. It provides the vital information about
who is in touch with whom and who knows what. If, for example,
American agents plant with the Soviet Military Attaché in London
a secret and ostensibly reliable report that in ten days the Americans will deliver an ultimatum to Pakistan to open its ports to
transshipment of Afghan goods, and two weeks later the French
Military Attaché in Kabul questions his American colleague as to
why the reported action did not take place, it does not mean necessarily that the French Military Attaché in Afghanistan is a Soviet
agent. It does mean, however, that there is a connection, however
tenuous, between the Soviet Attaché in London and the French-

man in Kabul. It could mean any of a number of possibilities, from mere idle leakage, to a Communist cell in the French Defense Ministry, or a Soviet network in Afghanistan with some connection to the French Embassy. It is one of the functions of CE to trace these possibilities whenever they seem promising enough.

When the purpose of planting of information or the taking of actions to create a desired impression is to influence the enemy's decisions and actions, they become one of secret operations' most vital and complex activities—deception. Although good cover deceives, this is not what is meant by the technical term "deception." One of my colleagues once spent nearly a year trying to devise a good definition of deception, and finally concluded that it means merely luring your opponent into doing voluntarily and by choice what you want him to do. The history of human conflict is filled with the use of deception, such as the crude but effective Trojan Horse, or the famous gesture of the Dame de Carcas, who, when her citadel was under siege in the Dark Ages, threw her last remaining food supplies over the walls to the hungry besieging army, which thereupon, in the discouraged—but false—realization that she could not be starved out, withdrew. (The ensuing victory celebration, with unceasing ringing of bells, changed the citadel's name to Carcassonne, of modern tourist fame.)

The Second World War provided recent history's most classic known example of deception in the Allied invasion of Normandy. In his superb *The Struggle for Europe,* Chester Wilmot wrote of the prelude to Operation Overlord:

All the guile and ingenuity of . . . Intelligence were being turned to the devising of a scheme of strategic deception, far more subtle in technique, far more sinister in design. The object of this plan, which carried the code name FORTITUDE, was to convince the German High Command *before D-Day* that the assault would come in the Pas de Calais, and *after D-Day* that the Normandy landing was a preliminary and diversionary operation, intended to draw German reserves away from the area north of the Seine so that the main Allied attack might be delivered there at a later date. By this bluff it was hoped that an army of a quarter of a million men might be kept, idle but expectant, between Le Havre and Antwerp until the Battle of Normandy had been won. . . . The seeds of deception was sown in fertile ground. . . . To the Germans the Pas de Calais was of vital importance and they made the common German mistake of assuming that it must therefore bulk equally large in the eyes of their adversaries. In working to strengthen these preconceptions, the British played upon the notorious tendency of German Intelligence Officers to approach problems with a card-index mind, indefatigable in collecting information, but incompetent in assessing it. . . . The aerial plan was shaped accordingly. For every reconnaissance mission over Normandy, two were flown over the Pas de Calais. For every ton of bombs dropped on coastal batteries west of Le Havre, two tons were put down on batteries north of it. In the bombing of railways 95 per cent of the effort was directed against targets north and east of the Seine. . . . The impression created by these operations was confirmed by information which came from the English side of the Channel—from [German] air reconnaissance, wireless interception, and the reports of spies who were surreptitiously provided with appropriate data. . . . Preparations in the southeast [of England] were discreetly revealed, but those being made in the south-west were hidden as carefully as possible. . . . The presumption that the main invasion forces were assembled in the south-east was reinforced by deceptive wireless traffic. By another radio subterfuge the idea was conveyed that the two follow-up armies (First Canadian and Third American) were in fact an assault force destined to land in the Pas de Calais. The Germans were allowed to learn that this Army Group was under the command of Lieut-General George S. Patton, who was an ideal bogey . . . [and] this set-up carried conviction to the logical German mind.

Wilmot, writing in 1952, still did not have access to the operation made public later which was a notable feature of the same Allied deception. This was the famous and delicate British operation of putting ashore on the north coast of Spain a corpse clothed as a British officer carrying secret papers—containing false information, naturally—concerning the forthcoming invasion, which the Spanish, as foreseen, quickly turned over to the Germans. Here was proof, if ever needed, that there are an infinity of ways of reaching and influencing the enemy's mind.[2]

Deception, like CE, is concerned with intimate, controlled, and purposeful contact with the enemy. While its objective is more specific than CE, it is a broader type of operation, being aimed at

the total range of elements which make up the opposition's think
ing and decisions, rather than only his intelligence organization. I
therefore frequently happens that the ultimate stage of a CE opera
tion, the ability to mislead the enemy, is subordinated to the re
quirements of a deception operation. In this case, the CE operation
becomes known as a deception channel.

Deception, because of its immediate relevance to action, is prob
ably the ultimate secret operation. But even if this evaluation is no
universally accepted by professionals of the secret war, there is no
doubt that strategic deception, whether in peace or in war, is the
most secret of secret operations. Accordingly, the less said about i
here the better.

1. While I was doing this annotation, a retired CIA friend, of a theoreti
cal bent, said to me (the quotation is *verbatim* because, not understanding i
when spoken, I wrote it down): "The ultimate philosophical rationale fo
intelligence as a function of government would lead inevitably to the hypo
thetical establishment of liaison between the Russian and American intelli
gence services," and quoted a former colleague, "Then I could talk to my
opposite number in Moscow!" This arose in connection with my emphasis
in the introduction to this edition on diplomacy in reading, and coming to
terms with, the adversary's procedures and aims. Admitting that we are a
long way from such liaison, but asserting a CIA advantage in being less
politically beholden to the Administration in power than is the Department
of State, my friend inquired, "Why not direct exchange?" Some clear
headed observers who are also first-rate thinkers might usefully leave be
hind the scorn these ideas will surely provoke in our day, and play around
with them a bit.

2. An unnamed British reviewer of this book, writing in *The Times Lit
erary Supplement* in 1963, pointed out that the operation with the corpse
clothed as a British officer—the reviewer specified as a "Marine"—was not
connected with Overlord (1944), but with Husky (1943) and the invasion of
Sicily.

CHAPTER IX

Political Operations

It is a misfortune that most of what has been written about secret operations is concerned almost exclusively with intelligence operations and their related functions. The result is a very misleading picture of the secret war—sometimes affecting even those actively engaged in it. For the central and decisive battles of the secret war are fought in the vast realm of covert political operations. One proof of this statement is that I must necessarily be somewhat less explicit in this than in preceding chapters.

Secret intelligence is essential, indispensable; it is also, as previously pointed out, inseparable from political operations. But it is not, and should not be allowed to become, an end in itself. The ultimate national aim in the secret war is not simply to know. It is to maintain or to expand national power and to contain or to reduce the enemy's power; it is the exercise of power, itself a dynamic not a static thing.

Intelligence gained by the Soviets about the atomic bomb would have been a pointless drill had they not had the intent, the technical knowledge, and the industrial capacity to create their own nuclear arsenal. In brief, they converted knowledge into power by means of action. Similarly, the most precise intelligence available to the United States about dissension within the satellite Communist Parties and unrest among the satellite masses is of only potential value until the moment when we can combine an intent to exploit that intelligence with effective forms of action in order to weaken Soviet power in the satellites.

The exercise of power, the transformation of intelligence and policy into power by means of action, takes place daily and visibly in strategic policy, economic policy, diplomacy, defense, propaganda—all the overt aspects of international relations. It also takes place daily, but invisibly, in the secret war in the form of covert political operations.

The range, both functional and geographical, of secret political operations is almost unlimited.

Geographically, secret political operations have marked human history in all lands. The only new feature produced by our own times is the universal extent—Antarctica excepted—of a single conflict, that between the Communist and non-Communist blocs. The human conflicts which employ secret political operations have always been limited geographically by the transport and communications technology of the age and by the power of other nations not involved in the conflict. Englishmen fought Spaniards simultaneously in the Netherlands and in the Caribbean; Frenchmen fought Englishmen in Flanders, North America, and India at one and the same time. Today, Communist and non-Communist maneuver in combat all over the globe—a measure not only of modern transport and communications, but also of the historically unprecedented emergence of but two great power centers whose preponderance relative to the rest of the world is such that, until other nations or combinations of states can achieve some parity with them, they inevitably tend to divide the world between them.[1]

The first great post-Second World War engagement between East and West in the sphere of covert political operations was the Italian national elections of April 1948. With all of Eastern Europe already in the Soviet grasp, with civil war raging in Greece, the West awoke to the fact that Italy could be lost to the Soviets by political action. Hastily improvised operations, a number of which could barely be dignified by the adjective covert—certainly the vigorous speaking tours of the American Ambassador to Italy were anything but covert—narrowly saved Italy for the West that year. (The elections of 1958 in Italy had, once again, a similar air of urgency, suggesting that not a great deal of progress had been made in ten years in cutting back the inroads previously made there by the Soviets.) After Italy, the lines were swiftly drawn on either side of the military division of Europe. From there the conflict spread to the Far East, to the Middle East, to Southeast Asia, to Latin America, to Africa. (The effort to keep the Cold War, in the sense of hostile blocs of nations aligned with East or West, out of Africa is a sound, even noble one; it does not and cannot eliminate the secret war, as a talk with any African trade union leader, from Morocco through Nigeria and Tanganyika to Madagascar will show.)[2] In all these areas the secret war is waged not by intelligence agents, but by agents whose function is, in the broadest sense of the word, political.

The functional range of covert political operations is so vast as to defy listing. It runs from the simple, obvious "spontaneous demonstration"—in Tokyo or Caracas, in New York or New Delhi—through the quarrels of an international labor organization, the speeches at an international conference of intellectuals, the resolutions of a congress of lawyers, the organizational maneuvers of churchmen, the patient and persistent pressures of exiles, and a staggering variety of publications, to the Viet Cong guerrilla hidden in the jungles of South Vietnam and a Cuban prisoner captured at the Bay of Pigs.

(Contrary to a widespread impression, there is a more or less tacit understanding between states today to refrain from including political assassination in political operations. Stalin used it, but only against those he considered renegades from his own authority, e.g., Trotsky, Krivitsky, et al. Alexander Foote has pointed out that Stalin could easily have had Hitler assassinated before the Russo-German Pact, but refrained. Smaller nations sometimes resort to it, as in Trujillo's attempt on the life of President Betancourt of Venezuela or the prewar assassination of King Alexander of Yugoslavia, the work of Croat terrorists who had Italian and Hungarian support, or the Puerto Rican attempt on President Truman's life and attack on the U.S. House of Representatives. It should, however, be clear to observers on both sides that the existing conflicts between the great powers can in no way be resolved by political assassinations—which is at least some advance toward civilization.)[3]

These varied activities have a common political objective: the organization, exploitation, and direction of existing human passions and purposes so that they contribute, no matter how indirectly, to the fortunes of one or the other side in conflict. It is the substance of power, wherever and in whatever form it may exist, which the political agent pursues, recognizing that all organized or social human activity has a political content and significance.

If this seems obscure it is because of general acceptance of a too narrow definition of what is "political." As used in covert political operations, "political" is not limited to the complex of activities surrounding the gaining and holding of public office, of the constitutionally designated seats of power. It refers instead to a much

wider concept—to politics as the general and infinitely varied
struggle for and the exercise of power in human society. Under this
concept all organized or social human activity represents potential
or actual power ultimately transformable into control of the state
and the society.

To claim that the scholar, the artist, the philosopher are apolitical is to deny the interrelation between human thought and action;
it is to regard the founders of the United States as illiterate but
dexterous constitutional carpenters, the upheaval of the French
Revolution as an outburst about bread, the conscious theoreticians
of the Bolshevik seizure of power in Russia as unlettered bombers
who had never read a book, and the Chinese Communists as
merely envious of Chiang Kai-shek and the Kuomintang. By the
same token, the allegation that the businessman with foreign investments is apolitical because he "doesn't mix in politics" is naïve
and implies two things which are patently untrue: that national
wealth is not a part of national power, and that the businessman
will under no circumstances seek his government's protection for
his business.

The narrow definition of "political" can have serious consequences in international affairs. In the overt domain it can lead to
the false and vulnerable position of appearing to back corrupt,
tottering, or tyrannical regimes, as with the United States in South
Korea and in South Vietnam (see also Latin America until very
recently), or to the waste of vast amounts of economic aid aimed at
reinforcing the viability of the regime, as in Laos and Iran. In the
covert domain it can lead to futile involvement in mere palace
intrigues (and to the even more grave error which I call the "our
boy" theory— "Look, let's just put our boy in there and he'll run
this show for us"—of which more below). The inherent limitations
of palace intrigue, that is to say, exclusive involvement with the
official center of power, are no modern development. In the sixteenth century, Don Bernardino de Mendoza, Spanish Ambassador to Henry III of France, was fully aware of these limitations in
the operation which he conducted and which successfully immobi-
lized France while Spain prepared to attack England. Mendoza
was fully active at court; indeed, his intrigue in support of the Duc
de Guise against the King and his bribery of Catherine de Medici
were essential elements in his scheme. Nevertheless, he spent almost as much time and money on petty nobles, merchants, and,
almost as importantly, on the organizers and instigators of the

arisian anti-Protestant mobs, who were to defeat the King where
ourt intrigue could not.

The sixteenth century, so akin to our own, also gave us another
f history's finest recorded examples of a sustained covert political
peration in the Jesuit underground in England. Over more than
ve decades the Jesuits sent covert missionaries to England to per-
orm rites for the Catholic families, to make converts, and to re-
ruit additional agents for training in the English College at Rome.
heir story is a textbook of covert and clandestine techniques;
unted men, they were experts at disguise, cover, escape, secret
nks, safe houses, hiding places, and all the paraphernalia and
ricks essential to their mission. When caught they gladly suffered
he penalty of death, regarding it as enviable martyrdom. But the
ltimate purpose of the Church of Rome in mounting this covert
peration was political: it was to return the rebellious Church of
ngland to the authority of Rome. The fact that the issue was
eligious authority does not alter the fact that the purpose was the
nhancement or recovery of power, meaning that the operation
vas political.

That even the Christian churches have not forgotten their an-
ient heritage of secret operations was illustrated by a bizarre inci-
ent which occurred in 1950. There was living in Paris at that time
he Metropolitan Vissarion of the Rumanian Orthodox Church.
his elderly prelate had two distinctions: one was that he had been
t the Tiflis Theological Seminary with Stalin; the other was that
e was the senior Orthodox hierarch in exile from the lands under
oviet control. It was the latter which aroused the interest of the
Churches of Rome and of England. At stake was the Roman aim
o draw the Orthodox Churches even closer to recognizing the
uthority of the Pope, and the aim of the Anglican Church to align
he Orthodox Churches firmly with Protestantism against Rome.

The Metropolitan was quite content to remain in Paris, where
radually, under the guise of brotherly assistance, he was being
ersuaded to accept Catholic offers of priests to minister to the
xiled Orthodox who suffered from a shortage of priests. (The
chism between the Orthodox and Catholic Churches is many cen-
uries older than that between Rome and Canterbury, but in cer-
ain sacramental respects much less profound.) There then ap-
eared in Paris one day an Englishman who presented himself to
he Metropolitan, showing credentials as an emissary of the
Church of England. He extended to the Metropolitan an official

invitation to come to England to live, as a guest of the English Church. For days the Metropolitan vacillated, and finally agreed to leave. When the time came, however, he had once more changed his mind. This was apparently too much for the British agent, whose instructions one can only surmise must have been quite categorical. For at this point he proceeded to kidnap the Metropolitan, bodily spiriting him away to a house outside of Paris preparatory to transferring him to England. Probably fortunately for everyone concerned, several Rumanian Orthodox communicants became suspicious, with the result that the French police, after several days, found the Metropolitan and his abductor.

Notwithstanding this misfire, the Church of England succeeded in its aim: the Orthodox Churches, including finally in 1961 the Russian Orthodox Church itself, became members of the Protestant World Council of Churches. Rome's position in any eventual negotiations for the reconciliation of the Christian churches is obviously thereby weakened; a unified opposition is much more formidable than a number of separate adversaries—provided, of course, that the opposition is genuinely unified.

It is this political—in the broad sense of power—characteristic of all organized and social human activity which imposes the extraordinary variety of secret political operations. My own diverse but not unusual experience in this field has run the gamut from organizing a literary evening in New York to directing the operation of a clandestine radio transmitter; from providing speakers for five different groups in the same national election to arranging for a gift to an important tribal leader; from organizing a political committee of exiles for the infiltration and invasion of their native land to reorganizing the same group some years later to eliminate their military activities; from supervising a dozen publications in half a dozen languages to rewriting a manifesto; from persuading twelve men representing as many different nationalities to agree on a single point to working a resolution through a congress of three hundred men representing thirty-five different nations; from subsidizing summer camps for children to running an escape chain out of Soviet-occupied territory. This partial list is not intended to demonstrate virtuosity on my part, but the ubiquitous quality of the political element in human affairs.

(That by and large the West recognizes this quality only to the extent of covert political operations, rather than openly proclaiming it as a justification for subjecting all organized human activity to the direction of the state, as in totalitarian systems, is a tribute to the steadfastness of purpose of democratic leaders and the resiliency and resourcefulness of our societies.)

The relevance of some of this variety to the secret war is not always evident at first glance. Those summer camps for children, for example, seem a far cry from political conflict. And yet they were the answer to a situation in which a Communist state arranged for summer vacations in their native land for children of exiles at less than a quarter of the cost of similar vacations in their adopted land. The fact that the parents were voters in a country in which there existed a strong Communist Party and in a district in which they had, until the advent of the Communist offer, constituted an important non-Communist force seemed to justify the subsidy of local camps, precisely as it had moved the Communists to their original plan. That in present conditions of greater prosperity in their adopted land, and of greater American public awareness of the importance of these problems, genuinely private assistance could probably be forthcoming does not alter the conditions as they existed at that time—which were that timely and adequate assistance had to be, if it was to be at all, in the form of a covert governmental subsidy for a definite political purpose.

The foregoing illustrates a point about covert political operations which distinguishes them sharply from secret intelligence operations. In the vast majority of political operations the true function of the operation itself is overt and acknowledged. This does not necessarily mean that it is publicized, but it is at least not hidden. If, for example, it is decided to strengthen a political party in a neutralist country which is wavering in the face of Communist subversion, the reinforced efforts of the party are not and cannot be hidden or disguised, nor is it even desirable to do so. What is covert is foreign government involvement in the process, whether it be in the form of subsidies or advice—and the two are rarely separated in practice. Since cover is limited to but one essential point—relationship to government—it is obvious that the choice of cover, the choice of agent, the forms of communication, and the nature of the case officer-agent relationship are all affected. Generally speaking, the cover possibilities in political operations are more flexible than in secret intelligence, the choice of agent is more difficult, the forms of communication are equally restricted, and the case officer-agent relationship is less prone to duplicity.

A clear understanding of the simultaneous unity of purpose and variety of forms of secret political operations is frequently obstructed by loose and conflicting terminology. Much is spoken and written, for example, about political warfare, psychological warfare, guerrilla and unconventional warfare, as though these were all separate and arcane fields of action.

Political warfare is a term sanctioned by frequent official usage. It embraces the same field of activities as the term political operations, but my own feeling is that it has a narrower connotation. Its inevitable emphasis is on war rather than on politics. It suggests a state of war and the existence of a specific enemy, but does not convey the full scope of activities or the existence of multiple rivalries as does political operations. I doubt, for example, that assistance to non-Communist parties in the 1948 Italian elections could be considered political warfare—although the signs posted in Rome in 1961 after the Twenty-second Congress of the Soviet Communist Party falsely summoning Italian Party members for a full discussion of Stalinism might be so considered. In any case, official labels cannot be taken too seriously. During the Second World War what were in fact deception operations and even mere publicity gimmicks were labeled political warfare, and what was a genuine case of political warfare—Allied involvement in the bomb plot against Hitler—came under the heading of intelligence.

Psychological warfare is another wartime term which has spread confusion. It has been widely used to signify political operations, but it hardly does justice to their real content. The blunt realities of a political operation aimed at the overthrow of a government can hardly be called psychological warfare. There is, however, a wartime operation which is highly useful and which is properly termed psychological warfare. It embraces a host of actions, from leaflets dropped to enemy troops, through broadcasts to the enemy, to the manufacture and spread of demoralizing rumors in enemy territory, and its sole aim is to weaken the enemy's will to resist. What is called psychological strategy, that is, the co-ordination and exploitation of a government's actions for maximum political effect, is, obviously, a political function, covering a government's overt as well as covert operations.

Guerrilla warfare has lately been the object of considerable attention. As guerrilla tactics themselves are as much a part of open war as of the secret war, the term unconventional warfare has been coined to describe the peacetime use of guerrilla tactics—among many other techniques—in bringing about the overthrow of a government and the capture of territory and populations. Taken as a whole, unconventional warfare is a political operation, initially covert, then clandestine, and finally overt.

The Communists successfully utilized this technique in French Indochina and continue it today in Laos and South Vietnam. The Soviets have made sporadic efforts to use it in Iran and Iraq, without success, and they have failed in its use in Greece, Malaya, and the Philippines. The F.L.N. mastered it successfully, and indigenously, in Algeria, as did Castro in Cuba.

Very briefly, the technique involves infiltration, agitation, recruitment, harassment of the civil and military power, and, finally, open assault. From the first day to the last, however, the entire structure rests on ever-widening control of the local population. Territory is a secondary and only ultimate consideration. But it is the population which provides food, recruits, and intelligence. (Experts estimate that a successful guerrilla force requires from at least five to ten or more times its own numbers as an intelligence screen, that is, sympathizers or agents in the local population who will provide reliable information on government troop movements.) This control of the local population is achieved by persuasion, by indoctrination, and by terror, i.e., reprisals and the threat of reprisals against those who will not co-operate. Thus the vital element on which the success of unconventional warfare rests is a political one.

Authorities on unconventional warfare without exception recognize its political character. In his *Problems in the Guerrilla War of Resistance Against Japan*, Mao Tse-tung wrote:

There are often military elements who "care for only military affairs but not politics." Such one-track minded military officers, ignoring the interconnection between political and military affairs, must be made to understand the correct relationship between the two. All military actions are means to achieve certain political objectives, while military action itself is a manifested form of politics.

(An interesting contrast to General Marshall's letter to Eisenhower concerning the British proposal to press eastward in Germany and take Berlin if possible: "Personally," wrote the U.S. Chief of Staff, "I would be loath to hazard American lives for purely political purposes.") Mao continues:

There are, of course, differences between political and military affairs, each with its special characteristics, but the one should not be disconnected and isolated from the other. . . . Only those who misinterpret the significance of guerrilla warfare would consider that "Guerrilla warfare is not a political problem, but one purely military in nature." This type of simple military viewpoint causes the loss of the political objectives of guerrilla warfare and must inevitably lead to the abandonment of political work, the dissolution of popular support, and the eventual defeat of guerrilla warfare. . . . If guerrilla warfare is without a political objective, it must fail; but if it maintains a political objective which is incompatible with the political objectives of the people, failing to receive their support, participation, assistance and active cooperation, then this too must fail. . . . This is because guerrilla warfare is basically organized and maintained by the masses, and once it is deprived of these masses, or fails to enlist their participation and cooperation, its survival and development is not possible. . . . There are those who cannot imagine how guerrillas could survive for long in the rear of the enemy. But they do not understand the relationship between the people and the [guerrilla] army. The people are like water and the [guerrilla] army is like fish. How can it be difficult for fish to survive if they immerse themselves within the mass of water? But if the water is taken away or dries up, the fish must also die and pass away.

Franklin A. Lindsay, an American expert who learned his basic lessons with Tito's Partisans in Yugoslavia during World War II, writing—somewhat less picturesquely, but just as realistically as Mao—in *Foreign Affairs* on "Unconventional Warfare" has the following to say:

Where the effective political control of the country has passed to the Communists, it will not be enough to conduct long-distance propaganda activities or to make plans on the assumption that the very real and very considerable dissatisfactions with the Communist regime will automatically result in a popular uprising as soon as the guerrilla forces appear. Clandestine support of at least a part of the villages and the countryside is an absolute prerequisite to the employment of guerrilla forces, for they must have local intelligence support and supplies if they are to survive in areas in which superior enemy forces are openly in control. In Jugoslavia, for example, in World War II, the Communist partisans had in many ways as favorable a situation for guerrilla warfare as might be expected anywhere. The main German forces were engaged by powerful allies on other fronts. Tito's partisan forces had as overt allies not only the Soviet Union but the United States and Great Britain. And from the latter two they received massive air support. In Slovenia, where there were no Cêtnik forces of Mihailovich to contend with, the political commissars of the Communist-established National Liberation Front could represent themselves to the people as the only force fighting the invader, and as having the complete support of all the major powers fighting the Germans. Yet they still found it necessary, in the words of one commissar, to "prepare the area intensively by the introduction of clandestine political organizers for a period of several months before we dared to introduce guerrilla forces."

Lindsay makes the point even more precisely:

The first step in mobilizing a civilian population against Communist subversion and guerrilla attack is to establish a set of political goals in terms that the average person can understand. They must be goals that strike a sympathetic response and that aim to remove the inequities in the existing society and the grievances which they have caused. Through mass communications these reform programs must be communicated effectively, and repeatedly, to the population. . . . But this is only the beginning of the task. Political organizers must be recruited and trained in sufficient numbers to reach by direct contact nearly every family in the land. They must be as thorough as the best of ward or district leaders in American politics.

In this light, the suggestion, heard after the Cuban debacle, that American responsibility for unconventional warfare—or paramilitary operations—should be vested in the Pentagon is revealed as something less than logical—or politic.

As a matter of record, in the general proposition—however crude it may sound—of overwhelming governments by remote control, the United States has had about the same proportion of successes as the Soviet Union. However, this is not a statistically measurable subject. Where the Soviets have failed it has been at an enormous cost to us in the application of overwhelming military might, as in Greece—and even there the Tito-Cominform dispute played a large role in stopping the conflict. On the other hand, where we have failed it has been because of too great a reliance on military force and too little attention, if any, to the vital political elements. Our only real success in this ultimate field of covert political operations was Guatemala—and there we displayed our customary tendency to get things over with in a hurry and to substitute might for politics.[4]

Guns, however, at best only act as a temporary substitute for sound and patient political preparation. In one American operation other than Cuba which failed, political preparation was, to put it mildly, hastily improvised. In another our impatience was such that when the operation did not immediately succeed in the military sphere, we abruptly switched sides. (This at least earned us the gratitude of the Head of State whom we were trying to overthrow.)

Since political operations are concerned with human beings, they have an organic development of their own: for real rather than merely apparent results, their timetable can at most be hastened, but it cannot be artificially imposed from without. Notwithstanding the rapid changes which mark our epoch, the long view of history is still the key to international politics in our time.

Secret political operations are based upon three major characteristics which dictate the potentialities, the timing, and the working relationships of such operations.

The first is that any political operation must be based on something real, something which in fact exists. Secret political operations are neither skulduggery nor legerdemain. It would be, for example, the height of futility to undertake an operation in Switzerland to bring about the abandonment of Swiss neutrality in order that Switzerland should join NATO. There would simply be nothing effective to work with, even if the idea were sound. One of the greatest wastes of American time and money I ever encountered was the success of a Hungarian Catholic in persuading the appropriate authorities to send him to London to agitate against the decision—already made—of the Anglican Church to sponsor the invitation to the Russian Orthodox Church to join the World Council of Churches. The decision having been made in the highest councils of the English Church, after full deliberation, and having been duly accepted by British opinion, this agent's mission was largely an exercise in talking to himself.

For a thing to be real it need not be organized or even coherent, but it must exist. A sentiment, an opinion, a movement can be exploited, developed, organized, even astutely exaggerated, but it cannot be created out of thin air. The Communist Peace Campaign was a masterpiece of organization and exploitation of an unorganized sentiment. Again, in 1954, the Soviets organized in East Berlin a cover organization called the Mikhailov Committee—named after the Russian general who headed it. The announced purpose of this Committee was to assist the return to their homelands of Russian and Eastern European political exiles. The formation of this group was greeted with hoots of derision in the West, since a more unlikely undertaking seemed inconceivable. Nevertheless, a certain success—rapidly capitalized upon by the Soviets—accompanied the Committee's efforts, for what they were able to exploit to a considerable degree was simple nostalgia and the economic suffering of many refugees in the West.

The Mikhailov Committee illustrates a corollary to the rule that an operation must be founded on a reality, however tenuous. It is the corollary that is, in fact, the foundation of all political operations. It is simply that in human affairs there is no such thing as a monolith. There may be repression, there may be terror, but there is no uniformity. Ingenuity in political operations consists in recognizing dissent, however hidden, and then in devising ways to exploit it. Viewing the Communist Empire in 1947, for example, a serious observer was entitled to weigh the measurable dissension in Eastern Europe and assume that Yugoslavia would be the most loyal of the satellites. History records, of course, that it was the first—and so far only—Eastern European satellite successfully to declare its independence of Moscow's domination. It was a fundamental Leninist doctrine—in his application of military doctrine to politics—to insist on the "monolithic unity" of the Communist Party. But what has happened? Today there are three major brands of Communism within the Communist bloc—the Soviet, the Chinese, and the Yugoslav. In this sense, of course, Chou En-lai was right when he spoke at the Twenty-second Congress of the Soviet Communist Party and asked that the differences between the parties not be made public, to be exploited by the enemies of Communism. And Khrushchev knew it as well as he. But the pressure of dissension in human affairs will prevail, and Khrushchev's only choice was to jettison—without openly acknowledging it, of course —the myth of monolith.

This does not mean that any and all dissension is directly exploitable. The West cannot at this stage persuade any of the Communist dissidents into alliance against one or both of the other two. But political operations are, in most cases, infinitely more subtle than that. To exploit a disagreement between Mao and Khrushchev it is no more necessary—or possible—to enter into direct contact with Khrushchev on the subject than it is for him to capitalize on differences between American Democrats and Republicans by secretly offering financial aid to the Democrats. Khrushchev does not have to enter into alliance with the German industrialists who think enviously of the Eastern markets in order to exploit their impatience with the inflexibly pro-NATO and pro-European stand of Adenauer. Nor does the West have to make agents of the Eastern European intellectuals in order for their discontent with rigid Soviet control to create real problems for Khrushchev and some easing, however slight, of the satellites' plight. In both cases it suffices to recognize the dissension and then, by ingenuity and indirection, to nourish it.

The second basic characteristic of secret political operations is that they must be performed by others. Obvious as this sounds, it is all too often overlooked in the directions given to political agents. If the objective is to have the Socialist International take a particular stand, to have a neutralist conference adopt a certain policy, to have the Liberal Party of country X support a given step, or to have the progressive opposition seize power from a tottering, corrupt regime, then for the desired action to be valid it must be the Socialists, the neutralists, the Liberals of X nationality, or the members of the opposition who themselves take the desired action. This obviously puts the highest premium on the arts of persuasion and indirection and on individual qualities of personal influence, tact, comprehension, forcefulness when necessary, and resourcefulness.

These necessities have direct implications for the case officer-agent relationship in political operations. While discipline must still be present, there cannot be the ambiguity of purpose and motive which most often characterizes intelligence operations. In a political operation the case officer must have arrived at a clear and workable accommodation of interests with the agent. Control by the case officer there must be, but not duplicity. The purposes of case officer and agent must have been presented with the maximum permissible clarity, and then a reconciliation of conflicts and limitations negotiated. In brief, the outstanding characteristic of the political case officer-agent relationship is that it must be an alliance, not a utilization of the agent by the case officer, as often occurs in intelligence.

In politics a "no" is acceptable, and even defeat is understandable. Highhandedness, particularly on the part of a great power, must often be swallowed; but irresponsibility carries with it its own destruction, however long the process may take. Irresponsibility in political operations is a readily identifiable fault: it can be measured against the cardinal rule of such operations—do not make unnecessary promises or promises you have neither the ability nor intention to keep. Once a promise is given, an agreement made, it must be kept to the best of one's ability. In the jungle of international politics this is the equivalent of "honor among thieves." The Middle East, whatever its complications, is a monument to British understanding and observance of this classic rule. In the First World War Lawrence, with full authority, extended solemn promises to the Hashemite dynasty of the Hejaz, in return for the help of the Bedouins against the Turks. The British could not, after that war, save the Kingdom of the Hejaz from Ibn Saud of Arabia. But today the Hashemite great-grandson of the last King of the Hejaz sits on the throne of Jordan as witness to a kept promise. The same promises were made in World War II to Idris el Senussi, in return for his help against the Italians and Germans. Today, King Idris I of an independent—even if economically unviable—Senussi Libya bears witness to another kept promise. The result is that even with all the vicissitudes of history, and the fulminations of Nasser, the British position in the Middle East today remains more solid and effective than the history of the last fifteen years would otherwise warrant.[5]

There is yet another implication of this second fundamental characteristic of secret political operations which may possibly be disturbing to Americans. It is the clear inference which can be drawn of a client-patron, an almost feudal relationship between lesser states and the great powers. This is a fact of international life which has always existed and continues to exist, but it is one for which the United States, by virtue of its isolation, was ill prepared when it almost overnight emerged into the world as a great power. It is a fact contrary to our understanding of independence, to our proclaimed ideals, and, we sense, to our own history. But our own history was a very special case. Washington in his Farewell Address warned not only against entangling alliances, but against the meddling of great powers in our internal and factional affairs. The United States grew to maturity free of this external meddling not because of innate American qualities, but because of a combination of historical, geographical, and technological accidents—and for many years behind the protective shield of British policy. New nations today are not so lucky.

However, the hegemony or domination of the great powers is not without its cost. The influence and power which the great powers exercise in the affairs of the smaller states work both ways. There is a permanent tendency for the lesser powers to factionalize the great powers. A prize example of this was Yugoslavia during the Second World War, which for a period was a source of acute friction between Great Britain and the United States, the British supporting Tito, the Americans favoring General Mihailovich. Similarly, in the Congo the British, for both European and African reasons, maneuver behind Tshombe and Katanga, and the United States, with an eye on what it feels are larger issues, maneuvers behind Adoula and the Leopoldville Government. An adept politician in a small country need not necessarily fear his own weakness; a political operation works two ways, and in return for accepting influence he finds he can also exert it.

The third fundamental characteristic of secret political operations is that it matters less what you do than how you do it. The wrong thing done well is always preferable to the right thing done badly. The principal British criticism of the American operation in Cuba which came to my attention, for example, was summed up in the observation of one Britisher: "Good Lord, man," he said, "if you're going to do things like that, then for Heaven's sake do them. Hard, and with everything you've got. No halfway measures in that sort of thing." It is a fact, however lamentable, that the Soviets were aware of this in Hungary in 1956. It is also a relevant fact that the Head of State whom we tried to overthrow—and failed, switching our support after the fact—is today, not many years later, one of the leading purveyors of enthusiastic statements about the greatness of the United States—which serves to show that bruises for doing the wrong thing heal quickly in the international arena. But ineptitude, which fosters loss of confidence, is not so quickly forgotten. One of the principal problems of international relations—including secret political operations—is simple communication across the barriers of linguistic, historical, and cultural differences. In international politics the *lingua franca* is the language of power. Talking with a nation which follows a bad policy, but executes it reasonably adeptly, at least permits communication if not liking. (South Africa comes to mind.) But communicating with a nation which is inept in the execution of its policy is like talking with a man with an insurmountable stammer—you don't know whether what he is saying is good or bad.

Americans are deeply concerned about the rightness of their national policies. This is healthy and useful. But too often the assumption is made that if the policy is right, its proper execution follows automatically. Vast improvements have been made in selecting and supporting the best-suited personnel for secret political operations in recent years, but there is still insufficient understanding of the fact that what is the American's meat may well be the foreigner's poison. I recall with a shudder the remark of an American responsible for a highly important Eastern European operation. "What I don't like about X," he said, seriously referring to a leading Czechoslovak politician, "is that he has none of that good old American get-up-and-go." The rejoinder is obvious: if he had it he wouldn't have been a leading Czechoslovak politician. (This same American, left inexplicably in his post for two years, was able, at the end of that time, to shock a Pole into disbelief with his remark that Poland had every right to all lands up to the Oder-Neisse line because, "After all, they were always Polish territory until the Germans took them away." The Pole was embarrassed, but he was a forthright man. "I am very grateful for your sympathy for our cause," he answered, "but, please, I beg of you, do not let it be known that you base it on that reason. I am obliged to inform you that historically it is simply not true.")

These things still happen, but the United States owes a not inconsiderable debt of gratitude in this connection to Allen Dulles for two reasons: first, he maintained, during his stewardship of the Central Intelligence Agency, and against strong and persistent pressures, the vital principle of civilian control of this powerful organization; and second, he instilled and developed, as rapidly as possible in the circumstances, precisely that sense of professionalism essential to the best conduct of secret operations. But the full process is a long one.

In the present transitional stage, the principal handicaps to

American secret political operations stem from the imposition on such operations of purely American standards which are laudable at home and inappropriate when exported. One such, for example, is haste. The result is what has been referred to, in some anguish, as the doctrine of immediate results immediately arrived at. In a field where quiet patience, the long view, and sustained effort are prime qualities the American bureaucracy is constantly pressed for demonstrable results to justify action. I recall spending two years creating a political organization whose ultimate purpose was the penetration of an already existing European institution. At the conclusion of the first meeting of the organization it was no closer in fact to its ultimate aim than at the outset. But it had at least been put into position to accomplish its mission. To my surprise I received high praise at this premature stage because, of all irrelevant reasons, two New York newspapers had published accounts of the meeting, and these clippings could be exhibited as proof of success. This impatience for quick and visible results leads also to what is generally interpreted by other nations as an American lack of tenacity. If results from a political operation are not almost immediately evident, the Americans will tend to lose interest, abandon the operation, or turn its personnel to other, frequently inappropriate uses.

The most common European charge against our operations, for example, that they are "not serious," stems from this same haste and its concomitant satisfaction with artificial results. As a Frenchman said to me in some disillusionment after watching the sudden turnabout of a highly complicated operation to a wholly new "priority" target, "The trouble with you people is that you only want to look good; you don't care about really being good."

This criticism also stems from promises too easily broken, almost always on the justification that high policy demands it or that overriding domestic American considerations require it. Under full authority I once made a careful agreement with a Western European political party which required guaranteed American participation for eighteen months. Five months later the American participation was canceled and the European personnel let go onto the street. In due course I found out that as a compromise in an American budget argument, this operation had been traded away for some funds for something else that now seemed more attractive. I had also to experience the quiet comment of a European Senator: "We shall never make the mistake of working with your organization again." The only saving point for the United States in this case was that he was speaking of a cover organization.

In a policy sense our operations also suffer from the application of purely American prejudices to situations where they are not applicable. The high Presidential adviser who once started to say that my residence abroad had made me "un-American," but who had the grace to pause and amend his sentence if not his thought, was exercised at the time over my proposal to bring an extremely well-known European Socialist into a European organization. "I don't understand why we can't just go along with our own people whom we've always worked with," he said. "You just don't understand that Socialism is a dirty word in this country." His observation about Socialism was no doubt true—notwithstanding the fact that it was by and large Socialist Governments in Western Europe which created NATO with us—but it was irrelevant to the fact that the organization we were discussing was formed to be effective in Europe, not in the United States.

(The bias is at least not one-sided. When on another occasion I proposed limited aid to an exiled monarch who had genuine popularity in his native land, the refusal was accompanied by the remark, "Surprised you'd even suggest it. What if Congress found out we were tied up with a *king*?")

The Presidential adviser's viewpoint was, of course, a close cousin of the "our boy" theory of political operations. I so label it because in a Western European country, functioning under a coalition of two dominant and independent parties—which meant greater effort on our part to maintain and develop our influence in this particular country—a neo-Fascist party was formed only a few years after the war. To my astonishment I encountered a serious proposal to back the neo-Fascist party with all our resources. The proponent of this plan ascribed my astonishment to ignorance. "Don't you see?" he said. "The leader of this party needs support; once he gets it we'll keep building him up until he throws out the coalition. Then we'll have our boy in there, and none of these headaches." Quite apart from the lack of political wisdom involved in this particular case, the "our boy" theory substitutes puppets for allies, corruption for viability, our prejudices for local reality. Syngman Rhee was "our boy," as were several others, now forgotten, in Laos.

In the purely technical aspects, our political operations suffer from an excessive prejudice in favor of intelligence objectives and procedures. When the inevitable conflict between intelligence and political objectives arises, the decision is too often in favor of the intelligence objectives. Similarly, the case officer-agent relationship in political operations is too often clouded by the duplicity and the type of rigid control characterizing intelligence operations. This prejudice arises from misunderstandings in Government departments other than the CIA of the value of political operations, with a consequent stressing of intelligence requirements, and from the fact that the great majority of CIA personnel are the products of training in intelligence rather than political techniques.

The heart of the secret war in our time, however, lies in the political conflict. Intelligence is essential and cannot for a moment be neglected. But we advance or we retreat, we make gains or suffer losses in proportion to our mastery of the details of the political struggle—meaning the living characteristics of men, the ever-changing human relationships within and among societies, from which flow the tides of power.

1. While the conflict "between the Communist and non-Communist blocs" continues, the world is no longer governed exclusively by this "single conflict." The "two great power centers" are no longer in a position to dictate unilaterally within their own spheres without recourse to force (which increasingly involves greater risks). Neither is even in a position in today's world to solve its own domestic problems with purely domestic solutions. (Note the Soviet Union's difficulties with productivity, and the United States' transformation in three years in the early 1980s from the world's greatest creditor nation to the world's greatest debtor nation.) No "other nations or combinations of states" have yet achieved "some parity with them" in terms of power, but the West European GNP now exceeds that of the United States—which has long exceeded that of the Soviet Union. While both superpowers meddle in the Middle Eastern conflicts, they certainly cannot now "divide" that "world between them," and the major shifts in the balance of power now originate in East Asia.

2. We can perhaps still agree that the "effort to keep the Cold War, in the sense of hostile blocs of nations aligned with East or West, out of Africa is a sound, even noble one," but the effort has neither succeeded (cf. Ethiopia, Angola, and Chad) nor failed. Where it has not failed much is due to the Africans' own rejection of bloc alignments. But, as the text states, this "does not and cannot eliminate the secret war" from Africa.

3. This was written before the revelations in the mid-1970s of the singular efforts to assassinate Fidel Castro. When the Office of Policy Coordination was established in 1948 the question of assassination arose, and was

promptly dismissed—one participant in the meeting observing, "Let's not get into that. They're so much better at it than we could ever be." This paragraph was written in 1962 with that in mind, and plainly in ignorance. I was therefore stunned (and appalled) at the 1970s revelations: Obviously my hailing of "some advance toward civilization" was premature. That "advance" then had to be legislated by the Congress. Still an "advance," of course, but not as much as would have been a voluntary decision within the Executive Branch.

4. Essentially the same can be said of the failure in Vietnam (which was only a cloud on the horizon when this was written).

5. Much has since transpired in this part of the world—including Qaddafi's overthrow of King Idris and, of course, the British withdrawal from the area. The basic point remains valid, however; note that the British still exercise important if inconspicuous (perhaps important because inconspicuous) influence in the Persian Gulf.

PART 2

Fundamentals and Forms in Action: The Seventy-Fifth Passenger

The reader who has come thus far probably feels that he has earned a story. It was my intention, in the account which now follows of an operation which I conducted in Soviet-occupied Hungary in 1946 and 1947, to provide him with a case history. But in setting down the case history, it turned into a story. A true story, but still a story.

The difference between the two is mainly an emotional one. Despite the intervening years, I found myself, in writing this account, immersed again in the sights and sounds, in the sensations and impressions, in my own emotions of the time—outrage, anger, worry, fear, suspicion, curiosity, pride, sympathy, hope, frustration, satisfaction, brief triumphs, occasional humor, and final sadness—all of which were as much a part of the reality of the operation as the events and actions themselves. As I said at the outset of this book, secret agents are not necessarily coldly unemotional. Thus this story may be a more accurate case history than a case history would have been.

Its accuracy depends in part, however, on the reader, on his willingness to view this account critically in the light of the principles described in Part I. For one of the strongest emotions experienced by any secret agent, both at the time of action and in retrospect, is, of course, the very human desire for self-justification. It is not absent from this account.

Nor is the reader spared the intrusions of my personal cast of mind. When, for example, in discussing courses of political action open to me at a critical point in 1947, I reject a particular course as "tantamount to buying an effort," on the basis of which, I state, "no long-term policy can be constructed," the reader will recognize that this viewpoint is at least historically debatable.

With the drawbacks of these personal desires and intrusions in mind, I have appended at the end of this account a brief, general critique of the operation. I still advise the reader, however, to follow the story without suspending his own critical judgment.

CHAPTER I

Budapest 1946

My emotional involvement, my shock, on the night of November 4, 1956, as Soviet troops assaulted Budapest, had their roots in a fight I had waged in that same city, in the same cause, ten years before. That fight too had been lost to the Soviet steamroller, but we who lost had emerged not entirely without honor.

I first saw Budapest in the summer of 1946. I came as a covert agent, member of an American intelligence organization—there then being no CIA—which has since ceased to exist.[1] I had been offered the mission because I spoke Russian and was primarily interested in Eastern European affairs. And Budapest in 1946 was as much a Russian as a Hungarian problem.

In the winter of 1944–45 three Russian armies had swept into the country from Yugoslavia, to the south, from Rumania, to the southeast, and over the Carpathian Mountains from Ruthenia, to the east. The Russians came, and were by and large awaited, as liberators. Nevertheless, the memory still lingered in Hungary of the last Russian invasion, ninety-seven years before, when, at the invitation of the Austrian Emperor, they had come to drown a revolt in blood, to maintain ideological purity, and to keep the virus of political liberty away from the borders of their empire—exactly as they were to do again only twelve years from this winter of 1944–45.

Remembering 1848, remembering Bela Kun's Communist regime of 1919, the Hungarian Government in 1943 and 1944 had established contact with the Allies in neutral capitals in the hopes of bringing about an Anglo-American invasion which would forestall first, a German occupation, and second, an exclusively Soviet occupation. A British colonel, in hiding in Budapest but in touch with both London and the Hungarian Government, had been secretly flown down to Allied Headquarters at Caserta. The Hungarian proposals were not acceptable to the Allies, who, in accordance with decisions taken at the Tehran Conference, told the Hungarians to approach the Russians. The military aspects of the proposals were in any case regarded as unfeasible in view of the planned Normandy invasion.

Knowledge of these maneuvers had been but one item in the German decision to occupy Hungary in March of 1944. A further effort in October by Horthy to surrender to the Russians had led to the arrest and kidnaping of Horthy—another successful operation by Otto Skorzeny, the Nazis' secret operations expert—and the installation in Budapest of the Szalasi Nazi puppet regime.

Less than a year after their seizure of the country, the Germans in Hungary were faced with the driving Russian armies, now broken out of the confinement of the mountains ringing the *puszta*—the Great Hungarian Plain. Here, a thousand years before, the Magyar chieftain Arpad had decided to settle his people, to cease their nomadic wanderings and plundering forays which had terrorized Christian Europe. As the Russian armies followed in the paths of the earlier Huns and nomad Magyars, their front-line Central Asian troops, with their rape and rapine, struck a special terror into the civilian population. (There was an atavistic ring to all this: Hungarians, with a thousand years behind them of Christian civilization in a beautiful and fruitful land, are sometimes wont to forget their own Asian origins.)

The Russians quickly cleared southern and eastern Hungary of the Germans, but it became clear that Budapest could not be bypassed: all the rail lines in the country passed through the capital. The Russians encircled the city on Christmas Eve, 1944, and attacked from the direction of Vienna, striking first into Buda, the more residential half of the city, lying on the western right bank of the Danube. The siege lasted fifty-nine days before the last Germans, holding out in the Var—Castle Hill—ancient seat of the Hungarian Kings and site of the Royal Palace and Coronation Church, and on St. Margit's Island, a wooded pleasure area slightly upstream, were finally slaughtered.

Their communications secured, the Russians went on to the west, to take Vienna on April 13, 1945, and to confront the Americans, at war's end less than a month later, at Linz in Upper Austria. Austria, while permitted a Government, was divided into four zones of occupation—with a fifth International Zone in the heart of Vienna—and the Soviet Zone was interposed between Hungary and the Western zones of Austria. Then the Hungarian drama, which the Hungarians hoped was ended, began.

The Yalta agreements had specified that Bulgaria, Rumania, and Hungary, although at war with the Allied Powers, were to be treated as "liberated" countries. Accordingly, as soon as Debrecen, the major Hungarian city in the eastern part of the country, had been taken from the Germans, the Hungarians had been permitted to form a Provisional Government there. An Allied Control Commission had earlier been established, chaired by none other than Marshal Voroshilov, and with American and British representation in the form of Major-Generals. The Russian Kommandaturas throughout Hungary operated in the name of the Allied Control Commission, which was run entirely by the Russian Chairman. At Potsdam the United States had proffered a set of proposed regulations for the Control Commissions, which the Russians, in one of their time-honored gambits, had accepted as a "basis for discussion." When some highhanded Soviet action in the name of the Control Commission provoked a British or American reference to the regulations, the Russian Chairman's reply was simply that they were merely a "basis for discussion" and that, in view of more urgent business, the chair would not entertain any discussion on that subject. When Budapest was freed, this comedy, along with the Hungarian Provisional Government, moved to Budapest, in the spring of 1945.

However, the Provisional Government was not a comedy, either from a political or an intelligence point of view. It was a coalition government, made up of the four political parties authorized by the Allied Control Commission: the Smallholders, the Social-Democrats, the National Peasants, and the Communists. A fifth party, predominantly Catholic, had been authorized in principle, but due to some dissension within the Church itself, did not succeed in organizing until late in 1947—which was, as we shall see, too late. Another minor group, the Civic Democratic Party, was authorized, but was not part of the coalition.

The Smallholders Party was a prewar opposition group which

sought agricultural reform in favor of small land holdings by the peasantry, but which also had some appeal among the small merchants and artisans of the cities and towns. It had a good resistance record and was conceded to be the majority party. The Social-Democrats, tolerated by prewar governments, were primarily a trade-union Socialist party; there was no Hungarian Socialist equivalent of the British Fabian Society or of the German theoretical Marxists. The National Peasants were more an idea than a party; the brainchild of a group of writers and intellectuals who sought to base Hungarian political life on the traditional values and preponderant numbers of the Hungarian peasantry, this was, in effect, the Hungarian version of the Fabian Society—romanticizing the tillers of the soil rather than the workers in the factories. The Communists—at least the presidium of the Party—arrived in the baggage of the Red Army, removed their Soviet uniforms, and set to work. Some 500 Hungarian Communists returned with the Russians. They didn't have much to work with: various agents who had been parachuted in during the fighting, and between 1,000 and 1,500 underground Communists who had managed to survive police nets over the years. The parties which had held power in the country during the previous quarter-century were abolished as responsible, in greater or lesser degree, for Hungary's Axis role.

By the time the curtain rose on the Hungarian drama, the same play, with the same producer, had already been on the boards for a brief time in Poland, Rumania, and Bulgaria. The plot had unfolded sufficiently in those countries so that the only question was whether the producer, a talented but mono- and megalomaniac Georgian, was going to open with the same show in Budapest. The David Merrick of his day, he knew that it was bad box office for the audience to leave in the middle of the first act. He was therefore reluctant to announce the name of the play—there were already faint stirrings among the critics—and it was plain that we would get nothing out of the producer's assistants—the Russians in Hungary. We therefore turned to the cast—the Hungarian Government—in the hopes that as the play progressed, they might slip us the title. In brief, we had to learn about what the Russians were doing in Hungary from the Hungarians. This was one part of the intelligence significance of the Hungarian Government.

The other part was the Government itself. If Stalin was putting on the same old show, it was the Hungarians about whom we would have to know in the future: the factions in the country, the trends of opinion, the personalities, who was prepared to oppose and who not, why, and what for, which people could work together and which not, the talents and motives of various leaders, actual and potential, who were Soviet collaborators and why, the resources and capacities of the country—the interminable and inexhaustible range of questions which go into assessing an entire nation.

Further, the Hungarian Government's interest to us was not only as a source of intelligence. The United States' interest in Hungary was a part of our objective of a stable peace in Eastern Europe, so long—and still—a major temptation and battleground for the Great Powers. With this end in view we would obviously seek to develop and maintain influence in the councils of the Hungarian Government. Also, if Russian intentions turned out to be of the worst—of which there was little doubt among experienced observers of the Russian performance—there would then arise the question of whether the American Government would oppose this development, and if so, how and to what extent. These were questions as yet undecided. But whichever way they would be decided, it was clear we would want the Hungarians on our side. The most direct, though not sole, instrument to achieve this was their own Government. Thus this hodgepodge Government, existing on sufferance of the occupiers, had a considerable political significance of its own in the international scene.

Insofar as the purely Hungarian elements in the immediate postwar scene were concerned, there was much on our side. To understate the case, the Russians were cordially disliked by the overwhelming majority of the population. All political leaders with any genuine following in the nation were oriented to the West; indeed, their major aspiration was to avoid being swallowed up in the Soviet Empire. While there was strong sentiment for political and economic reform, there was no class or group in the country interested as such in applying Communist solutions to their problems; the bitter taste of the short-lived Hungarian Communist regime of 1919 lingered. The American position was particularly strong: there were certain historical associations—Kossuth, among others; Hungarians of all classes were quick to recognize that the United States was now the leader of the Western world; and there were the innumerable ties resulting from the large Hungarian population in the United States.

Ranged against this was the presence of the Red Army. Its effectiveness was doubled by the fear it inspired. Its menace was reinforced by the hard fact that, except for the Allied Sectors in Vienna, the nearest Western outposts lay almost four hundred miles to the west of Budapest. To the north Czechoslovakia lay close, but the Czechoslovaks were hostile and had strong claims against the Hungarian state.

The Hungarian Communists, then, had little on their side, but what they had was implicitly effective—the Red Army had to intervene openly only once to assist the Communist take-over of the country—and decisive. Among their Hungarian opponents they had two allies: personal ambitions and dissension.

In November of 1945 Hungary's first postwar elections were held. They were free and unrigged, the sole such instance in Soviet-occupied territory and Soviet history. The results were striking: the Smallholders Party—which had interestingly enough also won a majority immediately following the collapse of the Hungarian Soviet Republic in 1919—received 57 per cent of the votes. The Socialists won 18 per cent, the Communists 17 per cent, and the National Peasant Party 8 per cent.

There has been much debate over the reasons for Soviet acquiescence in holding these elections. One theory is that they were misled by exaggeratedly optimistic claims of the Hungarian Communists. Another is that the decision was the result of factional quarrels among the Russian and Hungarian Communists—each Hungarian Communist leader had his own patron in the Soviet Politburo. Some students of the matter feel that the Russians desired to delude the Western powers as to their ultimate intentions while consolidating their hold on all of Eastern Europe. Matyas Rakosi, who directed the Communist seizure of power in Hungary and became dictator until his final fall from power in 1956, has stated, but without reference to the elections as such, only that the period from April 1945 to the end of 1948—distinguished for his famous "salami" tactics, or gradual take-over—was necessary to bring the majority of the workers and peasants to support the Communist Party, in accordance, so he claimed, with Lenin's teachings.

Whatever the reason for these unusual elections, the Communist 17 per cent was fully as striking as the Smallholders' absolute 57-per-cent majority. The fact is that a party comprised of no more than 2,000 members at the outset had, seven months later, at the time of the elections, 700,000 members. A minority of this number

was obtained from peasants who had benefited from the land reform, for which the Communist Party took credit, and from workers, particularly miners. The great majority was taken from the so-
called "small Nazis," that is, the rank and file of the Hungarian
Nazi Party which, in 1944, had numbered a million members.
These people were by definition subject to reprisals; their easy way
out and their safety were gained by joining the Communist Party,
which, by its control of the Political Police, could decide who
would be prosecuted and who not.

On the basis of these elections, a Government was formed which
was quickly granted full recognition by all the major powers—with
the exception of France, which chose to delay, ostensibly until the
settlement of certain property questions, but in fact as part of char-
acteristically De Gaullian maneuvers to assert the voice of France.
The leader of the Smallholders Party, Zoltan Tildy, was elected
President of Hungary—the second in its history, Count Mihaly
Karolyi having held the post in his short-lived republic at the end
of the First World War. The Prime Ministry devolved upon another Smallholder leader, Ferenc Nagy (no relation to the Communist Imre Nagy who was to become Prime Minister eight years
later and then again during the 1956 Revolution). The Government was a coalition of the four parties which had participated in
the elections, notwithstanding the Smallholders' absolute majority,
since a majority Government would have excluded the Communists from power—a solution the Russians were not prepared to
accept. Accordingly, Arpad Szakasits for the Socialists and Matyas
Rakosi for the Communists were each made Deputy Prime Minister. The various ministries were then apportioned out on the same
principle; of the key ministries the Smallholders received Foreign
Affairs and Finance, the Socialists the Justice Ministry, and, on
standard Communist insistence supported by the Russians, the
Communists—in the person of Imre Nagy and later Laszlo Rajk—
received the Interior Ministry, meaning, in Hungary as in the rest
of Europe, the police power. Within each ministry, in turn, each of
the coalition parties had its own representatives (although in the
case of the Communist ministries this participation was purely
nominal). In those days Hungary was so much a coalition that it
was scarcely possible to summon a plumber or have lunch except
on a coalition basis. The American Minister to Hungary at the
time gave it as his opinion that not even France, with its traditional

individuality and multi-party system, could compare for sheer complexity of partisan politics with postwar Hungary.

This ferment was not solely a political phenomenon, but was a reflection of the whole Magyar temperament. While it is true that Hungarians are given to streaks of melancholy, and even that Budapest had one of the world's highest prewar suicide rates, it is also a fact that as a people the Magyars are vivacious and resilient. The theater is probably their best art form; and the coffeehouse—kavehaz—astir with gossip, intrigue, and, above all, a flourishing and irreverent sense of humor, is the national institution. Their forthright, tolerant, highly appreciative, and continuous, but withal balanced, regard for the joys of the relations between the sexes causes even the most repressed Anglo-Saxon or dour puritan characters to realize almost exuberantly that life is much richer than they feared. The Hungarians are susceptible to a streak of self-pity, but they are also capable of laughing at themselves, and they combine with this a simultaneous streak of rashness often emerging as bravery. They are cynical of slogans, but they are beguiled by living.

The vitality of the Hungarians was nowhere more evident in the summer of 1946, when I arrived, than in the comparison between Vienna and Budapest. In Vienna, prostrate under four occupation armies, life just barely dragged along: there was no black market, the currency was stable, food was rationed and scarce, and people trudged through the streets, silent, gray, drab. In Budapest, which had suffered a degree of destruction comparable only to the major German cities and which lay at the not so tender mercies of the Red Army, there was whipped cream for the numerous daily coffees—and milk for the babies; reconstruction went on energetically —immediately following the siege the people of Budapest had voluntarily restored the famous and favorite Coronation Church on the Var, in Buda; the theater flourished wherever a stage could be found, and the night clubs were legendary in Europe for the period —one of the best being ultimately purchased with the profits of their loot by a consortium of nine Soviet officers; the currency entered upon the fastest and farthest inflation ever seen—rising in eighteen months from some 50 pengös to the dollar to a final quotation of 11,000,000,000,000,000,000,000,000,000 (27 zeros) to the dollar; and stimulating it all was one of Europe's liveliest black markets in which, of course, theft and hijacking played no small part.

The flavor of the Hungarian black market was well illustrated at the time by a statistic and a joke: statistically it was a fact that the number of automobiles in Hungary—without an automobile industry—increased tremendously in the first year after the war, while Austria, with several plants, experienced a sharp decline—to the point where the American Army in Austria would send a mission to Hungary from time to time to look for their missing cars. This was also the period when the coffee-house wags, seeing a friend in a new suit, would remark that he was "a Hungarian by day and a Russian by night." (These stories do not, however, do justice to the full range and flavor of the Hungarian genius: the story is often recounted of the meeting in Washington in the early fifties of the Scientific Advisory Board of the U.S. Atomic Energy Commission. When a count of the members showed a minority absent, but still a quorum, another count enabled the Chairman to say to his colleagues, in his faultless and native Hungarian, "Shall we conduct the meeting in the mother tongue?" Agreed and done.)

Notwithstanding all this variety and activity, the problem of my cover posed some special difficulties. The Russians controlled all entry into and exit from Hungary, and were most strict on this score. Entry was permitted only for members of official missions— and even they often had to wait a considerable period; for some correspondents—with similar delays; and a very few businessmen who had to be representatives of already existing American properties in Hungary. As the American companies with interests in Hungary—principally the manufacture of electrical equipment and the oil industry—needed whatever entry permits were available for their own people, and since it was a matter of policy to avoid jeopardizing either the American investments in Eastern Europe or the access of bona fide correspondents to Soviet-controlled territory, there was no possibility of a private cover which would give me residence privileges. It was therefore decided that official cover was the only possibility. This gave a choice of either the U.S. Legation in Budapest or the U.S. Military Mission, which was the American Representation on the Allied Control Commission for Hungary. As my functions involved some risk, it was, as is customary, decided to avoid any possibility of embarrassment for the Legation, our permanent diplomatic mission, and to attach me to the Military Mission.

The Military Mission was, of course, a temporary institution. It was not known how long such a mission would be maintained, for it was American policy to seek the departure of foreign troops from all occupied European countries except Germany at the earliest possible moment—which meant in practice, of course, U.S., British, and French departure from Italy; U.S., British, French, and Soviet departure from Austria; Soviet departure from Hungary, Rumania, and Bulgaria; and a limitation of the Red Army in Poland to supply and communications lines to Germany. (This was the effort and hope at the time, due to be blocked by the Soviet refusal to sign a State Treaty with Austria for many years, thereby giving them the pretext for continued stationing of troops—as supply lines to Austria—in Hungary and Rumania.) In support of this aim the Paris Peace Conference had already been convoked for the autumn of 1946, and it was thus hoped to be only a matter of time before the U.S. Military Mission in Hungary, like those in Rumania and Bulgaria, would be withdrawn.

With this time limit in mind, and with the enormous bureaucratic obstacles to transforming me into an Army officer at a time when our Army was to a large extent being disbanded, I was designated as an Adviser to the Military Mission, acting as a civilian. This cover not only gave me greater flexibility than if I had been in uniform, but it offered the possibility that, if circumstances turned out propitiously, I might, with the ultimate departure of the Military Mission, be readily able to transfer to some form of private cover. Alternatively, one of my tasks was to explore the ground and arrange or recommend a suitable cover for a successor if it should prove impossible for me to stay.

To explain to the Russians the somewhat unusual presence of a civilian adviser on the staff of the Military Mission, advantage was taken of the functions of the Allied Control Commission itself. There was at the time, in the U.S. Government, an operation known as "Safehaven," the purpose of which was to uncover hidden Nazi personnel and assets in areas outside of Germany. At the same time, one of the principal agreed functions of the Allied Control Commissions was to eliminate the last vestiges of Nazism in the countries where they operated. It was therefore explained to the Soviets that the tracing of refugee Nazi personnel and assets outside of Germany was a civilian function under our arrangements, and that, in effect, I would be at their disposition for whatever co-operative activity in this field they might find useful. It was thus hoped not only to explain my civilian status, but to give me a special access to the Russians themselves from which something of value might emerge. This manner of presenting things also served to provide a valid explanation for my command of the Russian language.

Communications were somewhat easier. I was instructed to enter into friendly personal relations with "Mark," a high official of the American Legation, who would, without knowledge of their contents, handle my communications. (The code names used throughout this account are obviously not those really used in the operation. Furthermore, none of the personnel of the network knew the code name by which I referred to them in my communications, although they had, whenever necessary, different code names for operational use among ourselves.) I would give Mark a sealed envelope addressed with only a code word for my organization, inside of which was another envelope with a code name for my case officer in Washington. He would forward all this by regular diplomatic courier in another envelope addressed to a cover office in Washington. Incoming mail arrived addressed in an outer envelope to him, which was the only one he opened; he then gave to me an inner envelope with the code word for the organization, which contained a final envelope addressed with only my code name. Telegraphic communications I simply gave to him already encoded in my own cipher. It was then encoded again in the Legation and transmitted to Washington. Messages for me came to the Legation, were decoded, and—since the Legation's decoded version ended up still encoded, but now in my cipher—then given to Mark, who would pass the message to me.

My instructions were specific and strict: I was forbidden to disclose to Mark any details of the network I was operating, nor could I reveal to him in any way actual operations in which I was engaged. I was to take political guidance from him as to U.S. Government policy; and, while I was not to withhold information from him of direct value to the Legation, I was to limit it insofar as possible to matters of urgency or of physical safety of the Legation itself, and then without revealing the sources. This was sound practice: the procedure may seem roundabout, but in fact all the information which I obtained, and which was considered to be essential to the Legation's functions, was in due course transmitted to the Legation in general or special Government reports and intelligence analyses. What was omitted, and thus protected, was the source. Thus the network and the agent were protected, the organization was shielded, the information which the network obtained was sub-

ject to the necessary control of who should benefit from it, and the
U.S. diplomatic establishment was not unduly compromised.

For full efficacy, such arrangements always depend upon the
human relationships involved; in this case, the key relationship was
that between Mark and myself. To everyone's good fortune it
turned out to be very nearly ideal: a genuine meeting of the minds,
as the lawyers say, and a due respect for the value of each other's
functions led to a most effective working relationship.[2]

In addition to these regular arrangements, I was also given a
connection with another agent residing in Switzerland. Facilities
were established whereby I could contact him directly in case of
emergency; in such cases I was entitled to take his word, if he gave
it, as equivalent to full authority from headquarters. This agent,
known as "Peter," traveled widely and often throughout all of
Europe. I was therefore authorized to discuss with him the details
of my work whenever a meeting rendered that possible. As important, it was also his function to provide me with funds. In the
Hungary of the period, this meant transfer by hand to me of cash
sums, either in Swiss francs—preferred—or American dollars.
This money I then cashed, either myself or through cut-outs, on
the Hungarian black market, which continued to flourish well after
the replacement in August 1946 of the pengö by the new, stabilized
forint, or, if my recipients so preferred, I simply disbursed to them
in the original currency. (In view of the nation's acute shortage of
foreign exchange, both non-Communist and later Communist
Governments were happy to blink at illegal transactions which
continued for long to bring in hard currencies. Thus my transactions aroused no suspicion. Even after the black market was later
severely reduced in scope, remittances via banks and such organizations as CARE from exiles and emigrants to their relatives, no
matter what the source, were—and are to this day—encouraged by
all the Soviet satellite regimes as a valuable source of foreign exchange.) Peter, in Switzerland, was the only other agent in Europe
—outside of my own network in Hungary, of course—with whom
I was in touch. While I could reasonably assume that there were
other networks operating in the various countries neighboring on
Hungary, I obviously never inquired about them—until an emergency did one day arise.

With cover, communications, and funds arranged, my headquarters had done all it could do. The rest could only be worked out on
the spot in response to what were bound to be rapidly changing

circumstances. What I didn't know, as I arrived in Budapest in late June 1946 and remarked, in the hot and lazy summer sunshine, the contrast between the pretty and chic Hungarian girls and the sullen and soiled Russian soldiery, was how fast and how far all would change.[3]

1. "Brigadier, U.S. Army, retired January of this year, sir, after some 35 years' service, 20 of which have been devoted to intelligence in various places; during the early days of the war, Deputy G-2 of the War Department, and Chief of the Military Intelligence Service. . . . About April, I believe, sir, of 1942 . . . it was decided . . . that the more active operational side of intelligence should go to . . . Coordinated Information [sic], that is, you know, the office that preceded the OSS, and that the regular intelligence services should proceed from there with their own intelligence activities. This gave the official approval for me to organize and set on foot the secret intelligence service.

"By December of that year this directive was expanded, perhaps it was October, was expanded to instruct me, which I in turn instructed my predecessor at this hearing [Col. John V. Grombach], that he would not only institute a secret intelligence service, looking to the needs of the current war effort, but that he would lay the foundation for a perpetual, a far-seeing, a far-distant, continuing secret intelligence service . . ." (Testimony of Brigadier-General Hayes Kroner, before the Committee on Expenditures in the Executive Departments of the House of Representatives, on H. R. 2319, National Security Act of 1947, June 27, 1947. *Hearing*, pp. 53–54.)

The crux of this Hearing was the question of whether to limit the collection of secret foreign intelligence to the Central Intelligence Agency in the new legislation creating the CIA, or to allow the Army, Navy, State, and others to engage in these operations as well, with the CIA as the central coordinating, evaluating, and disseminating authority. There were six witnesses before the Committee: Lt.-Gen. Hoyt S. Vandenberg, Director of the Central Intelligence Group; Allen W. Dulles (speaking as a civilian); Peter Vischer, former Secretary, Joint Intelligence Commttee of the Joint Chiefs of Staff, and author of a 1946 study on intelligence for the Military Affairs Committee of the House of Representatives; Brig.-Gen. Hayes Kroner, former Deputy G-2 of the War Department and Chief of the Military Intelligence Service; Col. John V. Grombach, Director, Secret Intelligence Branch of the War Department General Staff; and Rear-Adm. Thomas Inglis, Chief of Naval Intelligence. Vandenberg and Dulles spoke forcefully for a CIA monopoly of collection; Inglis was prepared to give the organized role to the CIA, with bits and pieces left for the services on an ad hoc basis; Vischer was opposed to a CIA monopoly role in collection, and for the rest wanted to maintain the Presidential directive of February 5, 1946, giving limited authority to the CIG; Hayes and Grombach had no objection to a CIA monopoly on coordination, evaluation, and dissemination of intelligence, but wanted to preserve independent secret collection operations and to exclude the CIA from collection. Although the final 1947 legislation went with Vandenberg and Dulles, other departments continued collection operations. (The 1947 Hearing was in executive session, and only one transcript was made. It was loaned to the CIA, where it was copied, and the original returned to the House Committee. In 1950 the Committee Chairman ordered the destruction of the original. The CIA copy was discovered during a House Intelligence Committee review, in 1981 or 1982, of CIA records [although it had been provided by the CIA in 1975, without House permission, to the Senate Committee known as the "Church Committee."] The House Intelligence Committee asked for its declassification in 1982, and the CIA concurred. Hence the thirty-five years between the Hearing and publication of its transcript.)

"The U.S. Secret Intelligence Branch . . . was organized just before the U.S. became involved in the war or a short time thereafter, but certainly long before the OSS. In fact, it began operating officially and actively under covers toward the end of 1941 and certainly by early January 1942 . . . I owe a great deal of credit to . . . members of the Secret Intelligence Branch, which I directed from January 2, 1942, to January 1, 1955, for the War and State Departments. . . . Credit is also due . . . for legal advice to me as director of the S. I. Branch in its friendly termination in preference to its being taken over and integrated into the CIA in 1955 . . ." (John V. Grombach, *The Great Liquidator,* Doubleday, New York, 1980, pp. 112, xi, xii.)

In late 1981, a year before his death, Col. Grombach was inverviewed by Professor Charles Gati, of Union College and Columbia University. In the course of the interview Col. Grombach gave to Professor Gati a memorandum which, though undated, contained internal references placing it in late 1954. Mainly devoted to Grombach's multiple grievances against the CIA, the memorandum does contain a brief section on the history of his "S.I. Branch," which states, *inter alia* [emphasis added], "This organization, tied in with the State Department for communication and necessary cooperation . . . scored many intelligence successes during the war. . . . In 1947, the newly created CIA, after first trying to take over and absorb the organization, forced the War Department to drop it . . . as part of a high level jurisdictional struggle for control and absorption of all . . . secret intelligence collecting agencies. This organization could not accept absorption by CIA. . . . *From 1947 to 1951, the State Department . . . secretly continued it* unknown to CIA *'as an adjunct to the Foreign Service.'* In late 1950 or early 1951 the State Department, against advice of the organization, revealed its continued existence to CIA. . . ."

2. I do not recall now what impelled me to describe this relationship as

"*very nearly* ideal." The adverbs were superfluous, since "Mark," at the time a career Foreign Service Officer, Second Secretary and Chief of the Political Section of the Legation, was James McCargar. (cf. Charles Gati, *Hungary and the Soviet Bloc,* Durham, Duke University Press, 1986, pp. 9 and 23; and *Foreign Relations of the United States, 1947,* Vol. IV, Washington, Government Printing Office, 1972, p. 398.)

3. April, not June. Should thus read, "bright spring sunshine."

CHAPTER II

The Network

Whatever my difficulties would be, I had one great initial advantage. I did not have to start absolutely from scratch, since I had a predecessor already in Budapest who had an established and functioning network. As his cover was considerably different from my own, I saw him only rarely and then always clandestinely. When we met in public we were, as two Americans in a foreign land, friendly and polite, but gave no visible sign that we saw each other apart from such chance encounters. Furthermore, his departure, which was a result of the need for arranging well in advance of future changes the possibility of a more permanent cover for either myself or my successor, was postponed for some four months after my arrival in order that no one should be able to draw any correlation between the two.

In this interval I settled in, so to speak, concentrated on establishing my cover, and began to move in as many different circles as possible. This is, of course, classical procedure. No agent—and least of all one with as broad an assignment as mine—is really of use until he is securely oriented in his surroundings. This involves a thorough absorption in the local habits, customs, traditions, and personal traits. Until this is achieved, any agent is ill advised to operate in any but the most limited or routine way. The alternative is to risk early exposure through simple faults of detail—such as, for example, a clandestine meeting place badly chosen for want of knowledge of local police habits—or a successful opposition penetration for want of insufficient familiarity with local personalities.

I was early able to find a small flat on the Var. This was probably the most destroyed area of the city, but that in itself gave certain advantages. The Var is a kind of bluff, with very steep sides, rising some 200 or more feet and running northwest from the Danube's right bank. It was in ancient times a fortified citadel, dominates the old city of Buda spread out around it, and overlooks the city of Pest across the river. The Royal Palace was on the Var, and most of the old city of Buda and its modern suburbs were residential areas, running up the flanks of the great wooded hills which here mark the west bank of the river. On the east bank stood the Houses of Parliament, somewhat similar in location and conception to those in London, although unique in style, and behind spread the city of Pest, on a great flat area signaling the start of the Great Hungarian Plain. In Pest was concentrated most of the city's business life, theaters, and, after the war, the Government.

My flat, on the northern edge of the Var, looked up the river, to the far mountains of Slovakia, and east onto the Houses of Parliament.[1] It also commanded a view of the single Danube bridge available to automobile traffic when I first arrived, as well as of one of the only two approaches up the Var itself. Nearby were the crenelated battlements and the winding terraces of the Coronation Church. The streets of the Var were obstacle courses of rubble piles, built up from the ruins of palaces and houses behind. To enter my own miraculously intact two rooms, it was necessary to traverse three tunnels dug through rubble, a series of confusing passageways, and then a small staircase leading only to my apartment. All of this added up to an area favorable to clandestine meetings, and reduced to a minimum the danger that one could be followed without it being known, for which I was later to be grateful.

In gradual stages my predecessor handed over to me the network which was already operating. It consisted at that time of eight persons.

"Leo" was a member of a noble family who had had an outstanding record in the Resistance. He had successfully avoided arrest by the Germans during the occupation, and following the liberation had entered into political life. He was a Smallholder Member of Parliament, and in numerous articles which he wrote for various papers he established himself as one of the younger spokesmen of a liberal group within the party who stood for various needed reforms, but who also sought to avoid Hungary's disappearance into the Soviet orbit. He provided steady and valuable information on the intrigues within the Smallholders Party itself and on the real policies of various party leaders as they reacted to the various Communist encroachments on the party's dominant position.

"Eugene" was likewise of a noble family, but without personal political ambitions. A man of conservative views and of eminently decent instincts, he had become mixed up during the war in a series of anti-German actions, including the saving of Jews, the operations of the Polish Underground through Hungary, and the abortive effort to surrender to the Western Allies in Italy. He had been arrested and deported to the Mauthausen concentration camp, which he managed to survive only through the intercession with the Germans of certain very highly placed neutrals. He had long represented a number of foreign firms, including American, in Hungary, and had resumed these connections after the war. He was able to provide valuable information due to his Resistance connections, with many of whom he did not share domestic political views but with whom he had shared the experience of a concentration camp, and he was also in a position to furnish useful information on developments in the business world.

"Paul" was a very high member of the Government, a Smallholder. A lawyer by profession, he also had an excellent wartime record of resistance. Besides his inside information on the high councils of the Hungarian Government, he also provided a transcript of all Cabinet meetings. (Since this was a coalition Government, and a growingly uneasy coalition, Cabinet meetings were inclined to be either a kind of formal battleground or a place for the final enactment of compromises already agreed upon outside in more informal, acrimonious interparty meetings. Even so, this material was obviously of very high value.)

"Simon" was a brilliant young economist. A non-party man, he was employed in the National Bank. As a Jew he had been lucky to escape with his life during the German occupation, and he was also vigorously anti-Communist. A gentle, scholarly man, he provided reams of detailed data on the Soviet plunder of the entire Hungarian economy, and valuable analyses of the means by which the Communists were gradually bringing the nation's financial institutions under their control.

"Jane" was a cousin of "Simon" and a close friend of "Paul." Although she worked in a Government housing office, she was herself a scholar. Her connections were due to her personal friendships in intellectual circles and not to her work. She functioned as a cut-out to both Simon and Paul, whom I rarely saw, which arrangement was facilitated by the fact that she lived not far from me. (Her role of cut-out was dictated by prudence concerning Simon and Paul, of course, and not by any need to protect identities.) It was also her function to provide likely recruits for the network.

"George" was a career Hungarian diplomat. While he had successfully undergone the "denazification" procedures for Government officials and employees, his position in the Foreign Office was not a senior one. Nevertheless, he retained the confidence and friendship of many of the higher career diplomatic officials and was thus initially able to provide useful information about Hungarian foreign relations, including notably those with the Soviet Legation in Budapest, and advance information on the planned assignments of Hungarian diplomats abroad. As time went on, however, he found himself more and more cut off from information, and eventually himself took a minor assignment abroad, from which he went into exile.

"Henry" was another aristocrat, a man of ebullient nature and many accomplishments. He had been a leading member of the Hungarian Upper House and active in Hungarian society, and his information, while never dramatic, reflected a wide range of interests and sources. In addition, he had had a bizarre experience at the end of the war. In hiding from the Germans, he had emerged when the Russians arrived, only to be arrested immediately by them and put in a Soviet concentration camp near the Austrian border, which was maintained by the Russians for Hungarians against whom they had no charges, but whose leadership potential was such that it was desired to keep them out of circulation until the postwar political structure had taken on the desired form. He was there for many months, and then, on his release, was required to walk the streets of Budapest, followed at a distance by Soviet agents, greeting anyone he knew and thus in effect providing the Russians with a quick file on all his numerous friends and acquaintances in all walks of Hungarian life. It was our hope that the

Russians might at some point try to use him again in more serious work, which would, of course, have provided us with a line into Soviet operations. In this we were disappointed—but Henry, understandably, was not.

"Louis" was a distinguished scholar. Although his field of study enabled him to provide useful works which bore to some extent on the general Hungarian economic situation, it was in fact neither that nor his status as an aristocrat which were of primary interest. Louis was the scion of a family which had for centuries occupied a decisive position in Hungarian history, and because of the role his family had played as recently as the past thirty years he was a figure of great prestige in the nation. He had been instrumental in bringing about the surrender to the Russians, and had himself played a part in the formation of the Provisional Government. He was not old enough to be an "elder statesman," but his prestige, his somewhat aloof, nonpartisan attitude, and his unquestioned patriotism put him in an analogous position. Furthermore, the Russians were not only cognizant of his prestige, but were also appreciative of his part in the surrender. They accordingly deferred to him to a certain degree—at least for a while—and even held what might be considered for the Russians as confidential conversations with him occasionally. These were clearly of interest.

Of these eight persons, none knew of my connection to a specific intelligence organization. However, Eugene, Paul, Simon, Jane, and Louis knew that they were connected through me to "American intelligence" in general. Leo, George, and Henry, although they must certainly have surmised the facts, were willing to look at the situation simply as being in touch with "the Americans." Of the eight, only Jane knew the identity of any other agent, and she knew, of course, in her role as cut-out, of only Simon and Paul. This arrangement meant that I had to hold most of the meetings with agents myself; this added risk was offset, however, by the greater security of confining knowledge of agents' identities to an absolute minimum—worthwhile in a city rife with personal intrigues and political gossip.

Not one of these agents received any kind of salary, and only Jane had need for expense money. I occasionally did personal favors for some—my predecessor was able to save a valuable library for Louis, and I would transmit gifts between some of the agents and their friends in the West, as my cover enabled me to do without risk—but these favors were never asked or performed as a form of compensation. Jane and Simon both had personal ties in America which gave them particular reason to assist the United States; the rest acted purely as Hungarian patriots in the framework of what each had personally concluded would best help to avoid the catastrophe of Soviet domination, if at all possible. In brief, political support was the motive of all of the agents in the network.

This network had certain obvious limitations—which was no reflection whatsoever on my predecessor, who had organized the group in a very limited time with what was readily available. It was outstandingly useful with respect to the Cabinet, the majority Smallholders Party, and Soviet seizures of property. It was satisfactory with respect to the Foreign Office, the economy in general, and informed opinion among center and conservative leaders. It had potentialities with respect to some Soviet activities, but not enough. On the debit side it was much too heavily weighted in favor of the former, ruling upper class. It was either weak or nonexistent so far as very important areas of Hungarian life were concerned: the other political parties, especially the Communists; organized labor; the Communist-controlled Interior Ministry, and in particular the Political Police, destined to become the organ of Communist terror; the military; and the Roman Catholic Church. (There is a sizable Protestant minority in Hungary, and a tragically reduced but still important Jewish population; but the Roman Church was of capital importance. Rome had granted Hungary the title of Apostolic Kingdom and its senior Catholic Bishop, the Archbishop of Esztergom, who in 1946 was already Cardinal Mindszenty, was also by law the Prince Primate, the country's chief personage after the Head of State. The Church's importance had in fact been recognized by the Allied Control Commission in its grant in 1945 of authority for the formation of a Catholic political party.) These limitations meant not only that the range of the network's intelligence was too narrow, but also that the intelligence was susceptible to a too uniform slant.

Notwithstanding the limitations of this network in terms of specific targets—and of partisan prejudice—the problem in Budapest was never, during this period, a lack of information. On the contrary, by the simple process of allowing others to do the talking, one lived in a veritable deluge of rumors. The daily crop of these rumors invariably contained some interesting kernels of truth, and the winnowing of the wheat from the chaff was a full-time process, involving innumerable conversations, checking, confirming, far into the night—a process made somewhat easier by the nocturnal habits of politicians in general, and Russians and Hungarians in particular. In addition, there was always the stray nugget of information that one stumbled upon by accident. (Later, toward the end of 1947, I found myself having a coffee one day with an American Government architect who was in town to discuss technical details with Hungarian architects about certain buildings purchased by the American Government. An excellent and thoroughly apolitical technician, he was discussing with me his impression of Hungarian baroque architecture. Offhandedly I remarked that the Government seemed to have plentiful resources for the atrocious Stalin Monument, but was averse to restoring the Royal Palace, even as a museum. "Oh, no," he said. "They're going to restore it. In fact, soon. The architect I saw in the Government Building Office today showed me the plans." I perked up and asked what it was going to be. "It's to be the headquarters of the Danube Federation," he answered. "Tito has already given the plans his approval." This chance remark led eventually, in conjunction with other items from elsewhere in the Balkans, to advance information on the Tito-Cominform dispute, which featured as one of its early phases an argument between Tito and George Dimitrov of Bulgaria, supported by Stalin, over whether a Danubian Federation should be based on the four states of Yugoslavia, Bulgaria, Hungary, and Rumania or—as Tito obviously desired—it should be composed of nine states: Hungary, Rumania, Bulgaria, and the six member states of the Yugoslav Federation.) Nevertheless, one could not rely on the stray nugget or on a spate of rumors. What was needed was reliable, steady information, keyed to all of the vital centers of power where the Hungarian fate was being worked out. To expand the network thus became one of my principal tasks.

During the autumn of 1946 I moved slowly, becoming thoroughly familiar with the city and the surrounding countryside, establishing contacts with foreign and Hungarian newspapermen, diplomats, politicians, always aiming, without notable success, at the targets I had set for penetration. My headquarters continued to be satisfied with the flow of intelligence and counseled caution in my efforts to expand the network.

But events were moving rapidly. In the city one could sense the steady pressure of the Communists, supported by their Russian backers. In October the peace treaty negotiations in Paris began. (These negotiations, in which the United States was obliged to assume a role, not entirely successful, of protecting Hungary from the maximum demands of its Czechoslovak, Rumanian, and Yugoslav neighbors, all egged on and supported by the Soviets, had at least one light moment. It seems the Hungarian Delegation, led by the Prime Minister, were holding highly secret discussions one evening in their hotel, when the door giving onto the balcony of the room they were using opened softly, and a strange man entered. Without a word he crossed the room and opened the door leading to the hallway. As the Hungarians sat thunderstruck, wondering what nationality of agent this eavesdropper was, the man paused in the doorway before disappearing. "Excuse me, gentlemen," he said, "but Monsieur returned unexpectedly.")

Meanwhile, in Budapest, there were enough light moments, but they were set to a counterpoint of people who simply disappeared one day or night, arrested by the Russians or the Hungarian Political Police, never to reappear; of trigger-happy and acquisitive Red Army patrols at night—shooting incidents between Russian and the few American soldiers in Budapest were not uncommon; of growing unease among even the smallest property owners; and of a general realization that the Soviet objective was to install the Hungarian Communists in full power. In September the Political Police were changed from being simply a branch of the National Police, which was directed by General Balassa, a Socialist, to an autonomous agency called the AVO—the Hungarian initials for State Security Agency—the head of which, Gabor Peter, reported directly to the Communist Minister of the Interior, Laszlo Rajk. The realization spread that a race was on: if the Communists could be prevented from seizing power in the period before the Peace Treaty took effect, that is, during the time when they would still have maximum support from the Red Army, then Hungary might be saved. This meant, for all practical purposes, that the coming year of 1947 would be decisive.

In these days I made the acquaintance of "Guy," the holder of an important post in the National—not Political—Police. As all responsible official positions required membership in one of the coalition political parties, Guy, on being offered his post in the Police as a reward for his Resistance record, had joined the Peasant Party. A city man, a prewar owner of houses and real estate in Budapest, his status as a "peasant," even a purely political one, was a perfect example of the fortuitous meeting of a wholly artificial system and an utterly cynical man. I liked Guy for his wit and intelligence, and he seemed to me at first glance to offer some professional interest. However, his work was exclusively preoccupied with criminal matters, and he spoke very little of it. By listening I gathered that he had spent much time in England, and I also noted that he seemed somehow apart from the people making up the circles in which he moved socially—circles which seemed more the natural result of the associations of his extraordinarily beautiful, aristocratic mistress than of his own. I realized eventually, however, that Guy was trying harder to learn what he could from and about me than I was about or from him. It did not seem plausible to me that he was a Communist agent; what struck me as more likely was a pressing need for money, to gain which I had the impression he was not likely to be too scrupulous. Despite my enjoyment of Guy's company, caution seemed indicated; it did not appear at all likely that this man would eventually be my most valuable agent in Hungary.

At this same time, I was still hoping for some more productive link to the Russians themselves. On my arrival, the Russians had indicated that a Colonel Tyushin was the appropriate officer for me to see if I had business to transact. Apart from an initial courtesy call shortly after my arrival I had barely seen Tyushin, who certainly seemed to have no business to transact with me. On our rare encounters, however, he was exceedingly affable; a stocky, barrel-chested man, he had an ease of manner and equanimity with foreigners unusual for a Russian official, suggesting either that he held high authority or had been much abroad. Whether the former was true or not was inascertainable, although he was popularly rumored really to be a Lieutenant-General in the N.K.V.D.—the equivalent, for sheer power in Stalin's and Beria's Russia, of a Field Marshal in anybody's army. As for his travels, he had been, he said, on numerous "trade missions" all over the world. It was Tyushin himself who suggested I see more of him.

In the late autumn of 1946, the Hungarian Government resurrected the annual Tokay Wine Festival, and at the invitation of the Prime Minister, practically everyone, Hungarian or foreign, with even the remotest connection to the Government, journeyed to the village of Tokay for a day of wine-tasting, sight-seeing, and speeches, to be followed by an official dinner at the college in the nearby town of Sarospatak. Tokay itself is an extraordinary sight: a lone, conical mountain, in shape something like a very large, man-made pile of dirt, rises from the plain. At its foot is the village of

Tokay; on its slopes is grown all of this magnificent wine, a little sweet for my taste, but so long famous in Eastern Europe that for centuries no King of neighboring Poland could be crowned without three bottles of Tokay at the ceremony.

Inside the mountain are long tunnels and caves where the wine is aged and stored. This year, however, they were empty. With Russians about, the villagers would describe how the Germans had looted the caves; when the Russians strolled on, the villagers would curse and say that the German looting was nothing compared to the thoroughgoing Russian job which followed it. There was, of course, the current harvest. This had not yet matured to wine, but was in the stage which the Hungarians call "must" (pronounced "moosht"), when the taste is somewhat sour, but an expert—and any villager—can already tell the quality of the vintage. ("Put this on your 'must' list," wrote one American on a postcard to a friend who had for years irritated him with cards from faraway places.) Once drunk, it continues to ferment, now more rapidly, in the stomach, and then packs a neat wallop—as a highly confused assemblage for the dinner at Sarospatak testified. It was in this melee that Tyushin sought me out to say that I should call him when we returned to Budapest; he would like to talk with me.

My headquarters viewed this invitation as a logical outcome of my cover arrangements and instructed me to pursue it. As it happened, the "must" at Tokay had so inspired one American Army officer that he had lost his way en route to Sarospatak. In this northeastern part of Hungary, as a result of the war and the generosity of the Benes Government in giving up the entire easternmost province of Czechoslovakia to the Soviet Union, the Soviet border was now across the Carpathian Mountains and onto the edge of the Hungarian Plain. The American officer was last seen heading in that direction. Accordingly, I persuaded the Military Mission not to take the matter up officially, and I went to see Tyushin. He deplored the officer's carelessness and regaled me with long stories of the ferocity and what he characterized as the bureaucratic stupidity of the Soviet border guards. Five days later, however, the officer reappeared in Budapest, no worse off for a week in a Soviet jail. This was an auspicious start.

I next saw Tyushin at a large American reception for the Hungarian Prime Minister. Any social function in Budapest, no matter how labeled, which started after 6 o'clock in the evening went on until the last guest had departed, which was invariably some time well after midnight. In the far reaches of this particular evening, when the guests had dwindled to perhaps a dozen, I saw a remarkable tableau. In one corner of a large room Tyushin was reclining on the floor, his head in the lap of an American girl, remarking to no one in particular on how excellent a solution this was to international problems, while in the opposite corner an American colonel, shortly to become a general, was being restrained by several others as he shouted, "Let me at him! We'll atom-bomb the bastards off the face of the earth!" I interposed myself between Tyushin and his view of the American colonel—Tyushin only looked bemused and asked, "What is he shouting about?"—and suggested we leave together. He accepted the suggestion, but, as we were about to get into my car, his driver came over and in effect ordered Tyushin into his own car. Tyushin reluctantly went with him, but turned as he got into his car and, pointing to his driver, said in heavily accented English, but with the lordly manner of an ancient boyar, "I shall have him horsewhipped." Not a very auspicious second round.

The third round was totally unproductive and went to Tyushin, as these things will. I encountered him at the November 7 Soviet celebration of the twenty-ninth anniversary of the Bolshevik Revolution. The Russian generals in their rich green tunics, gold belts, gold epaulets, barrel chests covered with medals, and scarlet-striped trousers were a reminder, if none other was needed, that those who ruled in Russia were determined to profit to the maximum from their victory in war. Tyushin, surrounded by his colleagues, was still affable but more formal, and in effect I found myself in a drinking bout with a coterie of Russian officers whose intent was unmistakable. I regret to say that I went down in just under an hour; I was then escorted, almost tenderly, to a waiting Red Army staff car outside, and the driver ordered to take me home.

At the foot of the steep, narrow road up to the Var, we were stopped by a Soviet patrol. They had been celebrating too and demanded that the driver surrender the car to them. He refused, saying he had an American general with him. I accepted my promotion without protest. The patrol insisted, and suddenly my driver cursed, slammed the car into gear, and we shot up the hill. He wasn't even in second gear before the patrol opened fire, the submachine gun among them sounding as though I were standing right next to the muzzle. The car was struck a number of times, but miraculously we reached the top of the hill and I was deposited at my door, intact and stone-cold sober.

I returned to the fray by calling Tyushin in a few days and accusing him of plotting my murder. He thought it a great joke. We agreed to lunch several days later—at the Russian hour of 5 o'clock. To my surprise, Tyushin suggested a popular, crowded political café right in the center of town. When we met, he started things off right away by ordering a bottle of cognac. I had learned long before, notwithstanding my lamentable November 7 performance, that a strong determination not to succumb plays a large role in this matter of liquor in such encounters; and I was fully determined on this occasion.

We talked for almost seven hours. My recollection is that we went through three full bottles of cognac in this time, and that we at some point lunched. But it was the talk which dominated. It was all political, and it ranged over the entire spectrum of the Soviet occupation of Hungary and the personalities, Russian, Hungarian, and Western, who were involved. Tyushin did not speak by any means as a disaffected Soviet citizen. When, for example, I raised the question of the Soviet plunder of Hungarian industry, he forthrightly proclaimed their right to restore Soviet industry and territory, utterly devastated when occupied by the Germans and their then Hungarian allies. When I observed that this surely did not include stripping the peasants' homes of furniture right down to mattresses and pillows, he said quite simply, "If the Russian peasant had only half of what the Hungarian peasant has I would be satisfied."

From the range and forcefulness of Tyushin's remarks it became clear to me that he played a much more important role than was indicated by his ostensible rank of Red Army colonel. Remembering the rumors which placed him as a high N.K.V.D. officer, I probed this by steering the subject around to arrests, concentration camps, and forced labor. He inquired as to my estimate of how many Soviet citizens were in concentration or forced labor camps. When I answered ten million, he smiled, paused for a moment, and then said, "Look, I know something about this subject. I have seen most of the camps. I can assure you, their population is not more than a million. One half of one per cent of our total population." While I had the impression that he wished this were so, more than he really believed it to be so, the important point was that he freely admitted special knowledge of the subject. Even more importantly, however, he admitted knowledge on a more immediately Hungarian aspect of the subject. It was common knowledge that, quite apart from the depredations of the Hungarian AVO, the Russians themselves were still occasionally arresting Hungarians. They repeatedly denied this and declared themselves innocent of all interference in Hungarian domestic affairs.

Only a few months before this, a notable case had occurred in which Count Geza Palffy, a very well-known Hungarian aristocrat, himself not active in politics, had been abducted by Soviet officers before numerous witnesses in broad daylight, on a crowded city street. I mentioned to Tyushin what was—in those pre-Khrushchev days—the unofficial loyal Communist explanation of the excesses of the Soviet purges of the late Thirties, namely, that Yagoda and Yezhov, Beria's predecessors as head of the N.K.V.D., had misled and betrayed Stalin, and suggested that perhaps the disappearance of Count Palffy was an indication that Yagoda and Yezhov's methods were being exported to Hungary. Tyushin did not deny Soviet involvement in the affair; instead, he reflected quite long and seriously, and then said, "That is a very serious case." I had the impression here of a distinct ambiguity in his answer; that is, that the seriousness of the case might be due to factors other than some act of Palffy's. Tyushin's manner and phraseology seemed to suggest that Palffy was not himself guilty of anything in particular, but that this was not the point or significance of the case.

Most importantly, the sense of Tyushin's comments and observations over several hours began to add up to a strong inference of disagreement among the Soviets themselves as to how to proceed in Hungary. Of all the personalities discussed in that long conversation the names of Georgi Pushkin—then Soviet Minister to Hungary, later Ambassador to East Germany, then Deputy Foreign Minister, and most recently Soviet co-Chairman of the Geneva Conference on Laos—and of General Sviridov—then Soviet Chairman of the Allied Control Commission in succession to Marshal Voroshilov, later Soviet Representative on the Allied Control Commission for Austria—were never mentioned by Tyushin. He was courteous and complimentary in his remarks about the American personalities in Hungary. He spoke very highly of the Yugoslavs, he having arrived in Hungary with the armies which came from the south. He exhibited marked impatience with Matyas Rakosi, the Hungarian Communist leader: "If you think he's one hundred per cent our man, you're mistaken," he said. (History proved him Stalin's man; the question was who was meant by Tyushin's "our.") Instead, he spoke more warmly of Rajk, Kadar, and Losonczy—Hungarian Communists who each had his own following in the Party, but whose common characteristic was that none of them was a "Muscovite," that is, a Moscow-trained Communist who returned to Hungary with the Red Army, as did Rakosi, Gero, Revai, Imre Nagy, and most of the Party leadership. Ten years is a long time in a man's life: in 1956 it would be Imre Nagy, the loyal "Muscovite," who would lead the revolt against Moscow, and Kadar, the "Titoist," who, having suffered imprisonment and torture, would betray that revolt back into the hands of Moscow.)

I left Tyushin that night aware not from any single remark, but from the total impression of hours of talk that there was disagreement among the Soviets. I did not think then, nor do I now, that this disagreement was over objectives. I believed then, and do now, that it was over tactics and methods: how far to go and how fast, it being recognized that the tactics of maximum speed would be bound to provoke opposition from the West. It was also clear to me that Tyushin, whatever his importance, was not a decisive element in resolving this dispute. But there were bound to be those behind him, in more decisive positions, whose views he shared or reflected. The difficulty was that I had no way of knowing, even with the frankness of much of Tyushin's talk, and even by the most correct deductions from his comments, what exactly were the alternative courses being weighed by the Soviets. Tyushin had given me some vague ideas of who the clashing personalities might be, but this, in the dark labyrinth of Kremlin politics, was far from enough to deduce the issues. In short, I felt I had recognized the hidden dissent, but I was at a loss how to exploit it.

The following day—fortified with aspirin—I dispatched a long report to my headquarters, recounting the conversation in factual detail. I added my personal impressions—labeled as such—and then decided to check with Louis. Without giving him the entire substance of my conversation with Tyushin, I explored with him the possibilities of strong policy divergencies among the Soviets about the Hungarian situation. My impressions turned out to be similar to his. For one thing, he recounted his experiences with the Soviets in the matter of the Armistice, when he said it was apparent to him that every Red Army Commander had a patron in the

Politburo, that every political commissar at army or corps level also had a patron in the Politburo—usually a different one from the Army Commander—that the same was certainly true of the diplomatic representatives, and that all this rivalry and dissension was deliberately encouraged by Stalin, who thus played all his subordinates and any possible rivals off against each other. For another, he had had similar indications in a series of conversations with various Soviet officials prior to the Paris Peace Conference, when it was his impression that they were undecided how far to go in supporting neighboring states' claims against Hungary. Louis took the Soviet stalling on an Austrian Treaty as a very serious sign, possibly negating any benefits from the Hungarian Peace Treaty, and pointed out that the strategic advantages to the Soviets of their continued occupation of Austria gave them time to resolve any differences over how to handle the Hungarian situation. He had no more concrete ideas than I had of exactly what alternative courses the Soviets might be weighing, or of the personal roles being played. "Anyway," he commented dourly, "by the time you figure all that out, and before you can exploit your information, they will have resolved their differences, most probably by force, and will run over us all with a steamroller."

Within three weeks Louis was proved right in this prediction. The first thing that happened was that Tyushin disappeared. On calling his office I was repeatedly told that he was out; the last time I called a brusque voice said that he had returned suddenly to Moscow. At a reception some days later I was standing with General Sviridov, Pushkin, the Soviet Minister, and others, when someone in the circle mentioned that he had not seen Tyushin for some time. Pushkin said quickly, "He returned suddenly to Moscow," and then added, with what I thought was singular casualness, "A death in the family, I think." As Tyushin has never since shown up on the international scene, so far as I know, one can only assume whose death it was. (The then Prime Minister, Ferenc Nagy, has remarked in his memoirs that he noted a distinct shift in the relative importance of the principal Soviet officials in Hungary at just this time.)

The second thing was that during December rumors began to spread around Budapest of important arrests made by the Hungarian Military Political Section—a Communist-controlled unit within the Army established at the same time as the civilian Political Police, and still theoretically separate from the AVO. Between

Christmas and New Year's, Leo gave me a partial list of those arrested, and next day Jane brought from Paul a complete list, which included the name of a Hungarian correspondent for a Western newspaper who had attempted to file the story. According to both Leo and Paul, those arrested were being subjected to torture, and the charges were of a "conspiracy" to restore the Horthy Government—about as harebrained a thought as could be mustered in Hungary at the time. Henry, who knew a number of those arrested, said the charges were pure fabrications.

The press, including the Communists, was still silent on the matter, and I thus at first took the "conspiracy" as just more terrorism by the Communist police. I was wrong. The Soviets had indeed reached a decision—with Tyushin most probably on the losing side —and the steamroller was getting under way.

1. Southern side of the Var. Quite different view than described—but pleasant. My occupation of this flat, which was actually my fourth and last residence in Budapest, coincided with the last and most active phase of my mission there.

CHAPTER III

Conspiracy

In early January Eugene reported a singular incident. In the early evening, in a crowded section of the city, there had been some shots fired in a nearby darkened street, and shortly afterward a Hungarian officer, wounded and bleeding, stumbled out onto the main avenue and managed to board a streetcar. Some fellow passengers helped him off, called an ambulance, and then stood about to protect him until it arrived. When it did, he was, at his own insistence, taken to the British Military Mission.

A casual comment to the man I had every reason to believe was my British opposite number produced only a very stiff upper lip. It took some time to find the answer to this mystery, but when uncovered it provided one key to the problem of the "conspiracy."

The Government was also, quite naturally, apprised of the arrests, and, after due consultation, the Defense Minister summoned General Palfi-Oesterreicher, Communist head of the Military Political Section, for an explanation. (The Defense Minister was a highly respected General, Albert Bartha, who had been recalled from retirement to reorganize the Army. Bartha had been with Kitchener at Khartoum, and still held, as he once told me with obvious pleasure, the rank of Lieutenant in the British Army.) Palfi-Oesterreicher at first refused any information, and then made allegations about a "conspiracy" against the "democratic regime." This being a political question, the matter was taken up with the Prime Minister, who ordered Palfi-Oesterreicher to make the prisoners available to General Bartha for questioning. At first Palfi-Oesterreicher agreed, but when Bartha showed up at the prison he was refused access to the prisoners on the grounds that the Soviets had forbidden it. The Prime Minister approached General Sviridov, who denied any such order. Accordingly, disciplinary action was instituted against Palfi-Oesterreicher. But the very same day this step was taken, General Kondratov, head of the Military Section of the Allied Control Commission, called on the Prime Minister and told him in no uncertain terms that if the proceedings against Palfi-Oesterreicher were not dropped immediately, the Soviet High Command would take the matter of the "conspiracy" into their own hands.

The proceedings were quashed, but in the meantime, in his rage at Palfi-Oesterreicher's insubordination, General Bartha had let drop the fact that his source of information about the arrests was the Socialist deputy head of the Military Political Section, a Colonel Viktor Kruchina. Some days after Kondratov's ultimatum, Kruchina was invited to tea by the Smallholder deputy head of the AVO, one Janos Gyurics. On emerging from Gyurics's apartment Kruchina was attacked by an AVO squad. Kruchina had been active in the Resistance against the Germans and the Hungarian Nazis, and had been in contact with the British during the war. He was thus experienced in these matters, and had gone to tea armed with two pistols—in some circles a more vital question than how many lumps of sugar. He fought his way out of the trap, was wounded, but escaped.

It was thus, by working through from an isolated if dramatic street incident, that we became aware of the extent of Soviet backing of the Communists' "conspiracy" maneuver. (The answer as to why the Government didn't tell us officially is simple: the Soviet Chairman of the Allied Control Commission had at the outset forbidden the Hungarian Government to communicate with the American and British Representatives on the Commission, and vice versa, except through the Chairman. To have told us unofficially would not have provided a basis for any American or British action—of the possibilities for which, in any event, the Government was, correctly, doubtful.)

Shortly thereafter, Rajk, the Communist Minister of the Interior, announced the "conspiracy" to the press. The Communist papers took up the cry. They thundered against "the fascists still in our midst." The Communist Party, in its press, in Parliament, in public speeches, had for some time been pursuing the line that the Smallholder majority in the 1945 elections was simply due to the fact that former Nazis had taken refuge in the party, and they had steadily been pressing for the expulsion of various Smallholder deputies from the Parliament and of certain Smallholder officials from the Government. They now shouted that the "conspiracy" at last uncovered was proof of what they had been saying for months.

All through the first weeks of 1947 the Communist press and speakers kept up a steady campaign against the Smallholders Party on the basis of the alleged "conspiracy." There was in fact no "conspiracy." There were discussions among everyone—including the Communists themselves, quite naturally—as to the situation which might exist in Hungary when the Peace Treaty went into effect. Such discussions among non-Communists—the great majority of the population, the Parliament, and the Government—were simply a meeting of the minds to the effect that the Communists should not succeed in gaining absolute power by the time the Occupation was legally terminated. (The opposite conclusion, basic to Communist discussions of the situation among themselves, was naturally not characterized as "conspiracy.") The question was how to avoid a Communist take-over, but no responsible Hungarian politician was under any illusions that the Western Powers would ever intervene by force to block such a seizure. They were, moreover, under no illusions about the neighboring and immediate power of the Soviet Union and the necessity to accommodate their foreign relations to the Soviet demands for security on their western borders; indeed, one of those initially arrested in the "conspiracy" was one of the three original signers of the Armistice with the Soviets. The outstanding fact, and the one which was ineradicably graven in my mind, was that among those arrested, and later among the hundreds accused, were almost all those who had distinguished themselves by active resistance to the Germans and to the Hungarian Nazis.

Nevertheless, the Communists, supplied by their police cohorts, continued to announce "confessions." These "confessions" were regularly alleged to have implicated more and more persons; these were in turn arrested, and then alleged to have themselves "confessed" and implicated still further persons. And so the pool widened, the rising waters claiming more and more victims; with each new victim, the hopes and future of those still on shore were also drowned.

The "confessions" were the result of interrogation methods which have since become well known. Notwithstanding the strict security surrounding the arrested, word began to come out of the prisons of these methods. Paul obtained a smuggled letter, signed by one of the accused, which warned that the "confessions" were false but were unavoidable in the face of the methods being used, and that the questioning was seeking to implicate the entire leadership of the majority party. (It was at this time that rumors first began to circulate of the use of drugs in interrogation. As I later learned, a Red Army medical major named Istvan Balint had come to the AVO at the end of 1946; he began using actedron, pentothal, scopalomine, and morphine on the political prisoners.) I informed Mark of these developments, about which I had a growing feeling of urgency and alarm. He shared these feelings, and shortly took the opportunity, while seeing the Prime Minister on other business, to express concern over the potential danger to the Government. Nagy answered that he and his colleagues were aware of the danger, but retained the hope that they could manage to keep the matter under control. What this diplomatic exchange really conveyed was the Prime Minister's knowledge of the Soviet willingness to support the Communists actively in the "conspiracy" affair, and his conclusion that, unless the Western Powers indicated that they would, and could, intervene effectively to offset Soviet pressure, he had no choice except to try by his own resources to minimize the damage.

In late January the Communist charges, which had already engulfed one Smallholder Minister and six of the most capable members of Parliament, spread out to include Bela Kovacs, the Secretary-General of the Smallholders Party. Kovacs, a peasant, a longtime associate of the Prime Minister, and a gifted organizer of enormous popularity, was the crucial support upon which the whole majority edifice rested. The charges against him were tantamount to accusing him of conspiring against himself. Nevertheless, they were pressed with all the vigor the Communists could muster —and with behind-the-scenes pressure from the Soviets.

This was the critical moment for postwar Hungary. The Parliamentary majority sensed this. Leo took the lead with several of his Smallholder colleagues in declaring that the affair had gone far enough. Independent of the leadership they introduced a motion for the creation of a Parliamentary committee to investigate the "conspiracy." The Communists raged and threatened to withdraw from the coalition if the measure passed the Parliament—a serious menace in view of Soviet insistence on their presence in the Government. The non-Communist Government leaders, who were aware, as the rank and file were not, of the Soviet presence behind the Communist pressure, sought to find a compromise which would save Kovacs—and with him Hungarian independence—and at the same time provide an effective sop to the Soviets.

On February 10 the Peace Treaty was signed—to come into effect ninety days after ratification. The hopes this aroused were used by the Smallholder leaders to calm the deputies. At the insistence of President Tildy, the Parliamentary investigating commission motion was withheld from debate and efforts were continued to negotiate with the Communists. These efforts were doomed to failure: the essence of the Hungarian position was lack of power; without it the concept of compromise is unknown to the Soviet vocabulary. Apparently the efforts dragged on too long.

On the night of February 25, 1947, Jane telephoned for an urgent meeting. We met—as prearranged for such emergencies—by the Coronation Church, from where I could see if she was being followed. She was not, but she was accompanied by Paul—agitated as I had never seen him. Earlier in the evening he had been on his way to see Bela Kovacs. Arriving at the block in Pest where Kovacs lived, he found the area sealed off by several companies of

Soviet troops. As he waited, he saw some Soviet officers emerge from Kovacs's apartment house. Kovacs was between them. He was shoved into a Soviet staff car and taken away. It was as simple as that—with the added benefit for the Soviets of a show of force to intimidate the Government majority.

I enciphered a message to headquarters, including my comments on the significance of the open Soviet intervention, and then telephoned Mark. We met in one of the city's livelier night clubs—it fitted well with the Communists' preconceptions of what Americans might be doing on a politically eventful night—and discussed the possibilities for the future. He knew as well as I that in one night all the implications and complications inherent in an intelligence network based on political motives had materialized. Political support as a motive naturally involves some reciprocity on the part of the nation benefiting from the intelligence. Whether Washington liked it or not, the Soviet challenge was political and strategic, and thus directly affected the intelligence potential of the network—as the questions of each member of the network in the next few days showed. What support will the United States give us to fight back now? To be able to assist the Hungarians effectively would require more than an attitude of disapproval by Washington toward the Soviet actions in Hungary. Similarly, expressions of sympathy to men whose lives or freedom were immediately endangered would be tantamount to refusal of assistance—with the consequent deterioration not only of an intelligence network, but also of American strategic and political interests in the area. For Leo and Paul, with the duties and possibilities of public office, these questions were urgent. But such questions can seldom be answered forthrightly in international politics.

In early March the American and British Governments sent notes to the Soviet Government protesting the Soviet unilateral interference in Hungarian affairs and the conduct of the Hungarian Communist Party. The notes called for a joint Soviet, American, British, and Hungarian investigation of the so-called "conspiracy" and of the role of Bela Kovacs. The anticipated Soviet rejection was followed by further American and British notes, without effect.

Prior to Kovacs's arrest, the United States had granted a $15,000,000 credit to Hungary for the purchase of surplus materials. On March 12, President Truman asked Congress for an appropriation of $400,000,000 for economic and military aid to Greece and Turkey. The accompanying statement, which proclaimed the United States' intention to aid peoples everywhere in resisting Communist aggression and was immediately labeled the Truman Doctrine, caused Americans in Budapest, increasingly somber these days, to walk in the streets with their heads held high.

These various moves were sufficient to restore some measure of courage among the Hungarians. Although Paul was more cautious, Leo felt that the American response now made it incumbent upon the Hungarians to move in their own defense. He felt that, at the minimum, they should make the position of the Hungarian majority clear, and that they should avoid any possible inference being drawn from their conduct that they had been supine before Communist and Soviet pressure and force. He resurrected, with the support of a numerous, rebellious faction among the Smallholder deputies, the proposal for a Parliamentary investigation of the "conspiracy." The leadership of the party was less sanguine about the possibilities for maneuver, and in mid-March the struggle came to a head. President Tildy summoned the dissidents to the Presidential Palace. There he cajoled, threatened, pleaded, blustered, and eventually succeeded in persuading the majority of the rebels to support the Government's policy. The motion for a Parliamentary investigation was abandoned. Leo was in tears as he told me of the session with Tildy and its outcome. It was indeed a turning point. When Seymour Freidin, then Eastern European correspondent of the New York *Herald Tribune* and an experienced observer of the westbound Soviet steamroller in Poland, Rumania, and Bulgaria, heard the news, he said, "That does it. At this rate I'll be filing my next dispatches from Hoboken—if I can make it to the ferry."

(In 1955 Bela Kovacs was released by the Soviets and returned to Hungary, his health broken. In the 1956 Revolution he reappeared as leader of the resurrected Smallholders Party in the coalition established by Imre Nagy. The contrast between the America of 1946 and of 1956 was most marked on the night of November 4, 1956. As the Red Army assaulted Budapest Kovacs appeared at the American Legation to ask asylum. On direct instructions from the State Department in Washington, which at the same time granted asylum to Cardinal Mindszenty, Kovacs was refused. There followed alternating periods of prison, hospital, house arrest, and limited detention, until his death in 1959.)

A lull now followed in Hungary. The Smallholders had been

forced to expel a number of their deputies and officials, and the party was demoralized. Most important, it was now clear that no one was immune from the "conspiracy" danger. Trials of a number of the accused were held, at which, as confession and self-denunciation poured forth from the defendants, the efficacy of the Communists' methods became apparent. (Retractions in open court—as occurred in the case of Balint Arany, a principal defendant—were followed by immediate adjournment of the case, to be resumed only when the defendant reappeared in court to retract his retraction.)

The trials, under the jurisdiction of the Justice Ministry, supplied a key to the critical question of why the other two non-Communist parties in the coalition collaborated with the Communist campaign of destruction of the majority party. Istvan Riesz, the Minister of Justice, was a Socialist—but this did nothing to protect the administration of justice from the Communist juggernaut. Furthermore, the Socialist Party, as well as the Peasant Party, throughout the whole course of the "conspiracy," had vigorously supported the Communist attacks. The answers to this suicidal policy were both overt and covert. The overt answer lay in a statement of Rajk, the Interior Minister: "Learn from Lenin," he said. "If you have five enemies, you should ally yourselves with them; arrange to incite four of them against the fifth, then three against the fourth, and so on, until you have only one enemy left in the alliance; you can then liquidate him yourself and kick him out of the alliance." But these tactics would not have worked alone; they were supplemented, as I was to learn in detail, by the covert answer: penetration, intimidation, and subversion on an enormous scale.

The Socialists, the second largest party in the coalition and with considerable strength in the trade-union movement, obviously could, if they so chose, act as an effective brake on the Communists. They were also in a position to know much about Communist plans and actions.

The deficiencies of my network which I had earlier remarked were by now becoming apparent. In the constant reshuffling of the Government Paul, himself long under attack by the Russians, had been removed from his post—although not from his seat in Parliament; Leo was becoming increasingly isolated after his defeat in the Parliamentary investigation question; Henry became less and less active as the danger increased; and George was now almost useless in a Foreign Office housekeeping assignment. Eugene was still active, but his sources were not in vital positions. Simon continued to provide valuable economic information, and Louis was still consulted by politicians of all parties, and by the Russians. Jane, of course, continued to operate effectively as a cut-out, but not as a source of important information. The situation was far from satisfactory and promised to deteriorate unless I could broaden the area of my work. However, the same events which had made my position more difficult had also gravely alarmed others; as I was looking for them, so they were looking for me.

In April a Hungarian newspaperman in whom I had full confidence, and who had been most helpful in arranging for me to meet persons in whom I was interested, came to me and said that certain important Socialists would like to talk secretly to an American. I arrived at the rendezvous given, which was simply a certain floor of an apartment house. There I was met by a young man who was intensely serious, but possessed of a sense of humor withal. He led me up one floor, around to the service staircase, into what I took to be an unused storage closet— "Sorry about the back entrance," he said—and there, hidden behind a curtain, was a door leading into the building next door, which fronted on another street. Unlocking the door, he explained that it had been cut between the buildings during the German occupation to assist the escape of Jews, including himself, and that now that the building was once again under surveillance it came in very handy. He led me into a comfortable apartment, where I found five other people. One of the group I recognized as Karoly Peyer, for many years leader of the Hungarian Social-Democratic Party, until his incarceration in Mauthausen by the Germans in 1944.

Peyer looked exactly as one would expect a Viennese tavernkeeper of the old Empire to look. Short, round, with shaved head, he sported magnificent handlebar mustaches, and his eyes frequently lit up with an irrepressible twinkle. He was shrewd, but there was no mistaking his ingrained decency. Peyer had been in the Socialist and trade-union movements ever since the beginning of the century. Under his leadership the party had managed to survive increasingly rightist regimes in Hungary, and for the average Hungarian worker the trade-union movement meant Peyer. On his imprisonment, one of his assistants, Arpad Szakasits, succeeded to the party leadership in his absence. By the time Peyer was liberated from Mauthausen by the American Army and had made his way back to Hungary, Szakasits had already entered into a close compact with the Communists. He relegated Peyer to a minor position in the party, which Peyer, for the sake of the party and notwithstanding his enormous popularity, accepted quietly. However, Szakasits's control was based on nothing less than bribery and corruption—a trip Szakasits himself had made to Western Europe at the end of 1945 in a private railroad car had been a scandal throughout the Continent—and Peyer, fighting all the way, had more and more come into active opposition while still within his party.

Peyer now saw the direction in which Socialist co-operation with the Communists was leading the country. His talk with me, although it took several hours, had basically but two questions: what is the attitude of the United States Government? And: what will the United States Government do in support of its attitude? Peyer was considering an attempt to reassert his leadership of the Socialist Party. His object was to deny Socialist support, automatically given by Szakasits, to the Communists, and thus block a Communist seizure of power before the effective date of the Peace Treaty; he was also anxious to save his party from the forced merger with the Communists which he foresaw in the Communist plan. But he was reluctant to expose his followers to Communist police reprisals and Soviet terrorism and abduction; against these only the West could provide a defense.

Now it was abundantly clear that the inexorable pressure of events, the effects of Soviet moves and the implications of American responses, were transforming my mission into a political operation. I had no aversion to such a development; on the contrary. I was personally enthusiastic, but I was nonetheless skeptical of what the United States was really prepared to do at this early juncture. Peyer had phrased his remarks with circumspection, but their burden was clear. I told him that the American attitude was summed up in the notes delivered to Moscow on the occasion of the Soviet arrest of Bela Kovacs, and I reminded him of the Truman Doctrine. For the rest, I said that I was not in a position to know what further steps the United States would now take in the case of Hungary, although I would see that his intentions and problems were made known in the proper quarters. I observed that questions such as his were not ordinarily susceptible to direct answers. To this he smiled and said, "Usually not soon enough."

On leaving, my guide— "Sam"—asked if I would mind coming

back in a few days: he and another young man— "Edmund"—who had been present but had remained silent most of the time, wished to talk to me about other problems. I returned on the agreed day, and what I heard was a considerable step toward answering my own problems. Sam and Edmund had both been active against the Germans and Hungarian Nazis: Sam had operated a clandestine radio station during the German Occupation; Edmund had been an Army officer and a member of the Hungarian Front, the clandestine organization of the Smallholders, Social-Democrats, and Communists, and had time and again risked his life saving Jews. Both had escaped imprisonment, Edmund on one occasion by shooting his way out of a police ambush. Sam was now an official in the Trade Union Council—a Communist-run organization used chiefly to dominate the individual unions and to organize "spontaneous demonstrations" for Communist political demands. Edmund, to my astonishment, revealed himself as an officer of the AVO—pointing out gravely that any carelessness on my part with this information would mean his instant death. He was one of the few Socialists permitted in the organization as a theoretical sop to "coalition."

Both were absolutely loyal to Peyer. However, as Sam pointed out, Peyer was working at the political level, in the situation as it was. He and Edmund, on the other hand, while they would work as hard as possible to help their party leadership, were convinced that the handwriting was on the wall. They believed it would not be too long before they would once again be forced underground by a totally Communist regime, and they wanted to prepare now for that eventuality. They emphasized that an underground network prepared now would have infinitely better chances of survival than one hastily assembled at the last moment. One purpose of such a network, as they conceived it, was to maintain contact with the West, and to this end Sam asked for the supply of radio sets. In the course of the afternoon they gave me vital details of the Communist and Soviet violence, blackmail, and intimidation behind the recent political developments, including the "conspiracy," and promised more.

I was curious as to why this approach had come to me. "Look," Edmund said, and mentioned the name of the newspaperman who had brought us together, "he vouched for you, as did several of the American correspondents he knows." I reflected that my hours spent with the journalistic fraternity had not been merely time pleasantly spent after all. "Furthermore," Edmund went on, "if you are not the man with whom we should speak of these matters, we can only trust you to put us in touch with the right man. It is in your interest as well." I did not acknowledge whether I was or was not the "right man."

I did ask a further question which puzzled me. "Why not the British?" I inquired. "Surely you have close fraternal ties with the Labour Government in England?" Sam laughed. "First of all, we don't trust the British because of their support for Tito," he answered. "Secondly, they seem to have no realistic conception of Soviet aims, and therefore they take Szakasits and his stooges as genuine Socialists, instead of the Communist tools they are. Thirdly, we suspect that the British, Socialist or not, don't really object to Soviet control over Eastern Europe—look at what they forced on Mikolajczyk and the Poles. Fourthly, America tried to help Hungary with the Peace Treaty; Britain couldn't have cared less." I remarked that I was glad the word had gotten around at least about American efforts. "Lastly," concluded Sam, "it is America that leads today." I thought it a quite complete answer. I looked at Edmund. "Quite a risk you're running." He shrugged.

I cabled my headquarters for a check on both Sam and Edmund. They had no information. Without telling her anything of my conversation, I asked Jane to make a few discreet inquiries. She came back with exactly the stories given me by Sam and Edmund of themselves, plus the fact that Paul had known Edmund in the wartime Hungarian Front and thought very highly of him.

At just this time, George decided to take advantage of the possibilities of a foreign diplomatic assignment. He went abroad, and in a few months resigned and stayed on in exile. But before leaving, he brought to me a woman whom I listed as "Sara." She had worked in the same administrative section with George, but was shortly due for transfer, because of a nominal Peasant Party membership, to the Political Section of the Foreign Office, where she was to have a position giving her access to all of that section's most confidential correspondence. Sara was forthright: she was convinced that the Communists would soon seize power; she was determined to do what she could to obstruct that, and when she could do no more, she planned to leave the country for a Western capital where her fiancé resided—a fact unknown to the Communists, she pointed out.

I now had three potential new agents, with easy access to highly valuable material, all of whom were motivated by political support. Furthermore, the initiative had come in all three cases—although less in the case of Sara—from the prospective agents themselves, which was not undesirable in my role, vis-à-vis them, of case officer. I began to feel somewhat encouraged as to my ability to ride through the changes which were bound to come in the succeeding months with a minimum of damage to the work and with some hopes for a future for the network.

While I was in this frame of mind, Guy came to see me one evening at my apartment. He did not seem personally concerned about the political situation, but told me, quite casually, that he had resigned from the Police. He made no comment about this, but proceeded to a proposition he wanted to put to me. It was astoundingly simple. If I would make available to him an American Army truck for two afternoons a week—a thing I had only to lift up the telephone to do—he would guarantee me $12,000 per month payable in any currency and in any bank anywhere in the world that I wished. I was stunned.

My first reaction was to throw him out of the house. I realized that this would accomplish nothing, however, so I asked him for further information. I could get nothing from him, except that the trucks would be used to cross into Slovakia, to the north, and his insistence that there was no danger. I finally gave up probing and told him simply that I was not in a position to help him. He seemed offended and deeply disappointed.

The next day I told Jane I wanted to see Simon. When we met, I told him of the offer I had received, but without saying who had made it. He laughed uproariously. Finally recovering himself, he said, "That would be the perfect deal. You working for the Communists. Take it. You'll be rich." Again he was overcome with laughter, but I finally got the explanation from him. The Communist Party had, the previous year, as one of the brainchildren of Zoltan Vas, the Communist economic wizard, formed something called the West Orient Corporation. It was, quite simply, an enormous and privileged black-market outfit. They stole cars in Austria and sold them in Hungary; they imported scarce goods from the West and sold them at enormous profits in Hungary; and they capitalized on Hungary's few products of export value by means of the Party machinery throughout Europe. The traffic to Czechoslovakia was simply the smuggling of Hungarian tobacco and cigarettes. At a time when cigarettes were still a medium of exchange everywhere in Europe, the income from this traffic swelled the Communist Party's coffers. Obviously they had been having trouble of late with the Czechoslovak border guards, not yet Communist, and an American Army truck was the ideal solution. I had to laugh myself. They could well afford the $12,000 monthly.

The implications were less worrisome than they looked. If the Communists had suggested me to Guy, it was a good sign that they took me for just another American profiteer—a not entirely unique specimen in Europe at the time. If Guy had come to me on his own, simply because I was the only American he knew who could help him, then there was also no danger. But I decided to keep Guy at arm's length.

For some time past I had been communicating to my headquarters the increasing and unavoidable political implications of my operations in Hungary. No guidance had been forthcoming. Now the Communists had begun to agitate for new elections, which could only intensify the pressures on me. My inability to take a line one way or another in the circumstances would sooner or later jeopardize my usefulness, even for intelligence work, let alone its effect on the willingness of Hungarians to continue to resist. I therefore asked for permission to meet Peter in Switzerland, under the guise of a holiday in Italy, to discuss these problems urgently. In reply, I was told to let it be known that I was going to Italy on vacation, but to come to Washington instead. I accordingly set out by car for Italy, driving to the southwest toward the British Zone of Austria. Apart from being arrested in Veszprem by a Russian sentry who, speaking mostly Ukrainian himself, took my imperfect Russian as proof that I was a Russian deserter, I arrived safely in British-occupied Graz, continued on over the Grossgluckner— then Europe's highest road, where I encountered more Russians, but this time former Russian prisoners who refused to return to the Soviet Union—and went on down to Salzburg in the American Zone, where I took a plane to Paris and thence to Washington.

Washington seemed unreal and excessively comfortable. In just under a year I had become accustomed to the ruins and rubble of Budapest and to the sense of danger in the air. Washington was alive with movement and confusion, but the sense of danger was noticeably absent; the general atmosphere was still that of victory in the war, and there was seemingly no public awareness of the erosion of that victory being so harshly pursued in Eastern Europe. I went over every detail of my operations with my chief and his assistants. My use of Sam and Edmund and of Sara was authorized, although without any intimation to them of the organization for which I worked. There was an obvious CE interest in Edmund, but I pointed out that, as a Socialist, his position in the AVO was too much on sufferance to offer any opportunities for operations more complex than secret intelligence. Sam's request for radio sets was turned down cold as too dangerous at this stage. I was instructed to continue to seek out new agents in the areas not covered. They themselves, presumably working through the Hungarian Legation in Washington, gave me the name of an agent, Anna, who would satisfy my requirements concerning Church affairs.

On the matter of political action, I presented my ideas for covert support of a wide range of Hungarian non-Communist groups. Here I encountered sympathy, but I sensed that I was considered to be somewhat alarmist, and in any event this was not a matter for decision by my organization. There seemed to be a general feeling that such techniques were wartime measures only and inappropriate to the postwar period. It was assumed that the results to be achieved by such action could be more properly obtained by direct negotiation with the Soviets. It would take another year, the fall of Czechoslovakia, the Tito-Cominform break, and the narrow victory of the Italian elections of 1948 before the United States Government realized the need for a political arm in the Soviet war.

I was, however, permitted to state my case to a high official, a Presidential adviser. He agreed with my analysis of Soviet intentions in Hungary, but, he said, the American people were in no mood to take serious steps to stop them. "The American people have just finished a war," he said, "and they will not stand for us taking action which seems likely to provoke hostilities with the Russians." I pointed out that the net result of this was not simply Soviet domination of Hungary, but a slaughter of the nation's entire leadership—beginning first and foremost with those who had resisted the Germans. This would mean, I said, that if the Soviets were allowed to pursue their course unhindered, they would have in their hands a nation without leadership, from which in the far future we could expect nothing except support of Soviet aims. "You are too pessimistic," he answered. "You should read the reports on the popular initial reaction of the Russian people to the German invasion. After almost a quarter century of terror, they still rose up to welcome the Germans in the naïve belief that they were being liberated. Even the Jews of Moscow, kept in the dark by Stalin as to Hitler's anti-Semitism, rioted in the streets as the Germans approached—convinced that they were to be liberated. These Russian reactions were pathetic, and when they found out the truth, the people fought for Russia. But their initial reaction is proof that people do not forget freedom as easily as you fear." I had little faith in this view at the time, but history was to prove him right. The Hungarian Revolution, in which a whole generation raised on Communism were to fight Soviet domination, was just under ten years away.

"At least we can save some of the people," I argued. "We cannot just leave those whose principles and courage will be our assets and their doom to prison, torture, and death." He thought awhile. "And can you save some of them without embroiling us in a series of clumsy mishaps that will only worsen their fate?" he asked. My answer, "Yes," may have been only bravado; it was still the only answer possible. "Well, we'll give that one some thought," he said, rising to signal the end of our talk. Before returning to Europe I drew up and presented a plan to my headquarters for a series of escape operations, designed to save political leaders whose resistance to the Soviets put their lives or freedom in danger, but with sufficient leeway to allow the inclusion of some persons who may not have been politically active, but who nonetheless merited our help. My headquarters received this without comment.

However, my chief had comments on another score which amused and at the same time irritated me for what it revealed of our confidence in our own agents. A large man of imposing appearance, quite the general he was, he took me to lunch just before my departure. Over the coffee I noticed that he was talking on at great length, seemingly without saying anything. I paid closer attention and finally realized what he was trying to say, with almost embarrassing discretion and a show of great personal interest in me. He was obviously well informed that in Budapest I saw a great deal of a particular Hungarian lady. I was embarrassed for him, but also annoyed. "You are afraid I will give something away to her?" I asked. "No, of course not," he demurred. "But you know how it is —blackmail and all that sort of thing." I felt genuine pleasure at what I knew I could answer. "You should have consulted the FBI," I said. "You will find that the Russians tried to blackmail me and failed. Where they failed their Hungarian stooges aren't going to succeed." He looked surprised. "I didn't know that," he said.

He appeared somewhat mollified, but still not completely happy. I gave him the rest. "What your informant was unable to tell you," I went on, "is highly relevant, however. It is true that I see a great deal of the Hungarian lady, but what your man apparently doesn't know, and the lady does, is that I am planning to marry someone completely different—a Frenchwoman, as it happens." His discomfort vanished in a flash. "Wonderful," he cried, and we parted in backslapping mutual confidence. What I had not done was to find out who was watching me in Budapest: whether I was the incidental object of some CE operation, the deliberate subject of a security surveillance, or merely an item of gossip.

I flew back to Europe. As I arrived in Paris I was met by the news that the Hungarian Prime Minister, Ferenc Nagy, on vacation in Switzerland, had been implicated in the "conspiracy." It seems that he had, with the agreement of his Cabinet, including Rakosi, requested the Soviets to turn Bela Kovacs over to the Hungarian authorities—obviously in the thought that even that was a lesser evil than imprisonment and possible death at the hands of the Soviets. General Sviridov had replied—in Nagy's absence Rakosi was acting Prime Minister—that the Soviets were unable to surrender Bela Kovacs, but included with his reply a copy of Bela Kovacs's "confession," which he noted showed that the Prime Minister was also a "conspirator." I hastened to Salzburg and drove on to Budapest. The day I arrived the Prime Minister's four-year-old son, left behind in Hungary during his parents' vacation, was handed into his father's arms at the Swiss-Austrian border by a Communist functionary in direct exchange for the Prime Minister's resignation.

CHAPTER IV

The Opposition

The Soviets and the Hungarian Communists had made their point: no one was immune from the "conspiracy." To eliminate anyone who opposed them the Communists had merely to announce in their press that he had been implicated in some "confession"— imprisonment, torture, death, or at best exile were the rapid consequences. For the sake of temporary appearances, the Communists found men in the other parties who were either utterly intimidated or of limited attainments and ridiculous ambition who would serve them as figureheads. In this way, they replaced Ferenc Nagy with another Smallholder Prime Minister who was but a puppet. The Smallholder President of the Parliament, Monsignor Bela Varga, surely the next on the list for elimination, disappeared—we learned only weeks later that he had escaped to Austria. He was replaced by Imre Nagy, a Communist, since the battleground now shifted from the Cabinet and Government to the Parliament, where opposition still existed.

Shortly after my return I met with Sam and told him that for the time being I would have no radios for him. I still had hopes that my headquarters would shortly see things in a different light. He was disappointed, but urged me to press the matter. He then told me that Edmund was working on a series of reports for me about the AVO, but it being too dangerous to meet with me, they would be passed to me through Sam. I received the first of the series that day. In due course I had the complete report; it came to several hundred pages, setting forth in detail the brutality, treachery, and corruption which was the Soviet version of "liberation." I confess it made me feel neither confident nor comfortable.

In January of 1945, while Budapest was still under siege, Gabor Peter, a Hungarian who had been a Soviet agent working with the

Red Army during the war, established the Budapest headquarters of the Political Police—a branch of the newly reorganized National Police. Peter's liaison to the Soviets was a man named Janos Kovacs, a Hungarian major and simultaneously a Soviet colonel. The ostensible purpose of this organization, proposed by the Communists and agreed to by the other parties of the Hungarian Front, was to uncover and bring to prosecution the Hungarian Nazis. About one month after getting into operation, Peter and his men in Budapest caught one Janos Kessmenn, head of the Hungarian Nazi organization charged with exterminating the Jews. (Even during the siege of Budapest, when it was no longer possible to ship them to Germany for extermination, the Hungarian Nazis continued to round up Jews: they were lined up on the quays of the Danube by the hundreds and shot, their bodies falling into the river.) The Political Police promised Kessmenn not only his life, but freedom from prosecution if he would show them the hidden cache of property confiscated from the Jews. Kessmenn produced about $90,000 in foreign exchange, some 1,500 carats of diamonds, and more than 10,000 different gold pieces. This became the Political Police secret fund. All during 1945 the Political Police added to this by simple robbery, theft, and extortion—mostly from small shopkeepers. They did not hesitate to murder, and countless innocent persons disappeared during this period. In the confusion of the time it was impossible to tell whether a person who had disappeared was a victim of Russian looting, Russian deportations for forced labor, the settlement of grudges, or the Hungarian Political Police. Nonetheless, Edmund's report contained quite a list of those known to have fallen into the latter category.

During 1946 the Political Police worked closely with the Soviet MVD; as often as not someone arrested by the Hungarians was turned over to the Soviets for interrogation. In such cases it was rarely that he was ever seen again. In 1946 it would appear that the Soviets concluded their tutelage had produced satisfactory results; in September the Political Police were reorganized out from under the National Police and established as the State Security Authority —AVO—with Gabor Peter responsible in theory to the Minister of the Interior. The AVO was, of course, directly responsible to the authority of the senior Hungarian Communists; but, as elsewhere in Eastern Europe, it became an integral part of the Soviet secret operations apparatus. It was a specially qualified local arm.

In the new AVO the coalition received lip service in the form of a

Smallholder deputy to Gabor Peter, one Aladar Gyuris, and a Socialist deputy, Istvan Bittmann. Neither of these two deputies exercised any authority whatsoever. Of the fourteen, later nineteen, Budapest districts, only three were under the command of Socialist AVO officers—and their authority was purely nominal. Of the seventeen divisions which comprised the AVO organization, only one was headed by a Socialist.

The structure of the AVO, quite apart from the vicious brutality which was its chief characteristic, was an interesting example of a painstakingly conceived and executed broad secret political operation. Against such a comprehensive and realistic—and ruthless—machine, ordinary political and diplomatic maneuver and negotiation—the mainstays of American policy at the time—stood not a chance. A study of this structure showed a notable disregard for administrative balance. From the point of view of American professional administrators such a structure would appear disperse, unwieldy, even sloppy; it would be difficult to reduce to the charts and graphs favored by Business Administration schools and Government bureaucracy. In fact, however, it was designed to perform with maximum effectiveness a special and precise function; to this end the factors of administrative balance and of theoretical organization were completely subordinated to the specific requirements of the mission. It was "bad administration," but it was a flexible and effective organization—even without rapine and murder.

As established in September 1946 the AVO had seventeen divisions, each with a special function to perform within the national life. Of these seventeen, the existence of only three was publicly acknowledged. The divisional functions were described and designated on the basis of what actually confronted the Communists, not on the basis of what they wished Hungarian national life to be. That came later, and only when it was achieved in fact. It should be borne in mind that beyond this AVO structure there also existed the overt political entity of the Communist Party—likewise politically trained—and, of course, behind both the menace of the Red Army.

The task of Division One was to infiltrate and ultimately to dominate Hungarian political life. Its director, Sandor Horvath, was a Moscow-trained Communist. Infiltration was accomplished in two ways—each for a different purpose. The first was the recruiting of informers in all the non-Communist political parties and their related organizations. Bribery was sometimes used—a principal Smallholder speechwriter who had a single session at AVO headquarters and thereafter submitted daily reports was one such case—but the favorite method was simply intimidation. Taken from their beds in the middle of the night, maltreated, threatened with a worse fate, then released on the condition of reporting, with the express threat of instant punishment for any disclosure, most people did as directed—suicide seemed the only available alternative for many, and such cases were not unknown.

The other form of infiltration was the introduction into the other parties of active agents. In the case of secret Communists no lure was needed; for the rest, entire "left-wings" of the Smallholders, Socialist, and Peasant Parties were made up of men who, as political opportunists, as victims of blackmail, or as recipients of various forms of bribery, deliberately worked under Communist instructions. At the highest level, two of them—Istvan Dobi of the Smallholders and Szakasits of the Socialists—were ultimately rewarded in a fully Communist Hungary with the Presidency of the Republic, Dobi first from 1952 and then again under the post-1956 Kadar regime.

As a part of its political responsibilities, elections in Hungary also fell within the competence of Division One—with final disastrous consequences for Hungary in 1947.

Division Two of the AVO was charged with infiltrating all foreign missions in Hungary—the Soviets obviously excepted. I noted one day to Mark that the receptionist at the American Legation seemed upset and on the verge of tears. "She's picked up every night after midnight and is interrogated until the morning," he said. "She's exhausted from lack of sleep and plain terror, but they won't let her quit her job here, and for us to dismiss her would only make them suspect her of a doublecross."

The target of Division Three was the churches. One of the traditional church activities in Hungary had been the support and direction of youth organizations, both Catholic and Protestant. These organizations were of considerable social significance, and were a prime obstacle to Communist aims for weakening church influence and dominating the youth. In the summer of 1946 two Russian soldiers, engaged in a gun battle between themselves on a main street of Budapest, were killed. Within twenty-four hours the AVO—still then the Political Police—fabricated a story that a young Catholic boy had done the shootings from a nearby rooftop. He was never seen again, and according to Edmund, his body was burned. Before his death, however, the name of a Catholic priest, Father Szalaz Kis, was extracted from him; Father Kis was killed in the 60 Andrassy ut headquarters of the AVO, and all the young Catholic men who were close to him were arrested and disappeared. (Among them was a Smallholders Party employee, which fact was used as an extra dividend to try to implicate the Smallholders as well.) On this basis, the Minister of the Interior banned and dissolved all religious youth organizations. Thereafter, the question of religious youth organizations came under Division Four, in charge of youth.

Division Three also pursued infiltration of the churches, and achieved some success in the Catholic Church because of differences within the Church itself. Cardinal Mindszenty, notwithstanding his merits as a churchman, was no politician—although he took an active interest in politics. His inflexible line had resulted in the failure in 1945 to form the authorized Catholic Party, and a temporary agreement had been reached whereby the Church would support the Smallholders, and the latter would represent Church interests in Parliament. As the Smallholders began to disintegrate, the disputes among Catholic politicians and within the Church began again; a group of Jesuits emerged in political opposition to the Cardinal and with a political program of their own. Division Three capitalized on this schism, and, obtaining, among other favors, a charter for a Catholic youth organization for the Jesuits, proceeded to infiltrate them.

Division Five, the only one commanded by a Socialist, had the duty of infiltrating the circles and activities of former aristocrats, Army officers, and politicians.

Division Six, using the same techniques as Division One, was charged with applying them to the Government and the entire apparatus of the state. They were singularly effective. The suicide of one young official in the Prime Ministry, who preferred death to becoming an informer, was one testimonial. Another was the reorganization under Communist dominance of the Defense Ministry, even in the presence of a Smallholder Defense Minister. In 1946 large-scale reductions in the Civil Service were undertaken for economy reasons. Those to be dismissed were put in category "B," so that the whole procedure became known as the "B" List. Making up the "B" List was obviously of great political importance to the parties. In each Ministry a commission composed of a representative of the Prime Ministry, a representative of the Minister involved, and a representative of the trade unions prepared the list. The trade-union man, being an appointee of the Trade Union Council and not of the individual unions, was always either a Communist or a complaisant Socialist. In the Defense Ministry, the Prime Minister sent a Smallholder deputy and the Minister delegated a trusted aide, a Colonel Daroczi, thus insuring a majority over the trade-union representative. Division Six, however, had reached Colonel Daroczi, and he voted all the way down the line with the Communists, thereby turning the Defense Ministry over to the Communists. Another notable success was achieved by Division Six with Jozsef Bognar, former Smallholder Party Secretary for Budapest. Even while Minister of Information, Bognar was secretly arrested by Division Six, shortly after the arrest of Bela Kovacs by the Soviets. Within a few hours Bognar went free, still a Minister, but now one of Division Six's chief informants.

Division Seven, headed by a former Hungarian Nazi, Gyula Princz, was charged with surveillance and kidnaping. Surveillance was of course a service function for the other AVO divisions. Kidnaping—as in the case of Laszlo Filler, a Smallholder member of Parliament, who was abducted and turned over to the Soviets, never to be seen again—was most often a service function for the Russians, to hide the Soviet hand or interest.

Division Eight was one of the publicly acknowledged activities of the AVO. Ostensibly its function was to track down remaining Hungarian Nazis; it was, in fact, a cover for the other activities of the AVO.

Division Nine was occupied with establishing and maintaining files on the entire population, for such later use as might become necessary. Under Soviet theory and practice, any information about anyone is of possible value. The result is history's most enormous dossier system (Division Nine was the Hungarian branch), which often turns out to be highly useful. One high Government official, for example, occupying a post which could effectively block Communist plans, was discovered by Division Nine to have been an illegal abortionist at one point in his early career; thereafter he was no obstacle to Communist aims. (The late John MacCormac of *The New York Times,* present in Budapest during the 1956 Revolution, claimed that one of the gravest errors of the Revolution was the failure of someone in authority, while the enraged populace was killing any AVO man caught in uniform, to destroy, systematically and thoroughly, the AVO files.) At least some reservoir of undischarged guilt feelings, no matter how sub-conscious, are acknowledged by psychological sciences as existing in almost all adults. The Communists recognize this too; they seek to know exactly what it is that every man is feeling guilty about and, when necessary, to what usable degree.

Division Nine also was charged with arranging false identities for AVO agents when necessary, and with the related function of forging documents. The microphone and wire-tapping services were also a part of this division. Mark told me later that an examination of his small office in the American Legation showed eight microphones in the walls and ceiling; but such installations were by no means confined to foreigners—they were everywhere. One of the more striking ironies of the situation was that this equipment in Hungary was all secretly manufactured by Communist workmen in the plant of the local subsidiary of the International Telephone and Telegraph Corporation—the same American company once lauded by *Fortune* magazine as an outstanding prewar model of successful American investment and operations abroad.

Division Ten was another overt group. It was charged with official documentation, including the issue of identity cards, and it maintained the legal personal files on the population, as distinct from the secret files in Division Nine.

Division Eleven was related to Division Eight. Its ostensible function was to assist in the prosecution of former Nazis before the courts. As such, it was located in special quarters at the Marko utca Prosecutor's Prison, but this was also a cover, since it insured continued AVO hold over prisoners who had been legally transferred from the AVO's custody. Division Eleven was also charged with the preparation and conduct of show trials.

Division Twelve was the AVO's own supply department. Apart from the usual supply functions, it was also charged with the raising—by any means available—and disbursement of secret funds. It also supplied apartments, furniture, clothing, cars, and luxury goods to the AVO high officials. The information thus obtained by this Division was later used by the AVO against its own officials when their liquidation became politically necessary.

Division Thirteen, also overt, was the Hungarian Passport Office. From the spring of 1947 it was directed by a Russian officer, Antal Weller. It provided a cover for the activities of other divisions.

The personnel department of the AVO was Division Fourteen.

This Division was also responsible for surveillance and security of AVO personnel. The Division's standards of performance might be described as utterly ruthless. Edmund emphasized to me the story of AVO First Lieutenant Mihaly Kovacs, an aide to Horvath, Chief of Division One. Kovacs was discovered to be working for the British. Both he and his wife were arrested and subjected to torture in the cellars of the AVO headquarters at 60 Andrassy ut. Ultimately, Kovacs was killed—with his wife forced to watch his murder. Only then was the hapless woman herself put to death.

Division Fifteen conducted surveillance of all high state officials. To this end, they appeared most often in the guise of "bodyguards" from the National Police.

Division Sixteen comprised the AVO sub-headquarters in the districts of Budapest. Originally these district offices had the power of arrest, but from 1946 on they were deprived of this and functioned as the eyes and ears of the Headquarters. The establishment of informer networks was their responsibility, and on the basis of the information thus obtained they were required to prepare blacklists of anti-Communists and "dangerous or hostile elements." These offices operated in the classical style and preferred a number of single key informers, whose responsibility was then to create their own larger networks of informers. In this manner they had, by 1947, 1,500 informers at the Budapest industrial complex of Csepel Island alone.

Division One-A performed the same function for the rest of Hungary as Division Sixteen performed for Budapest. By the autumn of 1947 there were, throughout the entire country, some 70,000 to 80,000 informers—out of a population of nine million.

This, then, was the "opposition." The relentless effort and the horrendous human cost which had gone into the AVO's organization showed this to be more than a mere cover to hide the Soviet hand; what had been constructed was a major line of defense, so that if the Peace Treaty, or if other diplomatic negotiations with the West, forced a Soviet retirement from Hungary, the nation would still be left, thanks to the AVO, firmly in Communist hands and tied to Moscow.

Following the forced resignation of Ferenc Nagy, the fragmentation of the opposition to the Communists was pushed with ferocious haste. Leo came to see me one evening in June. He knew that he was marked for arrest for his role in pressing the Parliamentary investigation of the "conspiracy." He had decided to escape, with

his wife and two children. I was deeply concerned about the risk,
but he assured me he had arranged it satisfactorily. I was dubious
and told him I was merely awaiting authority to establish an escape operation. "No," he said. "I thank you, but now one can
escape, with a little care and ingenuity. But in a few more weeks, or
at most a month or two, it will become impossible. You will see. I
must go now, while we still can." He left me his political papers,
which I agreed to send on to him when he should let me know,
writing under a false name, where he was. Four weeks later I had
word from him giving a Paris address. In due course he received
his papers, but I felt shame that I could not have rendered more
vital help.

Shortly after Leo's departure, Mark was confronted one day in
his offices by a member of Parliament whose immunity had suddenly been lifted and who had taken refuge from the AVO in the
Legation. Mark told me the man was verging on hysteria—but
Mark was forbidden to give him asylum. He had been obliged to
turn him out into the street, with only the advice, which he had
heard from me, to seek refuge with the Dominican friars and at all
costs to avoid the Jesuits. (An exact reversal of the situation which
had prevailed during the German Occupation, when the Jesuits
had distinguished themselves in rescuing those in danger and the
Dominicans had often refused help.) The deputy had left, never to
be heard of again. Mark was sick at heart from this incident.

I remembered it ten years later as I watched, with bitterness and
sympathy, the rending strain undergone by one of my colleagues in
Vienna, whose orders and role required him to answer "No" to the
pleas of Hungarian Freedom Fighter delegations from Budapest
for bazookas and ammunition to fight the Russians.

The deputy refused refuge was a member of the Freedom Party,
an opposition party led by Dezso Sulyok which had received in late
1946 an authorization from the Soviets, largely at the instance of
Prime Minister Nagy, to form and engage in political activity.
Nagy's theory was that there ought to be an opposition in Parliament, and he probably hoped in this manner to ease some of the
Communist pressure on the Smallholders. In this he was not successful, and, as the Smallholders disintegrated, the Freedom Party
gained in strength. The party had even attempted to publish a
newspaper, but its instantaneous success had led to a refusal by the
printers to set type for it. (Sam had told me the story of how this
was achieved by the Trade Union Council. The Council had issued

the order to the printers, who, favoring the paper themselves, had refused. They were then threatened with expulsion from the union —meaning also their jobs—and that was that.) Now the Communists were pushing through Parliament a bill for new elections. With the Smallholders in disarray, strong opposition to features of the bill was coming from the Freedom Party. Its deputies were consequently under constant harassment. A few days after Mark had been visited by one such deputy, Sulyok announced the dissolution of his party. Edmund reported that the AVO had quite simply informed Sulyok that when Parliament was dissolved for the new elections, all of his Parliamentary members, then without immunity, would be arrested en masse. Rather than expose his followers to this danger, Sulyok had given in; shortly thereafter he left the country.

We were doing pretty poorly. Not only was I without any effective political line in the circumstances, but even my proposal for an escape operation was still unanswered. While terror had silenced many, there still remained a number of politicians and leaders who were determined to fight the Communists in the forthcoming elections. At least some of them were going to require our help—and to earn the right to it. I therefore arranged to see Peter in Vienna. Since my return I had visited Vienna regularly, always going by car, in order to familiarize myself with the roads, the countryside, and to have continually in my possession a valid Soviet pass, the eternal *propusk*, without which one could not get by the Red Army roadblocks between Budapest and Vienna.

Vienna was still grim and gray, but by now my feelings had changed noticeably from the contrast so favorable to Budapest I had noted a year earlier. Arrival in the Western sectors of the city invariably produced feelings of relief, relaxation, and security. In an office where I didn't have to worry about microphones, I told Peter how rapidly the situation in Budapest was deteriorating, and emphasized the fact, which I found shameful, that I had been unable to be of any real help to Leo. I asked Peter to press Washington for the authority I had asked for escapes and for a political decision on which I could base some activity during the election campaign—which I pointed out might still result in a clear rebuff to Communist pretensions that they were assuming power legally and on a popular basis. It was my belief that such a rebuff might, at best, slow down the Communist timetable; at worst, it would still make clear to the world by what methods the Communists had achieved power in Hungary, a point which could be of great political value in future years if dramatized now. To my satisfaction, I found Peter in full agreement with my arguments, and there followed one of those typical conversations in which those working in the field commiserate with each other on the stupidity and myopia of headquarters.

Encouraged, I asked Peter to give me temporary authority to arrange a minimum number of escapes pending word from Washington. He insisted on pinning me down to an exact figure. I finally asked for ten outstanding political leaders and fifteen others as necessary, the latter to include members of the network. Peter agreed to this. I then pointed out that, assuming I could get my escapees over the Hungarian border, I could do nothing from Budapest about getting them safely through the 40-odd miles from the border to Vienna, nor through the 125 miles from Vienna to the American Zone of Austria. I asked for assistance from my opposite number in Vienna. Peter again agreed, and shortly I found myself introduced to our Vienna agent who was operating under the guise of an Army Colonel. The Colonel appeared eager to help, even while obviously studying the problem coldly and objectively behind a front of affability.

The Colonel's problem, it turned out, was bureaucratic, and bureaucracy won the day. He could help escapees from the Austrian border to Vienna, but from Vienna to the American Zone the facilities were in the hands of the local representative of the CIG—Central Intelligence Group, successor to the OSS, and predecessor of the CIA. To split the operation this way would risk revealing to the CIG representative both that our own intelligence agency was operating in Austria and the identity of the Colonel. I was stunned at this hapless example of wartime interorganizational rivalries living on into another age—but the Colonel, supported by Peter, could not be moved. However, neither he nor Peter had any objection to my approaching the CIG man—Hugh—provided that I maintained my cover with him and did not reveal any member of the network to him as being such. In brief, I could appear to him as a lone official of the Government who wanted to help some people in danger—a friendly but completely private secret operation. I accepted this way of doing it, being reminded in so doing of the German gesture of scratching the left ear with the right hand reaching behind the head, intended to describe either a deliberately complex brain or bureaucratic red tape. It was, of course, precisely this kind of bureaucratic conflict and artificial obstacle—markedly different from the innate, organic conflicts of secret operations, described in Part I—which the later creation of the CIA was designed—successfully—to eliminate.

I decided to await approaching Hugh until I had something definite in mind, and returned to Budapest. It was fortunate that I did. A week later Mark handed me a slip of paper bearing a name and a number. A man who said his name was Janos Majoros had called to see Mark at his office and had given him this much-worn scrap of paper. Majoros explained that he was a flier, that it was he who had secretly flown Hungarian negotiators and the British Colonel to Italy in 1944, and that an OSS officer, whose name and number were on the paper, had told him to use it at the nearest American diplomatic office if ever he were in danger or needed help. Majoros said he was now in danger of arrest and needed funds to arrange his own escape. I told Mark I would look into the matter for him, and then checked with Henry. Henry confirmed that there was indeed a flier named Janos Majoros, a genuine hero, but this of course didn't insure that the man who had come to Mark's office was in fact Majoros.

This was my opportunity to contact Hugh. I went to Vienna and called on him in his office. An intelligent and decisive man, Hugh was fully co-operative, and went immediately to the core of any problem. He checked the Majoros story, found it correct, and gave me the requested funds. Then he settled back to ask me a favor.

The Navy was interested in six Hungarian scientists and had, many months before, secretly signed contracts with them in the course of a Navy officer's visit to Hungary. The Navy was now extremely worried about their departure, and the scientists and their families, twelve persons in all, needed money and some assistance. Would I disburse $5,000 to them and if necessary help to arrange their departure? I could have looked on this request as a suspect gambit by Hugh to recruit me; instead I chose to regard it as a heartening example of interorganizational co-operation within the U.S. Government. When I left, Hugh and I were in business together: I had funds to disburse for him, but I also had the names of contacts in three Austrian border towns who would convey escapees to Vienna, and an address in the American Sector in Vienna where they would be housed before being taken on to the West by air.

(Highly personable and sensitive, Hugh's later career took an unusual turn. For some years he rendered most competent and effective, even distinguished, service in secret operations, but suddenly, while still in his early forties, he became sated and disillusioned with the world of politics and power. Renouncing his past for what he intensely felt was a wider and more profound perspective, he spent a year in a Trappist monastery and then went to Italy where, in a small seaside village, he devotes himself exclusively to work in ceramics. This kind of reaction among intelligent and sensitive men to the intense pressures of secret operations after some years is not infrequent, but few carry it as far as Hugh. However, I visit him from time to time, and of the many real and enduring friendships which this strange work nonetheless brought me, I value his highly.)[1]

Majoros and his money turned out to be a lesson in patience and relative values. Mark gave him the money and he disappeared. We heard nothing further from or about him. Six months later I apologized to Hugh for the loss of the funds; he dismissed it as part of the cost of doing business. But five years later a Hungarian airliner suddenly appeared one day over the Munich airport, asking permission to land. When it did, some fourteen of the passengers aboard requested political asylum in the West. One of them was Janos Majoros; he and another flier had taken over the plane while it was en route to Prague and had flown it to Munich. When asked about his disappearance five years earlier, Majoros said he was then being too closely watched. "I had to revise my plans. They took longer than I expected," he said, but with the confident air of a man who has worked hard to achieve his goal.

My own goal was far from being achieved. No one in the network was in a position to operate the kind of sure escape chain I had in mind. They were all tied to the city of Budapest by their work, and they had no forms of transport. I thought of Edmund; an escape chain operated by the AVO itself would be the kind of *tour de force* to make any agent's mouth water, but I rejected it as being much too dangerous and too susceptible to penetration. Both Eugene and Louis had told me of cases where the Russians themselves had arranged escapes. However, these were for money—the price was steadily rising—and the Russians involved were black-marketeers who were always in danger of being caught by their own troops or betrayed by rival Russian profiteers. Furthermore, these Russians were happy to take money from "capitalists," but would fear involvement with escapes of hunted political leaders.

There was one escape chain already operating through Budapest and tolerated by the Soviet High Command. This was the Jewish underground originating in Rumania which ran through Hungary and then alternatively by Austria and Yugoslavia to Italy. From there refugees were loaded onto ships for transport to Palestine. This operation had the tacit blessing of the Soviets since it contributed to British discomfiture and general unrest in the Middle East. In Hungary the operation was run by the American Joint Distribution Committee, the American Jewish organization set up for welfare work among the European Jewish survivors of the German slaughter. They were efficient—at a later stage they were reportedly running seventy-five persons a day through Budapest—but they categorically refused any non-Jews. In addition, Simon had obtained for me some time before several sets of the AJDC confidential monthly accounts, which showed sizable donations to the Communist Party in several districts of Budapest. I sympathized with their operation and admired the single-mindedness with which it was conducted, but it offered no possibilities for me. Even if I could persuade the AJDC to take some non-Jews, which was highly doubtful, it was not likely that they would risk their own people for the sake of defying Soviet and Communist political objectives, and the tacit co-operation of the Soviet and Communist authorities meant too great a risk of penetration.

While I was mulling over these problems, I gradually accumulated, in an unused garage in my building on the Var, a number of packing cases obtained from the American Military Mission, together with several tarpaulins and large sheets of the waterproofed, insulated paper used for packing large overseas shipments. To ship people out in boxes in the American Army trucks which regularly ran between Budapest and Vienna with supplies was not my idea of a discreet or desirable operation; but an emergency might necessitate something like it. I little knew how right I was.

In early July I went to dine at Guy's. I had not dropped him since his unwelcome offer to make me rich; I enjoyed his company and his wit, but I maintained a certain alert when with him. This particular evening we dined on the balcony of his apartment, overlooking a small, tree-lined public square. The people walking in the square, the summer air, and the night hum of the city hid the struggle and anguish which marked the day's reality. Guy, for the first time, spoke much of himself; I noted that, apart from a few sallies for their own sakes, he had dropped his cynicism.

He told me how he had resigned from the Police. The increasing Communist control had made him decide to leave, he said, but he knew that if this were to be interpreted as a sign of dissidence, he would only be putting himself in danger. He had therefore told Rajk, the Interior Minister, that he had to find some work which would pay him better while he awaited the award, under the land reform, of the 200 acres to which his Resistance record entitled him from a larger estate he had previously held. According to Guy, Rajk had intimated that he should act for the Communists in the Peasant Party to which he belonged, to which Guy had responded with a criticism of the Peasant Party which sounded at the same time like a eulogy of the Communist Party. He finished by saying how much he looked forward to working his land—obtaining a little bit of capital for this being the purpose of his looking for better-paying work. He then parted in most friendly fashion from Rajk, who told him to drop in to see him from time to time.

Guy paused here. "He's a murderer, you know," he said. I nodded agreement. Edmund had told me through Sam only a few days before that he had gone to see Rajk personally, on the basis of their Resistance work together, to intervene for another wartime comrade who was being tortured by the AVO. Rajk was expansive and assured Edmund that he could speak freely, as an old companion. When Edmund explained the purpose of his visit, Rajk's manner turned cold. Edmund reminded him of the man's wartime services. Rajk merely glanced at Edmund and, turning back to his papers, said, "The situation has changed."

Guy went on. "I didn't want Rajk hostile, and he was not, but that alone would not save me." For the ensuing two weeks, therefore, Guy had inserted anonymous personal want ads in the main papers, asking on each occasion if anyone knew the whereabouts of some ten or a dozen people. All the names Guy used were those of persons kidnaped or killed in the course of Political Police looting and robbery during 1945. He had then put the complete lists of these names, together with the date and manner of their liquidation by the Political Police—information he had carefully gleaned during his two years in the National Police—in a safe hiding place. He then resigned. Guy's idea was that if arrested, he would simply state that the lists detailing the fate of these people would be published if he did not reappear within twenty-four hours—he having arranged this with a friend—and that his proof of his threat would be the want ads. I could only admire Guy's imagination and his careful execution of his plans.

"So what happened to you and the West Orient Corporation?" I asked him. Guy laughed. "They came to me about a month after my resignation," he answered. "I decided to accept the offer," he continued, "because I assumed Rajk was trying to be helpful—and to ensnare me, of course. But even a month or six weeks of that would have given me enough to leave the country and live abroad.

"But I may have been wrong," he added. "It was perhaps just as well for me that I couldn't persuade you to give me an American truck. That at least showed I wasn't all that close to the Americans. To be perfectly frank with you, though, I was disappointed at the time. I didn't really care about this country then. I wasn't going to join the Communists, by any means, but I was sure the Smallholders weren't going to save the country, so I just counted myself out."

"So you're off to your farm?" I inquired.

Again Guy laughed. "My farm," he answered, "happens to be a plot of 200 acres adjoining the Austrian border. It took me a lot of intrigue to get just those 200 acres and not some others. People do escape now, but within a very few months they're not going to be able to. So, one day, working my fields, I'll just stumble through a bush into Austria and that will be that."

I laughed with Guy, but I was seeing him in a new light. "How soon will that be?" I asked.

"As late as possible," he answered. "I like life abroad, but now I have no money for it, and"—he paused— "when you're leaving for probably the last time you keep putting it off."

All that night I went over Guy's story. If he was not a Communist plant, he was the man to run the escape chain—provided he was willing. He had imagination, daring, and a conspiratorial cast of mind. The next day I checked the newspapers for the period he had mentioned. There were the personals. I then checked them against Edmund's list of victims of the Political Police. All of Guy's names were on Edmund's list. I then sent off a cable to Headquarters, asking for a check on Guy and explaining the purpose for which I wanted to use him.

The answer was both startling and encouraging. "Guy former British agent," it read in effect. "You may use him for stated purpose only provided you maintain your cover with him and provided you're satisfied he's not working with British." This was unusually generous. It left the responsibility on me to be sure he was not still working with the British, but at least his former service for them was not to eliminate him from consideration.

In about a week I invited Guy to dinner. He was unchanged from our previous encounter: always amused at some bit of irony, but more equable in temper than in the previous months. Politics took over our conversation, and I steered the subject gradually away from Hungary itself to the world situation. Guy made a number of remarks critical of the British. I responded with a defense of the British, always implying that Guy didn't really know or understand them. At last he said, "Look here, I worked with the British before and during the war. I know what I'm talking about. And I refused to work with them afterward." He then detailed his reasons; except that he was no Socialist I would have thought that I was listening to Sam's reasons for disillusionment with postwar Britain. I took no ostensible notice of what Guy had said, but I had what I wanted. It could still theoretically be an effort to penetrate my operation, but I felt the odds were against it. The decision was mine, as was the risk. I decided in favor of Guy.

The rest came easily. In a discussion of what could be done, as a practical matter, about Hungary now, we arrived together at the conclusion that an escape operation was the most necessary item. Guy was much less sanguine than I about the possibilities of the forthcoming elections, but he was personally enthusiastic about the prospects of saving those who would show the courage to fight in them. We bargained somewhat on the terms (in the circumstances the initiative to recruit Guy was in fact mine, however much it may have accorded with his own wishes). He wanted a veto on who would be taken out, and he refused to provide the names of those who would help him. The latter was contrary to the basic rules of secret operations, but to have insisted would have risked his concluding that I was a professional agent rather than simply an American wanting to be helpful. I gave in on that, in exchange for my insistence that he agree to take whomever I sent to him. Since I agreed to cover the expenses of the operation—an arrangement so obviously necessary in the circumstances that it provoked no curiosity—Guy agreed to inform me in advance of the identity of anyone he wished to transport. Finally, we agreed on occasional meetings at the same rate as in the past, but to utilize a cut-out for communications in the intervals between such meetings. He suggested a girl—Helen—a former countess now working as a barmaid in a popular bar who was known to us both as reliable. When we parted Guy's enthusiasm was unmistakable. It had much the quality of an adolescent who has found the perfect way of getting back at some hated authority. I realized that I had not seen Guy before as a lifelong rebel, someone always at the edge of his society, who welcomed an opportunity to flout that society in what had now become a desirable cause. Not at all a bad quality for the operation we had in mind. But I would be hard put even today to define Guy's motives: political support, certainly; the need for money (I realized Guy was making a small personal profit on each escapee); personal rebellion—but even beyond these factors, an important element of human decency which circumstances would bring ever more clearly into relief.

Thanks to Edmund, I knew the opposition we faced. Thanks to Guy, maybe we would give them some opposition of their own.

1. This parenthetical paragraph is a substitution for what was originally written. When the typescript of this book was submitted by the publishers of the first edition to the CIA—at my direction—the first response was a telephone call to the publishers from the Public Relations Officer of the CIA ("An oxymoron?" queried one editor). The message was a stern warning against publishing as "contrary to the national interest." Relations between American publishers and the CIA being very different in 1962 from what they are today, the affair then languished for months, as the CIA refused even to specify whatever might be objectionable in the text. "Hugh," who thought the CIA should try to obtain an Official Secrets Act from the Congress, and if unable to do so, live with the consequences rather than trying surreptitiously to threaten and harass publishers, at one point found himself discussing the matter with the Public Relation Officer. "But he's giving away all our trade secrets to the Russians!" the PRO protested. "Oh, come on," "Hugh" answered, "it's the other way around. We learn from them, not they from us." The PRO was quick with his rejoinder. "Yes, I see you got a favorable notice in the book," he retorted. When, finally, the CIA got around to specifying objectionable items in the book (having hurriedly put two new officers on the task over a weekend, was how I understood it was done), they produced a list of two dozen items. I rejected about a half dozen, modified another half dozen, and accepted about a dozen. The original paragraph concerning "Hugh" was objected to on the grounds that he was too easily recognizable. That was true. So the present paragraph was my amendment. When "Hugh," very much a worldly type, saw it, he

commented, "Never was a more untrue paragraph written." That may be. But part was and is true: the friendship does still endure, and I continue to value it highly.

CHAPTER V

Defeat, But Diluted

The same message which authorized me to recruit Guy also brought the instructions from Headquarters which I had awaited since my May visit to Washington. I was disappointed, and no little bit surprised, to see that I was given authority to organize an escape chain and disburse funds as necessary for a total of twenty-five persons, of whom ten were to be leading political figures and fifteen at my discretion, including members of the network itself. These were, of course, the minimum figures I had set when seeking Peter's temporary authorization. The limitation seemed artificial and unnecessary to me, but I decided not to look a gift horse in the mouth. Take it and worry about the limitation later.

I was also specifically instructed to insure that Paul was among those taken out, and it was suggested that the sooner the better. Obviously Paul had friends in high places. As I had never had any intention of abandoning Paul I thought the instruction gratuitous, but to mention the fact would serve no purpose.

Most serious, however, the instructions contained not a word about what steps might be taken in political support of those Hungarians still fighting the Communist seizure of power. I must admit that I didn't really expect such instructions, but I had come to hope very strongly for them. The elections had now been announced for August 31, 1947, as Headquarters well knew, but so far as my instructions were concerned it was as though they didn't exist.

In the state of innocence then prevailing in the American Government about the possibilities, even necessity, of covert political operations, such an omission was not surprising. In the circumstances all that could be done was to read between the lines of my instructions and to do some careful guesswork on the basis of known official, diplomatic policy. So far as my instructions were concerned, it seemed clear that if I was authorized to arrange the escapes of political leaders whose safety was endangered by their courage and persistence in resisting the Communists, then by implication I could certainly tell them before they undertook such risks that they could at least count on this much. But was the latter truly a logical implication of the former? The answer is that it was a logical implication, but it was not a correct political implication, as will become clear.

So far as determining official policy was concerned, I had my own conversations in Washington, public American pronouncements—not the strongest of all reeds—and the guidance of Mark on which to rely. Without mentioning the details of my planned operations, I took up with Mark the political dilemma in which I found myself. I was authorized to save lives for political reasons, but without a word having been spoken as to the nature, purpose, definition, or substance of those political reasons. This gave me a very free hand—the dream of every secret agent. But it left unanswered the question of what I could do in prior support of those very political reasons which were admittedly the prerequisite justification for my saving lives—and for my guess as to the answer to this question I would ultimately be myself held answerable.

Mark agreed that we had very little to go on. My skepticism of Washington's mood, based on my conversations there and on the fact of the peculiar limitation on numbers of persons, made me unwilling to risk what I had already gained in the way of authority by seeking any clarification of it. I therefore insisted we work it out on the spot, and I further insisted to Mark that I would take sole and full responsibility for the execution of whatever line we adopted. There is bureaucratic sin involved here, of capital degree —but bureaucracy cannot function, any more than life itself, without sin. The sin, of course, is that of apparently excessive local initiative. Today, with a functioning secret political operations apparatus, such improvisations would—ideally—be neither necessary nor possible.

There was every official and publicly proclaimed support for the basic thesis that the United States Government did not wish to see Hungary become the victim of a Soviet-backed Communist seizure of power. But it was also necessary to infer from the facts of American behavior that the United States Government was not willing to take truly effective steps to block such a seizure—whatever may have been the combination of domestic and strategic reasons for that unwillingness. In brief, the United States wanted the maximum result possible for the minimum price. Mark's and my task was to estimate what locally constituted the practicable maximum result and the minimum price.

The practicable maximum was not too difficult to define. It was any result in the elections which would either put an effective brake on the Communist timetable or would alternatively force the Communists to steps which would publicly demonstrate the falsity of their claims to have come to power through popular support. The former was doubtful, but the latter was possible. It was this which set the price, for it was precisely the matter of those "steps" the Communists would take which constituted the risk for those fighting the elections. To have encouraged men to incur those risks on even the implication that, if successful, the United States would be able and willing to nullify those risks—when it was apparently not—would have been political irresponsibility of the worst sort. It would have boomeranged in bitterness and hatred against the United States for years to come.

What we had in mind was the ability to offer to save the lives of a relatively few leaders. But to offer this in advance to such leaders, as a means of encouraging them to act, would have been a betrayal of the masses who were expected to support their fight and for whom no such rescue would be available. It would be tantamount to buying an effort. No long-term policy can be constructed on such a basis; in time its falsity and undependability will show, and the cost of defeat multiplied a hundredfold. Mark and I therefore agreed that I would refrain strictly from any such advance offers of rescue for political purposes.

Members of the network were obviously not included in this agreement. Furthermore, I was under specific instructions to inform Paul that he would be helped to escape—even though his role in Hungary had now become predominantly political rather than intelligence. I saw him, with Jane, to inform him of my instructions concerning him. He looked surprised. "No," he said, "that's not the way it is. I'll tell *you.*" And then his politeness came to the fore, and he smiled. "But do thank them, of course."

Mark's and my decision naturally did not preclude political conversations in advance of the elections with those anti-Communist leaders who sought them; obviously they would be necessary. As a leak of such conversations could be seized on by the Communists as evidence of American intervention in Hungarian internal affairs, we decided that Mark would direct any initiative for such talks to me. This naturally would tend to draw some attention to me, but at the same time I was, by definition, expendable: I could be disowned by the American Government; Mark could not. My line with them —weak as it was—was simply to be that the United States Government would favor any purely Hungarian efforts to stop the Communist steamroller and that it would co-operate with any democratically elected non-Communist majority in the future (were such a miracle to happen). If this seemed weak to them, and insufficient assurance on which to risk their followers, then that could not be helped. That was the true situation. However, I also decided to argue that the future of Hungary merited their efforts, if they could accept the inevitable risks. Hungary had suffered after the war because of the policy of her leaders to accommodate themselves to the Germans; the same error should not now be committed in the face of Soviet aggression and expansion. A clear expression of Hungarian protest against Soviet aggression might not stop the juggernaut, but it would be historically valuable to Hungary at some future date. Or so I argued. As it happened, millions of Hungarians felt the same way then, and even more millions were to feel that way in 1956.

Mark also agreed to refer to me any political leaders who might come to him seeking escape. The first such, shortly after our conversation, was one of Hungary's most extraordinary political characters. Father Istvan Balogh had been the priest of a small rural parish and active as an independent in local politics. He appeared in the Debrecen Provisional Government as Undersecretary in the Prime Ministry. Not a very tall man, Balogh weighed some 270 pounds. He was a Rabelaisian type in his personal tastes: he relished eating and drinking, and all the material comforts and pleasures of life. Politically he was a Renaissance priest-politician; he was, I personally believe, the master practitioner of politics in Hungary during the period. Cunning, shrewd, intelligent, he was an invisible presence in every intrigue and political maneuver, advancing and retreating, exploiting and conceding. His policies were perhaps too personal, but no accretion of genuine political power exists without at least one such genius as Balogh pulling important strings in some nominally unimportant office. (A few days after the initial success of the Hungarian Revolution in 1956, a Hungarian politician came to me and, more in seriousness than in jest, said, "This Revolution cannot succeed." I asked why he was so sure. "I do not see Balogh anywhere on the scene," he replied.)

Balogh gave me lunch in his luxurious villa in Buda. After lunch we strolled in the garden. Very matter-of-factly he said, "I am threatened with arrest. I do not have much time to decide. Can you help me to escape?" This was typical Balogh. He considered it unnecessary, maladroit, and impolitic to make the full statement: "I am threatened with arrest if I do not co-operate with the Communists in some plan they have for me. I do not have much time to decide whether I can stay here, play their game, and ultimately outwit them. But there is nothing to decide, really, unless there is an alternative. The alternative, if it exists, is escape. Can you tell me if it does exist? If not, the decision is made for me. If it does, I will make the decision."

I replied that I was willing to arrange his escape—although I reminded him frankly that his easily recognizable bulk would make the matter more than usually difficult. Guy had told me that he would be ready to operate in about two weeks from our first talk. I therefore told Balogh that I could do nothing about actually removing him from the country for one week, but that I would undertake to hide him in the interim if he was in immediate danger. He listened, reflected a bit, and then said simply, "I will let you know my decision."

Balogh had not specified how he would let me know. I in fact learned his decision when it was announced about ten days later that he was forming a new political party for the elections and would publish a newspaper.

I didn't see Father Balogh again until the late autumn. He sent for me, and this time I found him in a palatial apartment in Pest. I wondered if he had now reversed his decision. Not at all. He explained to me at length how his party was keeping opposition to the Communists alive; because of this, he said, they were squeezing him on newsprint allocations for his paper. His proposition was simple: he wanted me to arrange for the shipment of newsprint to him from the American Zone of Germany. "And how can you get it into the country without the Communists confiscating it?" I asked, curious. Again, matter-of-factly, "I can arrange that." He continued, "You understand, I am not asking for financial help. I can pay for the newsprint, although not in foreign exchange. You have perhaps heard of my art collection?" Indeed I had. He pointed to a small table behind my chair. "That, for example, should be worth a fair amount." I picked up a small painting in a standing frame. It was a Renoir. "Turn it over," he said. The reverse framed a Degas. In a way I was sorry to have to turn him down.

Father Balogh's was not the only new party to emerge for the August 1947 elections. The Smallholders being completely fragmented, those who had composed its 1945 57-per-cent majority now undertook action in other parties. In place of the five parties which had contested the 1945 elections, ten appeared on the ballot in 1947. Sulyok's Freedom Party was by now forcibly disbanded, an example intended to be menacing to those who would attempt the same maneuver of rallying the broken majority into a cohesive unit. Nevertheless, the attempt was made. The problem revolved around the necessary authorization to form a political party. In addition to the four coalition parties, such authorizations were already held, since 1945, by the Catholics—the Democratic People's Party—and by a small, intellectual and liberal group called the Civic Democratic Party. The latter was composed of followers of Karoly Rassay, a perennial prewar oppositionist, a man of great personal influence, and probably Hungary's soundest politician, who had himself been inactive since the end of the war.

I arranged to have a talk with Rassay. His party was taking advantage of its authorization, but he himself was abstaining from the campaign. In the confused situation I feared too many splinter parties, and Rassay, so widely respected, offered a rallying point for a broad spectrum of non-Communist opinion. A man of great charm, he heard me out politely. Then he came to the point. "Very well. Let us suppose that I get out in the square on my soapbox. I even draw a good crowd. So much the worse for them. For what can you do when either the Russians or the AVO come and cart me off to prison? For that is surely what will happen. Would you be able to save me?"

I answered that that would depend entirely on the circumstances. Rassay laughed. "Even that is not the point," he said. "Let us suppose that the circumstances were such that you could save me personally. What could you do to save all those who had gathered in that good crowd to hear me on my soapbox? They are the ones who would need saving, more than just one man. And there, I fear, you would be quite unable to do anything." An irrefutable argument.

I knew that Rassay was neither a coward nor a defeatist, and certainly no fool. "I assume, however," I asked him, "that we are speaking of certain personal situations—that you do not mean to say that no one should contest this election?" He smiled for just a moment, then was silent. Finally, quietly, he said, "No, I do not mean to say that." We parted, I feeling certain that Rassay's inaction ever since the war was the result of Soviet fear of his potential popularity and a consequent direct order to him to retire.

I had, shortly after my return from Washington, contacted Anna, the agent whose name had been given to me by Headquarters as a reliable source on Church matters. (It should be clearly understood that my interest in Church matters had nothing to do with religious doctrine or sentiment; it was concerned solely with the existence in Hungary of a vital political issue of Church-State relations and with the Roman Church as a European political institution. The same applies to my comments on Church personalities and policies.) Anna was a woman of outstanding character and great decency; nevertheless, I found her a bit fanatic. She was a Monarchist—not surprising in a country which had, until only two years before, been a Catholic monarchy for 1,000 years. To her, her religion and the Hungarian State were both bound up in the person of Cardinal Mindszenty, Primate of Hungary. She was part of a group who, selflessly and in ancient loyalty, gave of themselves and their remaining property to support the Cardinal in his role of unyielding last line of resistance to change.

It does not diminish the Cardinal's stature as a religious symbol, or the tragedy of his fate as a victim of wanton violence, to state that as a political figure he was unfortunately inept. Once, during the Paris Peace Conference, when the United States was laboring with little support to soften the harsh terms being imposed on Hungary, the Cardinal made a very strong public speech denouncing all of the claims of Hungary's neighbors against her. Mark had occasion at the time to talk with the Cardinal. On instructions from our Delegation at Paris, he pointed out the practical difficulties confronting us in our efforts for Hungary and asked the Cardinal what, in his opinion, posed the greatest danger for Hungary's

future welfare among three particularly severe demands being
pressed at Paris. The eyes flashed, studiedly graceful and impressive hands swept in great arcs, as the oracular voice intoned the
musical syllables. His priestly interpreter turned to Mark, speaking
with utmost softness and respect: "His Eminence speaks with the
moral authority and philosophy of the Holy Church. He says only
a cheap politician can answer your question."

From Anna it became clear that the Cardinal was at odds with
his own Bench of Bishops, who by and large in political matters
sought a less provocative and more liberal position in Church-State
relations. At the other end of the spectrum, the Jesuits pressed and
maneuvered for a radical policy which would permit them to co-
operate with the Communists. The issue at stake was which group
would control the Democratic People's Party—the Roman Catholic political arm which sought nonetheless to include Protestants
within its ranks, on the model of the predominantly but not exclusively Catholic Christian Democratic Parties of Western Europe.

In late July Mark suggested I talk with the Jesuits, who had
approached him. The arrangements for the meeting suggested that
I was dealing with an organization which knew my business better
than I did. I was instructed to wait on a corner at a certain hour; a
car passed, circled the block, and stopped to pick me up. The
driver mentioned my name, motioned me into the car, and, without a further word, drove off by a circuitous route to a walled
compound set in a forest in the hills of Buda. The security precautions were no less strict than those for the Vatican Secretariat of
State itself—without the Swiss Guards, of course. The only trouble
was that I knew from Edmund that this group was badly infiltrated
by Division Three of the AVO. This sharply limited what I could
say, but I was nonetheless curious to hear what would be said to
me.

I was received by two Jesuit fathers, who were courteous but
forceful in their discussion. (Hindsight touches this conversation
with stark irony: one priest was to end up in the AVO prisons; the
other—like Father Balogh—was to be defrocked and ultimately
excommunicated. God and Caesar are not everywhere easily rec-
onciled in our age.) They began by showing documents which they
claimed were proof of Papal support of their work. They criticized
all past non-Communist policy in Hungary and stated that their
projects provided a realistic answer to the problem of Soviet occupation and Communist domination. They were two: the Demo-

cratic People's Party, and a broad and vigorous youth program. They emphasized the latter most strongly, pointing out that they had the Minister of the Interior's permission for their program. Then they stressed their need for funds—which they hoped the United States would provide. Their program was summed up in the phrase which both repeated to me at frequent intervals: "We can create and maintain a Christian society in a Communist state." (This idea is still not entirely dead in the political debates within the Society of Jesus and receives its strongest current support, in various versions, from French Jesuits and, astoundingly enough, Spanish Jesuits who are interested in avenues for the exercise of Spanish national influence in Europe.)

My hosts' sure conviction of their capabilities in this regard left no room whatsoever for argument. Since I could not be certain but what my remarks would be promptly available to the AVO and the Soviets I had no desire in any case to argue. I therefore said that it would be quite impossible for the United States Government to assist any political party, since this would constitute an impermissible interference in Hungarian affairs. To this they responded that they could probably manage so far as the party was concerned, and they appreciated my view. But the youth organizations, they stressed, were the heart of their program and, they believed, the real answer to the Hungarian future. I suggested that this was surely a matter for the Church itself to aid, and I mentioned their assurances of Papal support. "The demands on the Holy Father are great," answered one. I did not mention that I knew that their difficulties with the Cardinal were blocking financial aid for them from both Rome and the Hungarian Bishops. I instead assured them that I would certainly see that the appropriate authorities were informed of their views and work, but that they would surely understand that in the United States the separation of Church and State forbade Government support for the social or religious activities of any denomination. The atmosphere grew frigid, and I was escorted out.

Within a short period Istvan Barankovics emerged as the leader of the Democratic People's Party. He was grudgingly accepted by the Cardinal, more warmly viewed by the Jesuits. A vastly cultivated man, of philosophical bent, Barankovics was essentially a compromise solution, but in spirit he was closer to the Jesuits. Nonetheless, as the election approached even Anna waxed enthusiastic about him and the party.

What with political conversations, a continuing flow of reports, encoding and decoding, the mechanics of clandestine meetings— mostly at night—and endeavoring to spend the necessary time at the Military Mission in support of my cover, I was not blessed these days with much leisure. Guy was wasting no time either. About three weeks after our last talk he informed me he was ready to operate. From his Police days he had found three unmetered-taxi drivers in Budapest on whom he knew he could count. In towns near, but not on the border, and in the general region of his farm, he had found three more. At a point midway between Budapest and the border he had established a safe house—the property of a local priest. The Budapest cars would take our passengers to the priest's house. There they would be picked up by the local taxis and taken to Guy's farm. In this way the suspicion which would attach to a Budapest car wandering near the border was averted, and the rural cars were spared the long absences from their towns which might also have aroused comment. Furthermore, a reserve of three drivers at each end would avoid using the same car too often, plus insuring that one would be available when needed.

Ideally, the trip could be done in about five hours, allowing for back roads and with no delay at the midpoint. However, it was preferable to have a delay of maybe twelve hours at the midpoint to avoid suspiciously frequent traffic at the priest's house. There was also the problem of notifying the rural drivers. Guy declined to use the telephone and relied instead on the mails, using a set of prearranged phrases. It increased the travel time to as much as three days, but it was secure.

In addition, Guy would visit his farm regularly to obtain information in the neighborhood about the border patrols, their habits and general state of watchfulness. It was not necessary for Guy to be at the farm to assist those escaping; he had a caretaker at the farm in whom he had full confidence who would guide them to the crossing point at a safe time. However, Guy also planned to secure alternative crossing points; he had no desire for his farm to be under suspicion when it came time to use it himself. To avoid possible compromise of the facilities across the border, the names, addresses, and passwords of Hugh's agents in the Austrian border towns would be given by me, never in writing, to the refugees.

Guy beamed with genuine professional pleasure as he outlined all this to me. I felt a pleasurable excitement myself. We soon discovered, however, that we had overlooked one important item.

In the first two weeks we sent out eleven persons, made up of three deputies of the defunct Freedom Party, whose immunity had been canceled by the dissolution of Parliament in preparation for the new elections and who knew that arrest was a matter of days, their wives and children, plus a Rumanian girl, known to Mark, who had escaped from Bucharest on the Jewish underground, but had been discovered by the AJDC in Budapest to be non-Jewish and refused further help. In each case we came up against our oversight.

It was that we had no way of knowing whether the escape was successful until Guy made his next trip to his farm, or I made mine to Vienna. Hugh had no secure communications with me in Budapest, nor any right to communicate with Mark, and the Colonel in Vienna, who could have communicated with me via Peter in Switzerland—a roundabout procedure—had no contact with Hugh, who was the only one to know whether or not the refugees had arrived. Telephone calls between Vienna and Budapest, saying "The package has arrived," would be absurd. At the same time Guy wanted no communications from the rural drivers direct to him, either by mail or telephone, since it would link him to them in case of surveillance. Nor did he want his caretaker corresponding more than usually with him, and in any event that could involve as much as five or six days between the time a car left Budapest and the word was finally received by Guy. There was nothing for us to do but sweat the time out, Guy scanning the papers every day for the announcement of an arrest of persons trying to escape across the Austrian border. It was nerve-wracking; I became an almost daily visitor to the bar where Helen, the cut-out, worked, to reassure myself that there was no disastrous news.

The anti-Communist Socialists were having great difficulties in preparing for the elections. I had one further meeting with Karoly Peyer and the others in his group. They knew perfectly well that they were worse anathema to the Communists than Nazis or the most reactionary landowner. They were fully aware that the most violent means would be used against them. Nevertheless, they were willing to enter the fight. Their theory was that by forming an Independent Socialist Party they would, given half a fair chance in the elections, break the Communist grip on organized labor and destroy the fraudulent claim of the Communists and their Socialist sycophants to a monopoly in speaking for the workers. They also hoped that in so doing they would mitigate the American anti-

Socialist prejudice and convey an authoritative warning to the Western European Socialist parties of the dangers of the Popular Front tactic. They asked me for no help of any kind. Indeed, in their difficulties I could have been of no help.

After breaking with the Szakasits leadership of the party, by means of a manifesto, Peyer and his followers had been refused authorization to form an Independent Socialist Party. Accordingly, Peyer had formed an alliance with Bela Zsolt, the leader of the Civic Democratic Party which already had an authorization since the days of Debrecen. They were now called the Radical Party, and Peyer and other Socialist leaders were running on that ticket, hoping that their personal popularity among the workers would counterbalance the lack of a Socialist label. (The Hungarian workers understood the maneuver; the slogan of "the solidarity of the working class" continued, however, to bemuse Western Socialist theoreticians, and for years Peyer's action was the subject of acrimonious disagreement in the Socialist International. Even Anna Kethly, a latecomer to the Socialist fight against Communism, but for which she spent time in prison, came out to Vienna in 1956 as a Minister of State and emissary of the Imre Nagy Revolutionary Government, still denouncing Peyer's 1947 "betrayal of the working class.")

It was only after the elections that Sam spoke to me on behalf of the Independent Socialists' leadership. He said that they had decided it would eventually be necessary to send an emissary to the West, and he asked if I could assist his escape. I assured him that I would do so, and asked who it would be. "I don't know," he answered. "They'll pick one from among themselves. The others will stay." And so they did, at heavy cost.

Paul meanwhile had left the Smallholders Party and joined in forming the Independent Party. This group was led by Zoltan Pfeiffer, a lawyer, former Undersecretary in the Justice Ministry and one of the principal Smallholder leaders in the anti-German Resistance. Pfeiffer, a man of outstanding courage and toughness, had acted as Bela Kovacs's lawyer up to the moment of his arrest by the Russians. It was the hope of the Independence Party leaders to re-create in effect the Smallholders Party and its majority, under a new name—leaving the name of Smallholders to the now servile group running that party. In an open political fight such hopes would have been subject to serious discounting by the ability of Father Balogh's, Barankovics's, and Zsolt's parties to appeal to the same elements. This was, of course, a major element in the Communists' tolerance of Zsolt, their encouragement of Barankovics, and their pressure on Balogh.

But as if this were not enough, the Communist-drafted election law, rammed through Parliament by threats and bribery, provided that 3,000 signatures were required from each district in which a new party wanted to run a candidate. The four non-coalition parties were therefore forced to compete against each other not only in the elections themselves, but for even the number of constituencies in which they would stand. (There were two additional parties in this same position, other than the four mentioned here, but they were fractional and of no numerical importance.)

Notwithstanding these odds, the Independence Party fought on. Their success was such that the Communists began to resort to the strong-arm tactics they had used against the Freedom Party. In that case they had sent squads of thugs to break up the offices of the party—with the police standing by under orders to arrest, when the thugs had left, the surviving party officers and employees for riot and disturbance of the peace. With the Independence Party the warning was even more direct. Paul reached me through Jane one night in August, some ten days before the elections. We met by the Coronation Church. As we looked out over the lights of the city, with the smooth mass of the Danube flowing past, Paul's story turned the warm summer night into a shroud for evil.

Paul had been with Pfeiffer on a speaking tour along the left bank of the Danube in the villages to the south of Budapest. In one village Pfeiffer was addressing an orderly and attentive crowd when two truckloads of men drove into the square. The men clambered out and pushed through the crowd, shouting about "fascists," and then assaulted the platform. Pfeiffer had been beaten into unconsciousness with bicycle chains; Paul had a severe gash in his left cheek and was badly bruised and sprained; one man had several broken ribs. Paul recognized one of the leaders as an AVO agent. With the speakers silenced and the crowd dispersed, the thugs departed. Paul had brought Pfeiffer and the others back to Budapest—Pfeiffer's courageous wife insisting that he be kept in their apartment, which was also party headquarters, as being safer for him than a hospital.

As if all of this were not enough, the Communists had stacked the cards even more in their favor, leaving nothing to chance. Two days before the election Edmund sent me a report which events proved absolutely and unfortunately accurate.

As long before as October 1946, the AVO had received orders to prepare a list of potential opposition within the country. These were specified to be: former aristocrats, former politicians, former landowners, former Army officers, "B"-List personnel (those discharged from state employ in 1946 ostensibly for economy reasons), those who "spoke against democracy," "Right-wing" Socialists (i.e., followers of Peyer), "deviationist" Communists, former Nazis and members of the German Volksbund. (The last two were *pro forma:* former Nazis belonging to the Communist Party were excluded, and members of the Volksbund had already, on Soviet instructions, been ordered deported to Germany.) By the summer of 1947 this list contained 1,160,000 names.

At the same time, the new election law authorized the Minister of the Interior to draw up new election lists, specifying several indisputable categories for disfranchisement—such as former Nazis, persons deprived of civil rights for criminal reasons, etc. Rajk's list of 1,160,000 names was sent to all the Communist district headquarters in the country, with instructions to challenge any voter on election day whose name was on the list. Meanwhile, the Minister of the Interior's official new list of qualified voters was published. The list of those qualified to vote did not, of course, show how many were disfranchised. The number, however, was exactly 1,160,000—out of an electorate of 5,000,000. (Among these were 168,000 "Right-wing" Socialists and more than half a million persons who had voted for the Smallholders in 1945.)

Not content with this, the election law also provided for absentee voting in the sense that a voter was not required to cast his ballot in his own district. However, in order to vote outside of his district, an elector had to possess an authorizing certificate, known as a "blue card." The AVO itself printed these, in the number of 750,000. These were then secretly distributed to local Communist Party sections—minus 150,000 which were, by secret agreement, given to the National Peasant Party's pro-Communist leadership. Not many ordinary citizens required a "blue card"—the election was on a Sunday—but those who did, for legitimate reasons, found them difficult to obtain. The Communists, on the other hand, rallied all the transport at their command—not inconsiderable—and truck- and busloads of Party henchmen went around the country, voting not just twice, but again and again, mostly, of course, in Communist districts.

On Sunday, August 31, the farce was enacted. Mark told me that all morning the American Legation—which had sent teams around the entire country to observe the proceedings—was deluged with calls from protesting Hungarian citizens. He had just received a call from a well-known and rather reserved lawyer, who spluttered in outrage that he had been disfranchised for "prostitution," when several British diplomatic observers trooped in and announced that they had visited four or five polling places, and never had they seen a more "orderly, well-conducted, and honest election." The senior Britisher wanted the American Minister to report jointly with him in this vein. The American Minister calmly suggested they wait until the election was over.

The Government figures were, to put it mildly, interesting. The Communist Party emerged as the largest single party, with 22 per cent of the votes. The Socialists dropped from their 1945 18 per cent to 15 per cent. The Smallholders dropped from their 1945 57 per cent to 15 per cent. The National Peasants, with their share of the "blue cards," stood still at 8 per cent. Barankovics's Democratic People's Party—with Church backing—obtained 16 per cent. Pfeiffer and his Independence Party took 14 per cent. Father Balogh's party had 5 per cent and Zsolt's Radical Party, on which ticket Peyer ran, obtained 2 per cent. The splinter parties accounted for the remaining 3 per cent. Even these fraudulent official figures showed that 40 per cent of the country voted against the coalition; 63 per cent voted against the Communist-Socialist combination. But the figures are, of course, meaningless; to give them any validity it would be necessary to take account of over a million disfranchised voters and of 750,000 votes cast no one knows how many times over.

The only figure which was meaningful was the Communists' own secret official estimate of their real vote. Edmund reported it to me from a source in Division One of the AVO ten days after the election. It was 7 per cent.

We had suffered defeat, all right. But its bitterness was diluted with the honor and colored with the courage of several millions of Hungarians.

CHAPTER VI

The President's Decision

The results fraudulently produced by the Communists from the 1947 Hungarian elections were cleverly conceived and just as cleverly exploited. Stalin was temperamentally susceptible to one serious tactical error—as Lenin had long before noted: he was prone to violate the rule that it is not always advantageous to take immediately all that is within your potential grasp. He was to demonstrate this failing six months later in seizing Czechoslovakia, which finally stirred the West to some sense of danger. In Hungary, however, whether because they realized that the rebuff to the Soviets of the 1945 elections could not be erased in a single stroke, or because more astute counsel prevailed, the Communists avoided the appearance of an overt seizure of power. Those who were aware of the fraud in the elections were, of course, stunned. But as no politician could safely stand up and publicly denounce the elections for what they were—Pfeiffer was to try, and to pay, for it—the masses were unaware of the vast extent of the fraud.

The Communists continued the comedy of the coalition, modestly nominating a Smallholder puppet as Prime Minister. For themselves, in the Cabinet, they added only the Foreign Ministry. The real power in the Foreign Ministry became the Communist Director of Political Affairs, György Heltai, an educated, cultivated, and intelligent man. (Imprisoned later as a "Titoist," Heltai escaped during the 1956 Revolution and now directs the "Imre Nagy Institute" in Brussels, a study and research center for "national communism.")[1] These changes in the Foreign Ministry were most welcome from the point of view of my network, since Sara, the agent recruited by George before his departure, was a trusted employee in the Political Department.

Meetings with Sara were difficult. She didn't dare use the telephone, and to have been seen together would have been fatal. Furthermore, she was wary of long or unusual absences from her normal routine. We therefore met by prearrangement at various street addresses and always after dark. These addresses were reasonably close to her normal route from work to home, or from home to evening lectures she would have to attend. Having ascertained that I was not followed, I would drive early to a point near the rendezvous, watching her arrival to see that she was not being followed. If all was clear, we would both get in the car, and while driving to a point near her next stop, she would give me oral reports. We never had more than fifteen minutes, but they were well worth it. On one occasion she had full information on the use being made by the Communists of the Hungarian Legation in Bern for espionage purposes, supplemented by the interesting information that the Soviets in Switzerland were using the Hungarian couriers for transmission of their own material. This information I sent to both Washington and to Peter in Switzerland; as the Hungarian couriers passed through the American Zone of Austria en route from Bern to Budapest, the information turned out to be of great practical value.

On the political scene, the seeming Communist moderation had the effect of lulling some of the opposition politicians into the belief that they would survive. Such hopes once again operated to prevent the kind of unity which alone offered any hope of saving the situation. The Communists could therefore continue their tactics of destroying the opposition piecemeal. For his temerity in questioning the elections, Pfeiffer and his Independence Party were the first targets for liquidation.

On September 20 Edmund reported to me that the AVO had received orders to visit all those persons who had signed the Independence Party's election petitions in the various districts. This involved thousands of persons, but it was done by the end of September. Under AVO threats, 70 per cent of the signers of the petitions withdrew their signatures. The Communists convoked a Parliamentary Committee, and the procedure was begun to declare all votes for the Independence Party null and void, and dissolve the party.

What was needed now was an authoritative voice to speak out honestly on the subject of the elections. Zoltan Tildy, the President of the Republic, was obliged by the Communists to make a public statement expressing his satisfaction with the conduct of the elections and their results. Any lesser voice could be calumniated and silenced, so, on hearing Tildy's statement, I concluded that was that. Or so I thought.

Two days later Mark, with ill-concealed glee, asked me to see Dr. Viktor Csornoky, the President's son-in-law. Csornoky had a not too savory reputation as a black-marketeer and general profiteer from his father-in-law's high position. He came to my apartment, quite openly, and notwithstanding his reputation I found him likable. He was of an ebullient nature and obviously enjoying his vicarious importance. He got to the point quickly. "The President," he said, "wishes to escape the country. Once safely in the West, he will make a statement finishing with these ridiculous elections once and for all. What can you do for us?" I was flabbergasted—but I felt an instant excitement. Tildy's role in the past two years could not easily be forgiven or forgotten, but the fact was that he was the President of Hungary. This single gesture, if it could be pulled off successfully, would compensate for at least some of his errors; its international effect would be tremendous.

"Why has the President already endorsed the elections?" I inquired. Csornoky shrugged. "He was forced to by threats," he said. "You know as well as I do that he is not a completely free agent." This was an understatement, and I refrained from mentioning that the chief hold on Tildy was the AVO's dossiers on the financial doings of both his son and son-in-law. "It is not an easy operation," I said. "Are you absolutely sure the President is firmly decided on this course?"

"Absolutely," said Csornoky. He then handed me a list of eleven names, including the President's. "These persons must accompany the President," he said. The list included what appeared to me to be all conceivable family connections of the President and his wife. "How much time can you give me?" I asked Csornoky. "Whatever you need to insure success," he answered. "But the President is extremely anxious that it should be done as soon as possible. He wishes to serve the country in this, and the sooner he can speak out in the West, the greater will be the international political impact." He then gave me some ideas of his own on technique, including his thought that the operation would be much more practicable from the President's country residence at Lake Balaton—a very long but narrow body of water—rather than from the city of Budapest. It occurred to me that if he thought so, probably the President's AVO Division Fifteen "bodyguards" thought so too. "Give me two weeks," I said. "And ask the President to spend several days at

Lake Balaton during the last ten days of that period." Csornoky agreed and said he would call on me again in exactly two weeks.

That night I dropped in to see Helen to tell her that I must see Guy the next day. The prospects of this operation both frightened and exhilarated me. Guy's initial reaction was one of disgust. "I wouldn't lift a finger to save any of them, and particularly not Tildy," he answered sourly after I told him of Csornoky's request. "It's not a question of saving Tildy," I reminded him. "The problem is to put the President of Hungary in a safe place where he can render the only valuable service to the nation left to him." Guy thought for a while. From the slow change of expression on his face I could see him being captured by the challenge of the thing. "Let's do it," he said. "It'll really be a good one." He decided to spend the next few days examining the possibilities of running the operation from Budapest, give me his conclusions from that, and then go to Lake Balaton for ten days. "I need a holiday," he said.

For once my Headquarters reacted with something approaching enthusiasm and displayed atypical restraint in not demanding full details of my scheme for the President's escape. As if to compensate for this, however, they sent a message insisting that the situation for Paul had become too dangerous and that I send him out of the country immediately. I sent this message to Paul through Jane, who promptly brought back the terse reply that he was holding to our agreement that he would tell me when he felt it necessary to leave. Jane left no doubt in my mind that Paul found the message offensive, and considered himself a better judge of his situation than Washington, with which I was inclined to agree. My reply, conveying this idea, produced a prompt rejoinder. "Failure to insure Paul's safety will be on your personal responsibility," the message kindly read. It was a comforting thought.

In a few days Guy brought the results of his survey of the Presidential Palace in Budapest. "It's out of the question," he said. "He's in there like a cigar in its wrapper. We'd never get him out, let alone more than three blocks away before the entire AVO would be on us. If we had him go to dinner out in Buda it would be even worse. That brigade of bodyguards he travels with surround him even more out than in." He then went off to Lake Balaton, about which he was more optimistic.

Two days later I was having a drink at my apartment with a correspondent of one of America's best-known publications, when suddenly Csornoky appeared at my door, unannounced and cheerful as ever. I motioned that I had someone with me, at which he nonetheless entered, introduced himself, and was immediately in lively conversation. Csornoky was no conspirator, for which he would ultimately pay dearly. To my consternation, in the midst of general conversation—I can only assume he felt reassured that my other guest was an American and felt this to be security enough—Csornoky handed me another list. "These three names must be added to those I gave you," he said. "They are people who have served my father-in-law well, and we cannot leave them behind." I tried to appear to attach small importance to the matter, but Csornoky went on. "As you asked, my father-in-law will spend the next four days at the lake. I will be there too, to look over the matter. I still believe it must be done from there." I agreed perfunctorily. After some further conversation, in which Csornoky let no opportunity go by to stress to my guest that his father-in-law was the President, he left.

My correspondent friend turned to me laughing. "So the President's taking it on the lam. What a nice story that is." This man had been an intelligence officer of no small accomplishments during the war; I decided that some frankness was the best policy. Giving him no details, I told him that he had stumbled on something about the importance of which he could have no doubt, and that he was under no circumstances to use this information in any way. I warned him that lives were involved, and United States Government interest as well. He assured me categorically that he would behave as though he had heard nothing. He left for the West the next day. It was not good, but it seemed the best possible in the circumstances, and certainly superior to a denial on my part followed by the correspondent's snooping about after a possible story.

At this point, the departure of the Navy's scientists, which had been bubbling along for two months, suddenly came to a boil. At their repeated requests, I had gradually disbursed the entire $5,000 to them. Some of this had been used for bribes to obtain passports, and they had assured me they would be ready to leave early in the week during which Guy was at Lake Balaton. Since they were leaving legally, I had arranged passage for them on the American military airplane which flew regularly between Vienna and Budapest, Bucharest, and Sofia. The day before their scheduled departure, two of the scientists came to see me. The AVO had categorically refused a passport for one of the wives.

The dilemma they posed was an unhappy one. The husband

refused to leave without his wife. The work of the entire group could not go forward with one member missing. And those with passports were certain they would be revoked or discovered to be invalid if they delayed their departure any longer. Guy was at Lake Balaton and would not be back for a week. Strictly speaking, I should not personally become involved in any operation while the President's escape was still pending. Nevertheless, for all I knew, the failure of these scientists to leave Soviet-controlled territory might ultimately be an even greater blow to Western security.

I told the husband that his wife must come to my apartment immediately after dark, but without having been seen either leaving her own home or en route to me. He was to spend his last night at home, and throughout the evening he was to talk as much as possible, giving his neighbors the impression that he was not alone. In the morning he was to have a tearful farewell at the door of his apartment, taking care that no one was to see that he was crying to an empty foyer. Meanwhile, his wife would have to spend the night in a box—but the box would be on the airplane with them in the morning. To my surprise the husband seemed delighted at the prospect of his forthcoming dramatic performance, and even promised a passable imitation of his wife's voice.

I watched the wife's arrival that evening on the Var—she had walked the entire distance and was not followed. I could only take her word that no one had seen her leave her home. Fortunately, she turned out to be petite. From my collection of crates I chose one that gave her room to turn from side to side, but not long enough to stretch to her full length. She was due for a rough fifteen hours, but she seemed to find that preferable to the prospect of years before her without her husband. I padded the crate with blankets and pillows to muffle the sounds of her moving and to make it slightly more comfortable. The joints of the crate were not quite flush, so she would have some air. I hammered down the top, stenciled "Fragile" and "U.S. Government Property" all over the crate, and addressed it to "The American Legation, Vienna." A muffled voice from inside said "Eet ees quite comfor-table." Fifteen minutes later a truck from the Motor Pool drove up, as I had ordered, and two GIs loaded the case aboard. I noted it was fragile and said, "Don't kick that around too much in the garage to-night."

"Nah," one of them answered. "It'll stay on the truck. The rest of this stuff is going on the same plane." That was something at least. It was going to be a long night for both husband and wife, but to have had the truck pick the crate up in the morning and go straight to the airport would have been too revealing, and any movement of such a crate later in the night would have aroused the suspicions of the Hungarian guards who stood by the Military Garage. Some American soldiers in Bucharest had pulled the same trick only a month before with three Rumanians; it had worked, but one week later the Soviet Command had requested by name the return of the three Rumanians who had left illegally on the American aircraft. I hoped the Soviets would assume we wouldn't be so stupid as to try the same trick again so soon.

The next morning, after the plane's departure, I dropped in to see Mark. I knew he had been out at the airport, and he knew that I had arranged the departures of the scientists. He gave me a very fishy look.

"Plane get off all right?" I queried him.

"It did," he said. "Took off right over my jangled nerves."

I looked at him.

"The military don't send cases marked 'Fragile' to the American Legation in Vienna. They send them to the military. But fortunately the Hungarian guards at the airport don't know that and the Russians can't read." He sighed.

"I thought it was more diplomatic that way," I said.

"Well, we will now hope and pray," he rejoined.

We never heard a word about it from either Soviets or Hungarians. But I heard from the Navy. Several weeks later when I was in Vienna Hugh introduced me to probably the most worried-looking Lieutenant-Commander I had ever seen. "Look," he said. "We appreciate all you did, and all that, but that $5,000 was supposed to get those people all the way to the *United States*! You blew all that money just getting them to Vienna. I can never face the Bureau of Accounts." I signed an affidavit certifying that the money had been properly and necessarily disbursed in Budapest and that, without that having been done, there would have been no scientists for the Navy. But I was far from pleased with myself. The operation had been sloppy, risky, and amateurish. Such methods could not be permitted with the President.

Guy returned the following week from Lake Balaton. "This is going to be very tough," he said, "but it can be done." He outlined his plan. It was complex and required split-second timing, but it was feasible. The only limitation was that with the very best of luck it could work for no more than eight people. It was quite impossible to approach the Presidential villa from the land side. The property had a considerable shoreline, however, and the only possible access was thus from the lake. This would involve crossing in boats, taking aboard the family at separate points along the property's lakefront, recrossing the lake to rendezvous points, and probably even traveling in separate groups to the frontier. This meant automobiles, boats, safe houses, and, most importantly, men. Guy was sure of only a sufficient number of all four to permit taking care of eight persons. To involve more men would risk a leak; to utilize more cars and boats would make the operation physically too conspicuous and unwieldy. Besides, eight people would take care of the immediate family.

I passed this information to Csornoky. His reaction was to express serious doubt that his father-in-law would be able to go with any lesser number than the fourteen he had already specified. Personally I felt him to be rather petulant about the matter. I explained the physical difficulties; and then I emphasized the national interest which was at stake. Csornoky promised only to consult the President and let me know as soon as possible. I spoke again with Guy about it. He was adamant and refused categorically to risk the enterprise with more than eight persons. His point was certainly valid: it was simply that with any larger number some people were certain to be caught; in the confusion he would not be able to guarantee that the President himself would not be among the unlucky ones. I began to worry. Tildy was not a man in whom I had had much faith up to now; if he ran true to form he would make the wrong decision again. But there was always the fact that in crisis men often rise above their usual form.

The next blow fell from an unexpected quarter. My correspondent friend's publication came out in America with a report that the President of Hungary was making plans to escape, in order to denounce the Communist frauds in the August elections. It wasn't even one of those "it is rumored" stories; it was all stated as fact, thereby showing how omniscient this particular journal was and giving the reader, safe at home, the sensation, cheap but so flattering, of being "on the inside."[2] In this case I was sure that no matter how cheap the sensation, the cost would be high. (My bitterness at this development is not necessarily at odds with my conclusions in Part I about the necessity to hide operations from the press as well as the public and the opposition. This correspondent was the recipient of a clearly labeled official confidence which he had given his word not to violate.)

The word spread quickly and was noted in Parliament. I briefly had the odd impression that I could sense the feelings of the entire country: the great majority of the population quietly—and hope-fully—watching to see if it would be true; the Communists maneu-vering quickly but silently to insure that it would not come true.

I did not expect to see Csornoky again. To my surprise he came to see me about a week later. His father-in-law was due to speak to the nation by radio that evening, and Csornoky arrived just as the President started to speak. "What is he saying?" I asked him. Csornoky laughed. "He's saying that reports that he is planning to leave the country are hostile fabrications against Hungarian de-mocracy; that the elections were honest and reassuring for the future of the country, and he stands proudly at his post to guide the nation to even greater democratic achievements," he replied. Then, as the President still orated on, Csornoky said, "Now you will understand that my father-in-law is more than ever anxious to leave—and quickly."

I understood nothing of the kind; here the danger had quin-tupled, but that seemed to make no difference. Csornoky contin-ued, "However, he cannot abandon those near to him and loyal to him to the fate that would surely come to them if left behind. Therefore, I must insist that we go as fourteen persons." This made no sense at all to me. I told Csornoky that the danger was now infinitely greater, and he should be talking about fewer persons rather than more. The danger and practical risks seemed to count not at all with him, nor was he really in the least disturbed by the American publication of Tildy's intentions. It was plain that he was living in some kind of dream world and felt no pressing need to adapt to reality; it was as though he felt himself in command of events. "I am sorry," I said. "Eight will be difficult enough, but I cannot take the responsibility for any more." Csornoky did not appear overly disturbed; he simply remained firm. "We are a very close family," he said. "It must be fourteen or not at all." With that he left. He had little more than a year to live.

(President Tildy stayed in Hungary. Some months later Csornoky was appointed Minister to Egypt. While there, ignoring his surveillance by his own staff, he made blatant attempts to get in touch with Western intelligence organizations. Summoned to re-turn to Budapest for consultation, Csornoky returned, was arrested, tried, and hanged. Tildy was obliged to resign the Presidency, which went to the Socialist Szakasits, who had merged his party with the Communists. During the Revolution in 1956, Tildy, his father-in-law killed by the Nazis and his son-in-law by the Communists, emerged as a Minister of State in the Imre Nagy Government. He is reported to have behaved courageously throughout, refusing to leave the Parliament building during the Soviet attack on the night of November 4 until all other members of the Government and its loyal employees had gotten away. There followed arrest, imprisonment, and limited detention until his death in 1961.)

1. Heltai came to the United States in the mid-1960's, initially to Columbia University, where he began by teaching history (and was somewhat taken aback by the educational attainments of American university students—twenty years before this became a matter of national concern and debate in the United States). He nevertheless followed an academic career, becoming Professor of History at Charleston College, Charleston, South Carolina.

2. *Time.*

CHAPTER VII

Escape

Except for Guy's ten-day absence at Lake Balaton, the escape chain had been operating smoothly. With members of Parliament the matter was fairly simple: as the Communists sliced away at the opposition, they would ask for waiving of the Parliamentary immunity of the various legislators under attack; between the request and the Immunities Committee's action—always as requested—

there was usually a lapse of two or three days. During this period the menaced deputy had to be moved out. At first this was not so difficult, but as more and more escapes occurred during this delay, the AVO began surveillance of their intended victims, even before the orders for arrest had been issued. The situation was further complicated by the understandable desire of deputies who planned to escape to make a final fiery speech in Parliament. As this was too obvious a signal of what was afoot, I was forced to insist that many such deputies whom we were moving out either make their "swan song" unrecognizable as such or forgo altogether their chance to have the last word.

The attack against the Independence Party was successful in early October, and then began the process of lifting the immunity of the various Independence deputies. On October 14 Pfeiffer himself, with his wife and five-year-old daughter, had to flee. He was being closely watched, but we managed successfully. Hugh told me later that Pfeiffer's escape was even complicated in Vienna, thanks to the Americans themselves. Pfeiffer arrived in Vienna in the middle of the night; the next morning, before Hugh had been able to move him on to the American Zone of Austria, the Vienna German-language newspaper published by the American Occupation authorities printed a large photograph of Pfeiffer on the front page, saying he was rumored to be in Vienna. Hugh thereupon had to alter his plans to have Pfeiffer and his family driven to the American military airport at Tulln, an enclave in the Soviet Zone, and instead have him flown out in a small plane from a landing strip in the American sector of Vienna.

With persons other than deputies, we had to rely on either their own knowledge of their danger or such information as Edmund was able to pass out from the AVO itself. I had informed the members of the network that they would be taken out whenever they felt the moment necessary or opportune. Henry, who had been inactive for some time, had already taken advantage of the offer. But these were not the only sources of our "clients."

In October Mark sent an American businessman, the representative of one of the important American interests in Hungary, to see me. I saw this man often; he was normally a cheerful, pleasant type of executive whose chief worry was, he thought, dickering with the Soviet representative of the confiscated German minority interests in the same company. This day, however, he was all nerves. Hesitantly, almost embarrassedly, he disclosed the fact that he had received word from his colleague in Bucharest that fourteen Rumanians would arrive two days hence, in illegal flight from Rumania. These were key employees of various British and American enterprises in Rumania, and the companies had decided to try to save them. My caller's task was to arrange their escape from Hungary, and he was worried sick at the thought. Fourteen in one group was something more than we were equipped to handle, so leaving him to cope with his nerves for forty-eight hours, I told him only to come back on the morning of the second day.

Guy was taken aback at the prospect of fourteen persons, but then the challenge interested him. As a result of his trip to Balaton, he had arranged additional safe house facilities there, so he decided to try it. He gave me three different rendezvous points in Budapest for the Rumanians for the day of their arrival. I gave these instructions to my American friend, and he gratefully resumed his normal coloration. The next night I checked with Helen, who said only— speaking for Guy—that "The lake has now become a very popular Rumanian resort."

Some days later I was lunching with Mark, and his telephone rang. He listened briefly, then looked at me and said, "I'll call you back in a few minutes." Sitting down, he said, "Now what are you up to? The Ministry of the Interior, strange to say, has just called the Legation to say that the Police in Győr are holding an American couple who were arrested near the border and who have neither money nor documents. They claim they were just touring Hungary and were supposed to go by train to Vienna tonight, but were robbed. The Ministry wants to know if we know anything about them. A Mr. and Mrs. Tompkins from Detroit. Do you know anything about them?"

I certainly didn't; an American couple "touring Hungary" at this epoch was too fantastic to be believable, and Mark knew as well as I that no such phenomenon existed. But obviously some unknowns were in trouble; whoever they were they merited a helping hand. I suggested to Mark that he tell the Ministry that he knew all about Mr. and Mrs. Tompkins, that they were distinguished American citizens, that it was an outrage to hold them under arrest after they had suffered the additional indignity of being robbed, and that he insist that the Police put them on the next train for Vienna.

Mark did so, and to our surprise the Ministry called back some hours later to report that they had released "Mr. and Mrs. Tompkins" and put them on the Vienna train.

I had to wait a week to see Guy to get the answer to this puzzle. It seemed that he had been moving the Rumanians from the lake to his farm in groups of two and four. His instructions were specific: no one was to carry either personal documents or any foreign money, and if apprehended they were to avoid disclosing, if possible, their true nationality, since Guy feared this would arouse too acute an AVO interest. "Mr. and Mrs. Tompkins" had been part of a group of four who were apprehended—fortunately not by the Border Guards, but by the Police in a routine check—in a village not far from the farm. The driver said he had merely been hired by his passengers in Györ to show them the countryside; he had been released. "Mr. and Mrs. Tompkins," having obeyed Guy's instructions, gave their story, speaking only English, and said that their companions were merely fellow travelers they had joined in Györ whom they did not know otherwise. Their companions, two Rumanian men, had unfortunately not followed Guy's instructions; they had both Rumanian documents and money and were accordingly taken to Budapest to prison. (Some months later they were expelled to Czechoslovakia and from there eventually reached the West.) "Mr. and Mrs. Tompkins," however, had put on such a good show of outraged indignation that the Police had finally telephoned to Budapest for instructions. Mark's response was so effective that the Police not only put "Mr. and Mrs. Tompkins" on the train to Vienna, but paid their fare and helped to clear them through the Austrian side of the border as well. It was a worthy and satisfying bureaucratic short circuit.

For most of the time that I had been in Budapest I had known and occasionally saw Lila, a cousin of Eugene. Herself an aristocrat, Lila was embroiled in an emotional vendetta against aristocracy which had its origins in the loss during the war of someone she loved, killed by the Germans. The tendency of many of the Hungarian aristocrats either to favor or at least not to fight the Germans had as a consequence appeared to her in an intensely personal light. She was not a Communist, but she had no objection to the Communist surgery on Hungarian society so long as it represented for her the destruction of the aristocracy. We often argued politics, in a very friendly way, for notwithstanding the force of her feelings, she was keenly intelligent and recognized the influence on her political views of her own emotional history.

During one such discussion, in October, I found her torn by contradictory feelings. She still supported the Communist program, but by now its execution had become distasteful to her. She lamented not at all the gradual destruction of the opposition parties, but she could not stomach the violence being wreaked on so many, most particularly on exactly those who had most courageously fought the Germans. I gave it as my view that this was a deliberate policy and an integral part of the system she favored, since it was aimed, not at remedying injustice in Hungary, but at rendering Hungary totally subservient to the Soviet Union. She reflected on this, obviously loath to concede the point. Nor did she. But after a considerable silence she said, "You know, I see Rajk once or twice every week." I knew she was friendly with the Minister of the Interior, but I did not know to what extent. "Yes," she went on, "I see him, and we talk, usually for an hour or so. He often tells me their plans for various people. I don't know why, but he does. So I often know who is in danger." She thought for a while longer. Then she smiled quickly. "So I will tell you when good people are in danger. Maybe you can discreetly do something about them."

I didn't press the point. I merely said, "Let me know."

This was an unexpected source of help, and as it turned out, most timely and welcome. By the end of October the campaign against the Independence Party had very nearly run its course. Paul and one or two others were still in Parliament, but the Communist aim had been achieved, and Paul's time was approaching. Meanwhile, Edmund was informed by a source in Division One of the AVO that the next on the list marked for destruction were the Socialists. The aim here was to achieve the merger of the Socialist and Communist Parties. To this end, the AVO planned to start a campaign against the Right-wing Socialists which would accuse them of conspiracy and then drag in any Left-wing Socialists who still held out against merger. Sam and Edmund, taking stock of their positions as Right-wing Socialists, Edmund's post in the AVO, and the risks of their connection with me, felt themselves seriously endangered. Lila, following her first talk with Rajk after our conversation, told me the same general story. Much as I regretted it, I told Guy we had two very valuable passengers with whom there could be no slip-ups. This was a nervous wait: the incident with the Rumanians had made us somewhat jittery, but at the end of a week Guy reported another successful operation.

In the disaster which was engulfing Hungary it was incomprehensible still to see those who felt they would succeed where others were failing. An American oil executive took me to task at this stage: "You Government people are too alarmist about this Communist thing. It's just a problem of working along with them. They need what we have so we'll be all right." Six months later, with two of his American colleagues beaten in prison and his company's properties taken over by the Hungarian Government, he hastily left the country. Some months before, an American newspaperman had expressed the view to me that American policy in Eastern Europe was "reactionary." He now returned to Hungary somewhat chastened, to replace his American predecessor who had been arrested and expelled, to find a substitute for his Hungarian stringer—who, having originally put me in touch with the Socialists, came to me for help and was taken out by Guy—and to try to arrange the release from prison of his own secretary whom he well knew to be innocent.

On November 7 I went to the Soviet reception marking the thirtieth anniversary of the Revolution. In one year so much had transpired that the Russians didn't even make an effort to be polite, but more or less ignored their American guests. I talked for a while with Istvan Barankovics, leader of the Democratic People's Party. I found him ridiculously confident and annoyingly condescending. He was now the leader of the largest opposition party and the second largest party in the nation. Far from being uneasy at such prominence, he parroted the same sure optimism which had animated the Jesuits. He even spoke of the gains he would make in the next elections. I had to laugh, but not from amusement. I do not pretend to be a prophet, but I was sure of what I said to Barankovics: "Within one year, most of us here who are neither Russian nor Communist will have fled the country, be in prison, or be dead." Barankovics laughed at my little fantasy. Less than eleven months later he was in flight to the West, his party smashed and his Cardinal facing trial.

I turned away to speak with Jozsef Kövago, the young and popular Smallholder Mayor of Budapest. He was, in contrast to Barankovics, utterly dejected; the mounting attack on the Socialists was, he knew, the signal that the end was close at hand. I told him of Barankovics's optimism. "Ridiculous," said Kövago. "Can't he see he's next?" Kövago seemed so certain of his own fate that I said to him, "If you wish to leave, I shall arrange it." He thought at length, and then he thanked me, warmly. "No," he said. "Someone has to stay." It was to be almost ten years before I saw him again. Then he had behind him eight years in prison and two weeks as Mayor of Budapest again during the 1956 Revolution. With the final Soviet attack on November 4 he this time chose exile.

Before their departure Sam and Edmund had told me that their leadership had decided to send Karoly Peyer as their representative to the West. The Communist press had by now mounted a full-scale attack on the Right-wing Socialists, and suddenly the State Prosecutor asked for the lifting of Peyer's Parliamentary immunity so that he could be arrested for plotting against the state. On November 15 his immunity was waived, but the day before—after considerable difficulty on my part in persuading the old man not to make the most fiery speech of his long career—Guy had spirited him out to Austria. The Communist press howled at Peyer's disappearance, and then reported it as officially known that Peyer was still in the country, in hiding.

Guy had been sufficiently interested in the case to accompany Peyer to the frontier himself. He had returned immediately to Budapest, and was so bemused by the Communist claims as to Peyer's whereabouts that he had gone to see his former chief Rajk, on the pretext of a friendly call. It was completely in character for Guy, and he told me of his interview with the Interior Minister with high glee. He had teased Rajk, saying that if he, Guy, were still in the Police, all these wanted persons would not be escaping so freely. Guy recounted how Rajk had leaped to his feet saying, 'We know where Peyer is. And we will have him in our hands within four days." Going to a map of Hungary, he showed Guy an area to the north blocked off in red marks. Stabbing with his forefinger, Rajk said, "He is hiding somewhere in here. But he won't escape us." Guy noted silently and comfortably that the marked area was nowhere near his farm.

I recalled Guy's coup two years later when Peyer arrived in the United States and was not permitted to land in New York. He was taken into custody and transferred immediately to Ellis Island. Apparently neither his fight nor his flight had had much effect on the American "anti-Socialist prejudice."

But another vignette of the period also showed the weakness of dogmatic judgments. During a reception at the Hungarian Parliament for some visiting American Senators and Representatives, I watched Congressman John Davis Lodge of Connecticut engage in a rather showy harangue against the Communist President of the National Assembly, Imre Nagy. No one could foresee that ten years later the Congressman's brother, as U.S. Ambassador to the United Nations, would indict the Hungarian Government before world opinion for the death of this same Imre Nagy.

Ten days after Peyer's escape Paul sent word through Jane that he was already under surveillance and that he would have to leave within three days at the maximum. I went to see Helen, to leave word that I wanted to see Guy urgently, and found that she had the same word for me from Guy. I went to Guy's apartment, where I found him with serious news. "We cannot function for at least two weeks," he said. "Perhaps even longer." I said he had to be joking, but it was perfectly clear he was not. Guy explained that three days before the AVO had arrested a British agent, a woman. She had talked, and the result was the arrest of some one hundred persons. Even simple smugglers were lying low; no one knew how much wider the AVO would drag their net. In addition, since the escape of Peyer, maximum security precautions were being taken along the entire frontier. Guy's men had passed him word they would be unable to move anyone for an indefinite period; it was his own guess that it would take about two weeks for the dust to settle.

I didn't have two weeks to risk with Paul, and I did have the responsibility for his safety fixed firmly and inescapably on me. The timing couldn't have been worse, but there was nothing to be done about that. I told Guy to keep me informed of any new developments, and went home to figure what to do. With relatively inconspicuous people it was sometimes possible, provided they had a passport, to have them openly buy a railroad ticket to Vienna and then buy a ticket to Prague under another name. While the police checked for them at the Austrian border, they could sometimes cross the Czechoslovak border without difficulty. Once in Prague, they could fly to Zurich, thereby evading the Soviet controls at the border of the American Zone of Austria. But Paul was too conspicuous, and he would be actively sought by the police for arrest the moment his Parliamentary immunity was lifted. The problem was complicated by his already being under surveillance, no doubt precisely to prevent his escape before Parliament acted on his case. I was not prepared to risk the airplane again, and in any event it was not due soon enough. There was only one solution. I would have to drive Paul myself to Austria or to Czechoslovakia.

I settled on Vienna; as Paul had no passport, his fate once in Czechoslovakia was too uncertain, and the audacity of the more dangerous route to Vienna was in its favor.

The operation could be done only under cover of my official position, undesirable as that was. I could certainly not disguise myself as a Hungarian, and in any event to have done so would have instantly closed the border to me. Any other nationality was also out of the question: I had by now a fair collection of Soviet gray passes, which was the only thing which interested the Soviet sentries along the road, and I could forge the names on them easily, but the Hungarian Border Guards would insist on my passport, and a passport was not so quickly or easily forged.

I thought at first to take Paul and his wife in the trunk of my car, a small prewar German Mercedes, but then I realized that to leave Jane behind, known as a friend of Paul's and privy to the escape arrangements, would be fatal. When I told her she would have to come as well, she agreed, but asked that Simon, his wife and baby also accompany us. As I had by now decided on a Chevrolet delivery truck belonging to the Military Mission, I agreed. With Paul's wife we were now six adults and a three-year-old infant.

At this point I had a stroke of luck. I was loath to travel the road to Vienna in full daylight, but to travel at night—even though there were fewer patrols, the border posts were more negligent, and the contents of my truck invisible—would have aroused suspicion since American trucks always made the run in the daytime. However, at almost the last minute an agreement was reached with the Hungarians over an American correspondent who had been arrested: he would be released, provided he was over the border by the following midnight. As he was being driven out in the late afternoon, I let it be known that I would personally drive a truck containing his and his family's belongings, as a way of insuring that the Hungarians kept to their agreement. It was improvised cover, but it was cover nonetheless. And it meant moving Paul a day earlier than he had planned—but that was an advantage as well.

The afternoon of the day of departure, I dropped in to see Mark and left a sealed letter with him. It contained my resignation from the Military Mission, in case something went wrong and it became necessary to disown me. I didn't tell Mark its contents, but told him only to open it if he did not hear from me in three days. I then gave him a coded message for my Headquarters, telling them what I was doing. I was certain they would receive it too late to stop me even if they wished.

As soon as it was dark I went to the garage and picked up the truck. I drove to my apartment. There, hidden behind a pile of rubble, I loaded four large cases into the truck, threw in blankets and pillows, two large tarpaulins, and rope. It was a bitterly cold night, so I put on an Army parka, in one pocket of which I carried a Walther automatic and three clips of ammunition. I had no such dramatic intention as shooting my way through a roadblock; but the AVO was capable of methods other than an overt arrest, and drunken Russian troops were not to be confused with sentries on duty.

Jane was waiting for me at the Coronation Church. We drove to a quiet street in Buda where Simon, his wife and baby waited. Then instead of continuing on out the Vienna road, I turned up a high hill just to the north of Buda. A great forested knob, the unpronounceable Harmashatarhegy—Three Border Mountain—looked out over the entire city of Budapest, to the east to the Great Hungarian Plain, and to the north as far as Slovakia. A wild expanse, it was a favorite summer picnic spot, but in late autumn and winter no one went near it. Nine years from this night it was to be the last hideout of the Revolutionary Freedom Fighters of Budapest. It was there we would meet Paul and his wife—if they had evaded surveillance. If they had not, the rendezvous might include some uninvited guests.

I arrived at the appointed spot and made a wide U-turn, with my lights full on. They caught only Paul and his wife, behind a tree. It was 8:30, as fixed, and they had made it successfully—with no baggage. It was a long and steep walk up the mountain, and it had been preceded by crossing almost the entire city on foot. Nevertheless, the precautions were worth it. Paul had lost his "shadow" while still in Pest, and his wife, leaving their house in the morning, had not been followed. In the still night ours had been the only vehicle they had heard moving on the mountain.

By the light of a flashlight the five adults and the child slipped into the crates. Paul and his wife were in one, Simon's wife and the baby, who had been drugged, were in another, and Simon and Jane in a third. I then maneuvered the crates around so that the open ends all faced in toward the center of the truck. The fourth crate I put next to the rear door, blocking the access to the others. I then covered all the crates with the tarpaulins and arranged the rope to look as though the crates were all bound and lashed down. I locked the door, got behind the wheel, started the motor, and swung back down the hill and onto the Vienna road. There were six people only a few inches from me, but I felt very, very lonely.

From Budapest to the border I drove steadily. None of the road-blocks was manned—one advantage of traveling during the dinner hour—and we scarcely saw another car on the road. I had told my passengers that when I knocked three times they could talk among themselves softly; when I knocked twice they were to maintain absolute silence. As we entered towns I would knock twice—instantly there was not a sound. Safely out in the country, where a sudden stop was no longer likely, I would give three knocks, and the voices would resume their murmur and even, occasionally, there would be a laugh. In the talking periods, even though I was not in the conversation, my queasiness would disappear and I would become calm; but in the silences I became tense and worried.

At the border point near Hegyeshalom, I knocked twice and pulled up in front of the Customs. Here again luck. The Czechoslovaks had just taken over five Hungarian villages on the south bank of the Danube opposite Bratislava—granted them by the Peace Treaty. In so doing they had cut the main Budapest-Vienna road and taken over the old Hungarian border station. This one was a mere temporary shack, with no lights in front and no facilities for examining the cars. I left the truck in the dark and went into the building. In a few minutes my papers were cleared, with barely a word, and I was back in the truck. The guards didn't even look out as I drove off.

I had no sooner knocked three times and settled down to driving than I had to quickly knock twice and pull up before the Czechoslovak occupants of the former Hungarian border station. They were very put out that I had wandered into Czechoslovakia. I blamed it all on the Hungarians. They had not yet built a new road to avoid Czechoslovak territory, and they were so lazy that the necessity for a detour from the former main road wasn't even marked. The Czechoslovaks were mollified and, berating and abusing the Hungarians, permitted me to continue on.

I explained to my "cargo" what had happened and then knocked for silence. A few miles farther on, the Austrian guards checked me through politely. I wanted to ask where the Soviet roadblocks were on this night, but, on the assumption that the Austrian border guards in the Soviet Zone were handpicked by the Soviets, refrained from showing any such interest.

Between the Austrian border and Vienna there were usually three or four roadblocks operating, but one never knew where they would be, except for the final one at Schwechat, just outside Vienna. Some five miles from the border I finally saw the first one, but there were no sentries on duty. I knocked three times and drove on.

Just when I was beginning to congratulate myself on having chosen a good night, a dim light showed ahead. I quickly knocked twice and slowed to a stop as my headlights shone on a barrier and a Russian tommy-gunner.

I rolled down my window, and he came and leaned against the side of the truck, his gun slung over his shoulder. "Zdrastye." "Zdrastye." By a flashlight he studied my pass and then handed it back to me. He flashed the light over my shoulder into the back of the truck.

"What are you carrying?"

"I don't know."

"How is that—you don't know?"

"Listen, I'm just a courier," I answered him. "They tell me to drive a load to Vienna, I do what I'm told. They don't explain it to me."

He laughed. "But what is it?"

I shrugged. "How would I know? Diplomatic papers, some general's furniture, more papers. I don't know."

He walked around the truck shining his flashlight inside. I prayed for not a move from anyone and thought instantly of someone sneezing. Then I hastily obliterated the thought, for fear my six passengers might get the idea telepathically.

The sentry came back to the front of the truck. "Come on, let's look at it anyway," he said. I felt my gun. I couldn't tell how many more sentries, if any, were in the nearby hut, but it was a ridiculous thought. I'd never make it that way.

"Open it up," he repeated. But he was not very forceful about it, and he hadn't yet unslung his gun. I didn't move. Instead I sighed.

"Can't do it," I said.

"Why not?" he asked and leaned against the window.

I reached for my cigarettes and brought out a pack. I took one first myself. Russians can be bribed, but the worst mistake is to offer a Russian a bribe. For him a bribe must be either something he took by violence or a gift of pure friendliness. I saw him eye the cigarettes.

"For one thing, they don't allow me to, so I'll get in trouble," I said. While talking, I extended the pack to him. He took two cigarettes. As I kept on talking, I shook more cigarettes to the front of the pack, paying no attention to his lifting of cigarettes out two by two. "For another thing," I continued, "it's a lot of trouble. I get out on a cold night, unlock the door, then have to wrestle with all those lashings and tarpaulins. I've still got a way to go, and it's not early." He had now taken ten cigarettes. I still held the pack there, while ignoring it. He took two more and then stood back.

He grinned. "Spasibo," he thanked me. "You can go." He raised the barrier.

I smiled back at him and drove off—not too fast. I was so shaken I even forgot to let my passengers talk. My mind was totally taken up with the luck I had just had, and worry about the next checkpoint. Between the two thoughts I kept up a constant dialogue with Soviet sentries in my head, until finally I came under the glaring lights of the Schwechat roadblock. This would be the last one. The barrier was up, but a sentry with a tommy gun was in the roadway, motioning me to go on.

Never had the cobblestones of Vienna felt so good, never had the grimy buildings seemed so welcoming. As we drove into the Ring, I banged three times on the crates and shouted, "Becs!" Even the Hungarian name for Vienna sounded good. A muffled but rousing cheer came from the back, and then excited talk, in which I could hear the relief. I stopped at a hotel in the American Zone, called Hugh, and then drove to the address he gave me. In addition to providing lodgings Hugh thoughtfully brought along a bottle of French cognac. We had a small party—at which I regret to say I left very little cognac for the others.

The following day I exchanged my truck for the car which had brought the American correspondent to Vienna. I had no desire to promote any further public associations between myself and trucks, particularly when the AVO would be suspicious over Paul's departure. Then I telephoned Mark in Budapest and made irrelevant conversation about books; he had now heard from me and had no need to open the letter I had left with him. Also I had a plan, and might not make it back to Budapest before the three days were up.

I had heard from both Edmund and Guy that the Soviets maintained one road between Hungary and Austria for their sole use. According to what they told me, no Hungarian or Austrian checkpoints were maintained on this road, and there was only one Soviet checkpoint, at the frontier itself. Most importantly, they had heard that if traveling at night, it was only necessary to give a signal with the headlights—three flashes—and the barrier was raised without even the necessity to stop and show documents. I may have been a bit lightheaded from Paul's successful escape, but it seemed a timely moment to find this road.

Hugh knew of the road, but only that it was supposed to be slightly to the south of the main Vienna-Budapest road, and he did not know the signals. Studying the map, I realized that the Schwechat checkpoint's main purpose was to prevent unauthorized travelers—meaning everyone but Austrian citizens and the Soviet military—from reaching that road, since at Schwechat another road forked to the south, from which other crossings could be reached. By taking the main road and turning off to the south after the Schwechat checkpoint, one could reach the south road by country lanes—provided they were not blocked.

I started about 9 in the evening, fortified by a lively Viennese cocktail party. Rolling out of Vienna to the east, I paused at the Schwechat checkpoint and was again in luck. No sentry. I turned off to the south, and at a distance I could only guess as approximating the location of the road I had picked as most likely, I took the first turn to the east. The land began to be slightly hilly, which meant I was running too far to the south, out of the Danube Valley, so at the nearest crossing I turned to the northeast.

Passing through a village—every shutter closed and not a light showing anywhere—I remarked that the village seemed to go on for an exceptionally long time. Then I began to see shadowy figures moving about, outside the range of my lights. By now I was completely lost within the village, so I stopped and dimmed my lights.

I stepped out of the car. The houses in the darkness had strange profiles—high, thin, slanting chimneys rose black against the starlit sky. All around me was the deep hum of voices—speaking Russian. Of all places to be, I was in the middle of a Red Army tank park. The "chimneys" were the elevated guns of the tanks, and hundreds of Soviet soldiers were lounging and walking about in the dark after their dinner. My presence was, at best, subject to misinterpretation.

My first instinct was to get in the car, turn around, and get out as quickly as possible. I then realized that would look undesirably mysterious. Instead I approached a group of Russians. Nothing was visible in the dark except the vague forms of their greatcoats, and I knew I was only a dark shape to them.

There is a way of speaking in Russian which, when translated into English, is rudely offensive to Americans; to the Russian it most often signifies authority. Gruffly, impatiently, without greeting, I said, "Where is the road to Hungary?" A pleasant, respectful voice answered almost immediately. "You took the wrong turn. Go back to the second corner, turn left, and then keep straight on. Five kilometers."

Five kilometers to the east I made out the dim light of a sentry post and then the red-and-white striped barrier. I did not slow at all; one—two—three, I flashed my headlights. A small figure ran up to the barrier. Just in time the bar rose, and I swept past under it. The figure in the dark looked for the brief instant I glanced at him like an Austrian, not a Soviet guard, but it didn't matter. The road did exist, and the signal was three flashes. It was useful to know.

By now my own situation was precarious. The Peace Treaty had come into effect. The Military Mission was winding up its affairs prior to departure. I saw no prospect of arranging another cover for myself, and the possibilities of cover for a successor were no better. In this much of my mission I had failed. My failure was the opposite side of the coin of the Soviet success in winning their race against the time limit of the Peace Treaty. Even if a suitable cover could be found for another agent to follow me, he would not have much to work with. My network was now exactly half of what it had been. Furthermore, fear had now reached such proportions that it was highly doubtful that reliable new agents could be recruited for some time to come, and least of all those in key positions. The possibility of a "sleeper" network, such as Sam and Edmund had in mind, was always to be considered, although the recruiting involved grave risks in the atmosphere of terror which reigned.

All this I reported to my Headquarters, though with no immediate response. I did not report to them that I myself was becoming increasingly nervous. Several weeks after my return from Vienna Guy still maintained that it was too risky to operate. I felt an air of impending danger; I wondered whether in the last few months I had not exposed myself in some way of which I was not aware. I went over in my memory all of my conversations, their circumstances, my meetings, the various escapes. No single detail seemed wrong, but the whole added up to a pattern of excessive activity. I took to sleeping with my gun by my bed; although I had no illusions about its possible usefulness, it was reassuring.

In early December my premonitions took on a concrete form. Lila told me of her latest conversation with Rajk. In continuation of their pressure on the Socialists for a merger, the AVO was planning a show trial of various arrested Right-wing Socialists. The charge was conspiracy, but it was necessary that the victims be shown to have been in touch not merely with the West, but specifically with the Americans. The reasoning was simple but effective. This trial was addressed to those Socialists, not necessarily Right-wing, who still opposed merger with the Communist Party. To show the Socialist "conspirators" as being in touch with the British, with a Labor Government in power in England, would possibly have led only to further argument. To make the point unmistakably clear, involvement with the Americans was desired, since this would show the Right-wing Socialists as "traitors to the working class." To this end, the AVO was considering the possibility of arresting an American victim. Besides, Rajk had further confided to Lila, the AVO was certain that the Americans had been playing a large role in the numerous recent escapes of wanted persons, and he had hinted that they had a quite good idea of which American was responsible.

Lila was extremely agitated about this news, although not for exactly the same reason that produced a similar effect on me. Lila was devoted to her cousin Eugene, and she feared that, because of his associations with American companies and Americans, he was likely to be one of the victims. She had tried to persuade him to leave the country, but he had refused. She wanted me, as a friend of Eugene, to persuade him to leave. This I readily agreed to do, for plural reasons, of which only my friendship for Eugene was, of course, known to Lila. I also sent off a message to my Headquarters, reporting this latest information, but without comment. Rajk, I conjectured, could be as close to the identity of the American who was "responsible" as he had been to capturing Peyer.

Persuading Eugene to leave took a long night. Neither the wine nor gypsies playing lugubriously in the back room of a small café helped, but when we had alternated tears with laughter, and deep melancholy with surging optimism, in the exact proportions which Magyar custom demands for such evenings, Eugene finally agreed that he would not be of much use to anyone if he was rotting in prison and that this time no neutral intervention would save him as it had from the Germans. He had made a business trip to the West earlier in the year and still had his valid passport. I had the Military Mission buy a railroad ticket to Prague and wired Peter to buy an air ticket Prague-Zurich and mail it to Eugene at a hotel in Prague. Just before he left, I saw Eugene and told him to reserve me a hotel room in Zurich.

My Headquarters had become as jittery as I was. I had received a reply to my last message. It was simultaneously contradictory and explicit: "LEAVE HUNGARY WITHOUT CONSPICUOUS HASTE BUT IN NO CASE LATER THAN FOUR DAYS."[1]

I hastily consulted Guy. He considered the operation to be finished and planned to use his farm now for its original purpose—his own escape. He agreed, however, to take with him anyone I wished to send him, provided they did not exceed four persons. I had, in fact, five persons remaining from the network for Guy to take. I approached them all, hoping I could persuade Guy at the last minute to accept the extra person.

Lila was not a member of the network, strictly speaking, but she had certainly contributed to saving some lives, and I had come to trust her in her oddly correct role. She thanked me, but she was not interested; she believed the terror was a temporary phase, and after that would come the Hungary she wanted to see. At the time of Rajk's arrest as a "Fascist, American spy, and Titoist agent" in 1949, Lila was fortunately out of the country on Government business. She never returned.

Anna stayed for similar reasons of optimism and duty. Her optimism unfortunately was based on even flimsier foundations than Lila's. She was arrested when the final campaign against the Church got under way in 1948 and spent seven years in prison.

Helen made the same decision. Arrested in 1949, she also spent seven years in prison.

Louis had been elected to Parliament in one of the splinter parties. So long as his party was not under attack he did not feel entitled to leave. But he gave me his melancholy smile; "I shall join you before long," he said. Six months later his party was destroyed, and happily he did make good his escape to the West.

Sara well knew that she had but one place to go from the Foreign Office, namely prison. She also had her fiancé already out of the country. She accepted Guy's good offices with pleasure.

I made up my accounts in preparation for leaving, to be dispatched by Mark in the usual manner. It had been what one might call a bargain operation. The eighteen months had cost the American taxpayer, including my salary—well below half the total—some $20,000.

In reporting my expenses I was, of course, confronted with my insubordination. I had, by a considerable margin, disobeyed my orders and exceeded my authority. In doing so I had deliberately accepted the fact. Now I was obliged openly to state it. Headquarters had authorized me to remove twenty-five persons from the country. On one line of my accounts, including funds I had advanced to Guy for the escape of himself, his mistress, and Sara—which took place successfully two weeks later—but excluding both a scientist's wife and the cost of gasoline for one trip to Vienna accompanied by Paul and five others, I wrote a single comprehensive entry: "Expenses for escape of 67 endangered persons, at average $100 per person—$6,700." A total of 74 persons. I wish it had been more. But I was never reproached that it was not less.[2]

On a December night, cold and clear, I drove down from the Var for the last time. I gave a long last look to the Danube, which knew no politics—and all politics. I was deeply sad, with an ache I well knew would not quit me for years, if ever. On the way out of Buda I stopped at two cafés. But each delay was an empty tribute to those who could not go free; each glass, each effort to live again in these walls among these people was vainglorious; I finally realized that I had to accept my own frustration and live with my own sadness, respecting the suffering of those whose part was and would be greater.

As I rolled through the towns and villages and along the deserted highway to the West, I certainly found no solace in the knowledge of defeat. But in the frozen, waiting countryside I at least avoided bitterness; there was the minor compensation of having at least tried.

Two weeks later, the young and popular King of Rumania, ordered bluntly by Vishinsky to abdicate, would pass along the rails by the side of this same road into exile, signaling another final conquest. Two months later Czechoslovakia, just across the river which I glimpsed from time to time, would be swallowed into the Soviet Empire, under the threats of Zorin to call in the Red Army. We still pay for the pride which brought about these falls.

Beyond Györ, but before the border at Hegyeshalom, I turned off the main road to the south. Watching my mileage carefully, I turned again at a familiar crossing, this time to the West. Again I saw before me the red-and-white striped barrier and the dim light of the sentry hut. One-two-three, I flashed my headlights. I couldn't be sure, and my nerves were far from being as controlled as the first time. But I didn't slow down. Again it worked. The still undistinguishable little figure raised the bar in perfect but illegal co-ordination.

This time bypassing the Red Army tank park, I turned north on small country roads until I came out again on the Vienna-Budapest highway. Five miles later I halted at the Schwechat checkpoint. A sleepy and surly Soviet sentry looked at my documents—a valid gray pass and one that had the name and date forged. He looked only at the seals.

Rudely, he told me to go on. But I was not the least offended. As the buildings of Vienna swallowed me up, I knew that I was tired and that I was beginning a letdown which would last for months.

Nevertheless, my feelings were not undiluted. For myself, there had really been no need to take this surreptitious way out of Hungary. But I had not done it for myself. The Frenchwoman, my intended bride, was an invention for my chief in Washington. Common sense and my heart demanded that I bring with me, on my last trip, the Hungarian lady. Both were satisfied by the seventy-fifth passenger.

1. Cf. *Foreign Relations of the United States, 1947,* Vol. IV, Washington, Government Printing Office, 1972, p. 400.

2. On the other hand, as of forty years later, neither has any part of the United States Government proferred thanks of any sort. The Department of State has been steadfast in its refusal to consider the matter—or even to discuss its 1948 suppression of documentation amounting to such thanks. The final episode came in 1987 when the Honor Awards Committee of the Department of State, responding at last to a 1985 suggestion by an Administration official that some recognition be accorded these services, asserted, "[We are] not able to mobilize our procedures today to deal with a situation that far away." A curious reaction for a department which, almost more

than any other I can think of in the Government, is beholden to the historical sense. The State Department Committee's refusal to even consider this matter came in the same week in which the press announced the Department of Defense's award of a Purple Heart to a veteran of the First World War.

NEW YORK 1962

The operation described in the preceding chapters contains a number of illustrations of the reality of secret operations. For one thing, it shows the complexity of these operations and their close interrelationships. What started as a straight secret intelligence operation became, under the pressure of events, a political operation, and then concluded as an escape chain. Similarly, it shows the intricate but unbreakable web of human relationships in the secret war: the real and vital impact on the lives of persons in a distant land of an official statement in Washington, the effect on the people and future of an entire nation of the arrest of a single man, the chain of events by which an argument in a political party can lead to the final disruption of an intelligence network.

For another thing, it demonstrates the constant compromise with the ideal which is an unavoidable characteristic of secret operations in practice. Bargaining with Guy, improvising in the escape of the scientist's wife or of Paul—all involved necessary compromises with the classical principles and ideals of secret operations.

The reader may also have noted that this particular operation was characterized by a certain undesirable rashness. To cite a few instances: I twice exposed Mark to considerable risk. It was he, for example, who passed the money to Majoros without my having checked as to whether the man was in fact Majoros or merely an agent provocateur. *Again, I urged him to assure the Interior Ministry that he knew the identity of "Mr. and Mrs. Tompkins, of Detroit," without considering the possibility that this might be a trap set by the AVO. The escapes of both the scientist's wife and of Paul certainly involved grave risk, the clandestine elements far outweighing the improvised covert elements. Lila also represented a considerable danger; I was banking—correctly, as it turned out—on her innate decency, but she could have been an attempted AVO penetration. And, with the advantage of hindsight, I could, let us face it, have refused Csornoky admittance into my apartment when the American correspondent was present.*

It is quite true that in each of these individual instances the operation was successful or at least unharmed. (In the case of the American correspondent, it was the President's decision more than the correspondent's violation of his word which obstructed the operation.) Nevertheless, taking all these instances together, they form a pattern of rashness which is just the sort of thing bound ultimately to bring about the downfall of an agent. In emergency circumstances—which I believe these were—it may be necessary to entertain such risks; but neither the agent nor his case officer should be under any illusion, because of individual successes, that he is pursuing anything but a dangerous course.

In the intervening years I have sometimes reflected on the possibility that the 75 escapes, or a considerable number of them, may have represented a condonation, a tacit concurrence, by the Soviets and Hungarian Communists. For this to be so, however, it is necessary to assume that the Communists desired to avoid the opprobrium of the arrest and prosecution of these various persons. Nothing in their reactions at the time nor in their subsequent behavior toward those who did not escape even remotely suggests that this was the case. Furthermore, they would have had to have achieved a successful penetration of the operation, and nothing has ever come to light indicating that this occurred. (I still come across traces of the operation: twelve years after the fact I found myself at a dinner in Mexico City seated next to a delightful lady whose conversation disclosed her to be none other than "Mrs. Tompkins, of Detroit." It was only then that I also learned that a man I had known in Europe for some five years was one of her arrested traveling companions.)

As for my having exceeded my instructions, I can only repeat what I said at the beginning of this book: the secret agent's objectives are to him, necessarily, of paramount and highly personal importance. In this case, the rapidly deteriorating circumstances—and the absence of any subsequent reprimand—can only be presumed to indicate that the case officer, on due reflection, decided the agent's actions accorded with his own objectives—a happy outcome which is definitely the exception and not the rule.

It is quite possible that this book has posed more questions than it has answered. If that is the case, the reader may wish to pursue the subject at his leisure in the daily newspapers. In so doing, it is my hope that he will be aided in his understanding by the various criticisms—particularly of American practice—which have appeared herein. At the same time, these criticisms cannot be a source of comfort to any possible Soviet reader. In spite of their early advantages in the field of political operations, the Soviets are laboring under a severe handicap in the secret war. It is simply that their basic policy and objectives are false. The human condition does not support a single nation's rule of the world. No single set of ideas, no single catechism of beliefs, no single doctrine or purpose or scale of values can uniformly animate all men everywhere. Man's unity lies in his diversity.

Ironically, as through all of human history, we shall have to continue to fight for the right of diversity. That is what the secret war—international or individual—is about.